Visionary Evaluation for a Sustainable, Equitable Future

A volume in
Evaluation and Society
Jennifer C. Greene and Stewart I. Donaldson, *Series Editors*

Visionary Evaluation for a Sustainable, Equitable Future

edited by

Beverly Parsons
InSites

Lovely Dhillon
Jodevi Consulting

Matt Keene
The Silwood Group

INFORMATION AGE PUBLISHING, INC.
Charlotte, NC • www.infoagepub.com

Library of Congress Cataloging-in-Publication Data

A CIP record for this book is available from the Library of Congress
http://www.loc.gov

ISBN: 978-1-64113-833-8 (Paperback)
       978-1-64113-834-5 (Hardcover)
       978-1-64113-835-2 (ebook)

Printed in the United States of America

CONTENTS

Preface vii

1   Introduction: Visionary Evaluatives Co-Creating a Sustainable,
    Equitable Future 1
    Lovely Dhillon, Beverly Parsons, and Matt Keene

2   Visionary Evaluatives' Perspectives Part 1: A Conversation
    About Humans, Nature, and Technology 23
    Matt Keene, Beverly Parsons, and Lovely Dhillon

3   Visionary Evaluative Principles: Deepening Understanding 55
    Beverly Parsons, Lovely Dhillon, and Matt Keene

SECTOR VISIONING

4   Social Protection: Reframing Toward Individual, Community,
    and National Well-Being 79
    *Lateefah Simon, Charlyn Harper Browne, Ryan Eller, Bo Pryor,
    and Justin Speegle*

5   Nature: Connecting Well-Being and Conservation Praxis 95
    Kent H. Redford, Carly Cook, Duan Biggs, and Glenda Eoyang

6   Law: Living Values in Our Legal System 111
    Ellen Lawton and Joe Scantlebury

7 Business: Doing Well and Doing Good 127
Eric Barela and Bob Willard

8 Health: Building Our Power to Create Health Equity 143
Jeanne Ayers

9 Financial Investing: Valuing Social Returns 161
Georgette Wong

10 Transportation: Designing for Values-Based Mobility 175
Thomas Abdallah and Antoinette Quagliata

11 Education: Emancipating Learning 187
Elizabeth Kozleski

12 Design: Creating the Future We Want 205
Cameron Norman

13 Visionary Evaluative Inquiry: Moving From Theory to Practice ... 219
Beverly Parsons, Matt Keene, and Lovely Dhillon

14 Visionary Evaluatives' Perspectives Part 2: A Conversation
About Creating a Future of Well-Being 241
Matt Keene, Beverly Parsons, and Lovely Dhillon

15 Conclusion: Living as a Visionary Evaluative 261
Lovely Dhillon, Matt Keene, and Beverly Parsons

About the Editors 271
About the Contributors 273

PREFACE

Sparks of hope, possibility, opportunity, and energy are enlivening society and nature, bringing forth transformation and inspiration to a world filled with rapid and challenging changes. We can all be part of igniting life-giving sparks through our daily actions, thus shaping the future for all of us.

Join us as we use the art of storytelling to envision a future of well-being that we believe can bring life to values that revolutionize our thinking, actions, and outcomes for people, planet, and nature. Join us in turning in a new direction despite the turmoil of our times.

In this book, we use creative elements and a collaborative approach to encourage learning in a way that diverges from the norm. The story is set in motion by a conversation that occurs in low-Earth orbit in 2030. The book engages with three diverse scenarios about the future: the extension of current trends toward mass extinction; the extreme and rapid advances in all facets of technology including artificial intelligence; and the bringing about of a sustainable, equitable future.

We invited change makers from multiple sectors—social protection, nature, law, business, health, financial investing, transportation, education, and design—to envision the future by writing in terms of 2030. We use "Praxis Quests" to illustrate how diverse "questors" support one another to reweave a net of supporting theory, practice, inquiry, and more to enact the values of sustainability and equity. We bring the story together around the book's title: *Visionary Evaluation for a Sustainable, Equitable Future.*

As choreographers and orchestrators of this book and its story, we invite you to take the position of a "Visionary Evaluative," a term we coined to envision and experience our whole selves engaging differently in evaluative processes. We focus on the power of values in adjusting the trajectory of life. We anchor to two core intertwined values—equity and sustainability—as we adjust our personal and professional lives.

We especially call on our colleagues in the transdisciplinary field of evaluation—either as practitioners of evaluation or users of the processes and results of evaluation—to step up to the power of evaluative inquiry as a means of igniting a future of well-being. The book is intended to help us all reposition ourselves, not only in relation to evaluation, but also to our many other roles in this world. The book is not a toolkit, yet it can potentially revolutionize how we use tools of all types to engage in co-creating a sustainable and equitable future for people, nature, and the planet.

We believe in the goodness and power created by people who interlock their values with those of others to envision and create a desired future. We experience this daily as we work with inspirational people who are dedicated to the well-being of the world across highly diverse situations, sectors, geographies, and communities.

Before you jump into the book's framing and story, a few words about the backstory and the supporting steps beyond this book.

THE BACKSTORY

This book has its roots in our shared work around the theme of the 2014 conference of the American Evaluation Association[1] that bore the same name as this book. That year, I (Beverly) was the president of AEA and we (Matt and Lovely) were program cochairs. With the positive feedback we received from conference attendees and our diverse backgrounds, perspectives, and experiences connected to the evaluation field, we decided to write this book. We sought to push ourselves and others to move to another level of depth about what it could possibly mean to engage in visionary evaluation for a sustainable, equitable future. The development of this book has moved us far beyond our starting point in both understanding and action.

THE NEXT STORY

The next story is all of ours. We invite you to engage with your colleagues, community, classmates, friends, family, and us around the ideas in this book. Work with the Visionary Evaluative Principles to make them your own. Keep in touch with us via our website at www.visionaryevaluation.com.

We are committed to living as Visionary Evaluatives and will passionately join you in pursuing a flourishing future of life and equity for all. Share with others what you are learning, how you are living, and what you are do-ing to co-create a future that is sustainable and equitable. It is the intercon-nections among us all that will help elevate these values above the turmoil of our times and build momentum toward our united well-being.

ACKNOWLEDGMENTS

We thank the authors of the Sector Visioning chapters of this book who joined us in the artful adventure of positioning their writing in 2030 and connecting with the Visionary Evaluative Principles and living as Vision-ary Evaluatives. They represent the many colleagues with whom we have worked in multiple sectors who continually inspire us with their dedication to a flourishing and equitable world.

We gratefully acknowledge the decades of work by Michael Scriven that grounds our focus on values as the core of evaluation. We thank him for that significant contribution to the field as well as a grant from his Faster Forward Fund that made it possible for us to build connections among our contributing authors and enrich the overall presentation of this book.

Jennifer Greene, coeditor for Information Age Publishing's series, *Eval-uation and Society*, kept us on the path to completion with her ongoing en-couragement, her patience with our ever-evolving timeframe, and her feed-back on drafts of ideas, then chapters, then a full book.

We are ever grateful to our many colleagues who reviewed portions of the book and challenged our ideas, and to our family and friends who sup-ported us throughout the development process.

—**Beverly Parsons, Lovely Dhillon, Matt Keene**

NOTE

1. Learn more about the American Evaluation Association (AEA), its many topi-cal interest groups, and its 7,000+ members at www.eval.org. At this website, you can also learn more about AEA's connection to the international evalua-tion community. For more information about the many international evalua-tion organizations that exist, see International Organization for Cooperation in Evaluation at https://www.ioce.net/ and EvalPartners at https://www.eval-partners.org/.

CHAPTER 1

INTRODUCTION

Visionary Evaluatives Co-Creating a Sustainable, Equitable Future

Lovely Dhillon, Beverly Parsons, and Matt Keene

Welcome to the Anthropocene—a time in which humanity is exerting its influence on all of the earth's ecosystems. Humans are more interconnected than at any other time. With the addition of digital technology,[1] the significance, impact, and pace of these changes is unprecedented, leading us to new evolutions in our social and natural world.

Many of us are asking: What will the impact be on me, my family, my personal and professional communities, my country, and our world? What role and responsibilities do we have in this new era as individuals, organizations, and countries? How do we make progress on issues that have challenged humanity for generations, and work toward a future of well-being for all?

In this book, we ask you to join us in contemplating these questions and envisioning ourselves as "Visionary Evaluatives" (VEs)—those who utilize evaluative inquiry and a set of VE principles to contribute to a sustainable, equitable future. This approach recognizes the rapid ways in which the world

Visionary Evaluation for a Sustainable, Equitable Future, pages 1–21
Copyright © 2020 by Information Age Publishing

1

and society are evolving; the ways in which we can actively co-create progress through evaluative inquiry; and the ways that those conducting evaluative inquiries and those using evaluative inquiry results can join together as VEs to move the world toward a more sustainable, equitable future.

Visionary Evaluatives are guided by these principles:

1. Commit humbly and compassionately to a sustainable, equitable future.
2. Recognize the world as composed of living, entangled systems.
3. Discover, reveal, and respect intersectionalities.
4. Facilitate the transparency and understanding of human values.
5. Learn through iterative action and inquiry.
6. Engage in deep praxis.

The VE approach, described below, centers on values. The approach builds on the belief that humanity's best chance at well-being during the Anthropocene depends on purposeful and disciplined attention to human values.

LIVING IN THE ANTHROPOCENE

Humanity's impact on the earth has become so profound that some have called for the declaration of a new geological epoch—the Anthropocene.[2] The current officially recognized epoch, the Holocene, covers the 12,000 years of stable climate since the last ice age. It is during the Holocene that all human civilization has developed. However, the striking acceleration of humanity's impact in the mid-20th century marks the end of stability. The evidence of the impact envelops us—the creation of a new geological layer on Earth formed in part by sea level rise, climate change, plastic pollution, ocean acidification, population growth, extinction of species, nuclear weapons testing, deforestation, and urbanization.[3]

Although the Anthropocene has not yet been formally defined as a geological unit within the geological time scale, the current informal use of the term has proven to be helpful as scientists, artists, and citizens alike shift beyond seeing the changing conditions of the planet as isolated or disconnected events to recognizing that these and other changes collectively are setting a different trajectory for the earth system on which humans are, at least for the time being, wholly dependent.

Perhaps the Anthropocene began when human capabilities and intentions began to be offloaded to machines, initiating the acceleration of our influence on the world and ourselves. The dramatic change of pace marks a point of departure from the rest of evolution. Until then, the evolutionary forces of nature had been driving and guiding change on Earth for billions of years. Humans introduced additional avenues of accelerating change, not driven by the familiar forces of the entirety of natural evolution but instead by the force of human values. It is only in recent decades that humans, as a species, have considered and taken action for the co-evolution of nature, humanity, and technology for the equitable and sustainable well-being of the planet as a whole. In fact, currently dominant human societies most often consider humanity as the "whole" in and of itself and nature as only important to the extent it served a purpose for humanity. As a result of the lack of attention to the interdependence of nature and humanity, patterns have emerged in the relationships between human values, actions, outcomes, and visions that undermine the very things that may be most important for human well-being, even survival as a species—water, air, food, dignity, love, life, and connection with one another and nature. As human and planetary interdependence and sustainable boundaries for co-existence are better understood among citizens and leaders alike, humans are recognizing our responsibility for our impact and our future. More and more of us are recognizing our responsibility and potential to rebalance and co-create for a future that serves nature, and in doing so, serves ourselves as well.

Many scenarios are circulating about the future of humanity and the earth. This book engages three diverse scenarios for rich contemplation about the future: the extension of the current trend toward mass extinction; the extreme and rapid advances of all facets of techonology, specifically artificial intelligence; and the bringing about of a sustainable, equitable future.

Scenario 1—Path of mass extinction: Some declare that humans are on a path toward a mass extinction that is far more significant than any in the history of the Earth. Humans have so damaged the support systems of the earth that natural life is eroding and eventually nature, including humans, simply will not be able to survive. Such a scenario depicts a huge amount of destruction and suffering along that path for both humanity and all life on Earth.

Scenario 2—Technology and Artificial Intelligence: A second scenario points toward a technological takeover where life and reality is transformed through the expanse of technology such as artificial intelligence, synthetic biology, virtual existence, and artificial superintelligence (ASI). ASI, the most extreme example of this scenario, represents the emergence of a machine intellect that far exceeds current human cognitive abilities in almost every conceivable way. ASIs could be entities separate from humans or something that some humans attempt to integrate into themselves as they transform and transfer their biological selves into creations aimed at transcending current human limitations. In this second scenario, ASIs and/or enhanced humans will evolve independently of humans, and will take control of the future of humanity, the Earth, and all life on it. These new technological beings may determine whether humanity, in our current form, has enough value to be worthy of survival.

*Scenario 3—A sustainable, equi*table *planet:* A third scenario offers possibilities that humans can rein in the move toward Scenario 1 or 2, and shift away from the overpowering and excessive consumption, greed, and dominance that have been expressed through genocide, slavery, and colonization as well as moving away from a focus on constant technological "advancement" without considering the impact on nature and humanity. This third scenario builds on the patterns of nature's evolution, its right to exist, and also on the rights of all people. In this scenario, humans have the chance to turn internally, focus on values, and share those with others as well as learn of the values of others. In Scenario 3, we are moving in the spirit of a humanity-focused[4] approach which will inevitably lead to care for the planet, nature, and others. It is through this approach that we will be able to create a sustainable planet and a more equitable society.

In this book we encourage putting our energy into co-creating the third scenario while recognizing that the first and second scenarios may be playing out at the same time.We purport that, as we make choices among visions of the future, it is our human values that will guide our future, especially as we work to envision and contribute to it.

VALUES

Values have been described as trans-situational goals that serve as guiding principles in the life of a person or group (Schwartz, 2011). They emerge from a multitude of diverse relationships found at the nexus of, for instance, other values and related actions, outcomes, and visions. Each person has a unique collection of values co-evolving with, for instance, community, group, and family values and influencing perceptions and experiences. Expressions of values are dependent on context.

While human values have been studied and discussed historically, those discussions have not been in the context of today's complex world. We contend that values can be understood more deeply, and that they should be more systematically, transparently, and purposefully a part of our decision-making. Given the complexities of accelerating changes for humanity in an unprecedented future, we must attend to how we think about and address the potential need for changes to our values. At the same time, we must humbly acknowledge that even when we have the best of intentions based on our well thought out values, it is dangerous to assume that we can know or even recognize the full range of outcomes for ourselves and future generations that will result from our actions.

These recognitions call for attention to the intersection of planetary changes with social and personal value changes. We consider the time period between now and the year 2030 to be a critical window during which humans have to make collective, wise decisions about the values that they hold and take actions with careful attention to unanticipated and unknowable outcomes in order to bend the trajectory of humanity toward an equitable, sustainable future.

No matter which of the above-noted scenarios, or versions thereof, that the planet is headed toward, in this book we contend that the values of equity and sustainability are worthy of primary attention to give us and future generations a planet that supports well-being for all life. We are guided in our thinking by the statement of the Universal Declaration of Human Rights which begins, "Whereas recognition of the inherent dignity and of the equal and inalienable rights of all members of the human family is the foundation of freedom, justice and peace in the world" (UN General Assembly, 1948, Preamble, para. 1). We are also guided by the recognition that all life, all ecosystems on this planet are deeply intertwined leading to a growing Rights of Nature movement, which asserts, "nature in all its life forms has the *right to exist, persist, maintain, and regenerate its vital cycles*" (Global Alliance for the Rights of Nature [GARN], (n.d.); What is Rights of Nature? (section) para. 2)[5]

In this book, we take the position that values are at the heart of bending the curve of our current planetary trajectory toward a sustainable, equitable future. While recognizing their multiple meanings and expressions, some of which are discussed below, we put forth sustainability and equity as values that are essential to guide us through the Anthropocene.

It is in this context that evaluators and evaluation have a powerful role to play.

THE ROLE OF EVALUATION AND EVALUATORS

The field[6] of evaluation has a uniquely important role to play because of its connection to values and to systematic inquiry. Evaluation, as a field in the United States, has largely been considered to be the act of looking critically at a social intervention[7] to determine its merit, worth, and significance (Scriven, 2016). The field builds from the natural human activity of holding and acting upon certain values—those beliefs or principles, implicit or explicit, that are important in the lives of individuals or groups. Evaluation as a field is also grounded in the process of systematic inquiry (the basis of many fields, especially in the sciences) but it goes beyond systematic inquiry in intentionally conducting inquiry with certain ethical principles of respect for all people and nature as expressed in the guiding principles of the American Evaluation Association.[8] Evaluation, and its corresponding components of evaluative thinking and inquiry, is well positioned with systematic approaches to question assumptions and beliefs, test for their existence, and examine relationships between values, actions, and outcomes.

Evaluation, evaluative thinking, and evaluative inquiry mean different things to different people and fields. This book uses these terms in the following ways. Evaluation is a field that looks beyond whether something has happened or not to consider as well the influence of that change or lack thereof. Evaluation utilizes evaluative thinking and evaluative inquiry with a practiced consideration of values, methodologies, and use. Traditionally, an evaluator would collect data, analyze that data, develop an interpretation, and share information about that interpretation. This process would follow a mostly linear pathway, addressing the needs of decision-makers by generating inferences on how well-intended outcomes were reached. The underlying values that guided the thinking about desired outcomes were seldom clarified and, even if they were, rarely made explicit.

Today and into the future, evaluation is evolving in multiple ways to address the complexity of the world, the expanded means and uses for conducting evaluation, and the legitimacy of multiple audiences for evaluation. The significance of the underlying values of what is being evaluated, who is doing the evaluation, who is requesting the evaluation, who is using the evaluation, the stakeholders of the evaluation, and those values inherent in the overall process of evaluation is being recognized in the field, especially as it relates to equity.[9] Similarly, a consciousness of the importance of seeing environmental sustainability as a value that shapes evaluation is rapidly coming into the evaluation field.[10]

Evaluative thinking—a combination of critical, creative, inferential, and practical thinking focused on values and valuing—is essential when considering the difficult and complex issues of the Anthropocene. Everyone engages in evaluative thinking, though to various degrees, in considering issues and events in families, communities, organizations, and the world. This consideration and focus on values at multiple scales, though not nearly acknowledged enough, is at the heart of evaluative thinking.

Finally, there is evaluative inquiry which is a systematic process of using empirically derived and value-based data, as well as evaluative thinking, to move to action related to the issue at hand. People take their learning and integrate it into their work regarding the issue—such as modifying strategies, changing activities, and adjusting goals. For example, there may be systematic inquiry into the homelessness issue in a community through the gathering of information about the level of homelessness compared to other similar cities, having conversations with some of the homeless community members, considering the values that underlie what worked in the past and projecting how those values might apply in the future, and using that data and evaluative thinking to propose legal, health, policy, educational, and/or other avenues for addressing the homeless issue. Evaluative inquiry helps find potential pathways for change.

Evaluation crosses social sectors and academic disciplines. People across sectors and disciplines use evaluative thinking and inquiry to various degrees. Sectors and disciplines as well as individuals within them may differ in their assumptions about the role of values, the appropriateness of various inquiry methodologies, and the purposes and use of evaluation. Each discipline and sector has its own theories and assumptions about the world as well as their histories of the use of different inquiry methodologies. These differences affect the role evaluators can play or expect to play in addressing societal and environmental issues. In this book we call on evaluators to open their thinking and practices to the breadth of methodologies and theories from multiple disciplines and sectors about how evaluative inquiries are conducted that can inform the links among values, actions, outcomes, and visions of the paths that move us all toward well-being. It is what is needed for these times.

Evaluation, as a field in the United States, has tended to look to the past to see what worked and has assumed that what worked in the past will work in the future. That may be appropriate if the intention is to keep on the same path into the future that we were on in the past. But if as a species we are recognizing that humans are creating conditions that can lead to our very collapse, do we want to continue down that same road? Instead, evaluators and others who engage in evaluative inquiry can use the past to help humanity understand what needs to be changed while working to design a future that includes respect for the well-being of all people and nature. The understandings derived from inquiries of the past about the complex interplay of values, actions, and outcomes can be projected wisely and carefully to map out a new path guided by a vision of a different future. In this book, that future is framed as equitable and sustainable for many generations of life to come.

The belief that evaluators and the values that they hold should be (and can be) distanced from the evaluative inquiry process is another important belief of many evaluators relevant to this book and our concept of VEs. In this book, we take the opposite position—that evaluation practitioners and users of evaluative inquiry should, with conscious attention to their values and those of others, be far more personally connected to, aware of, and active in their roles; that more methodologies should be considered; and that a broader spectrum of sectors and individuals should collaborate in considering the pervasive issues of the Anthropocene.

Those involved in evaluation, as well as all of humanity, cannot approach the future with the same mindset that has gotten us to this dangerous position. That mindset has been one of assuming that change happens in a steady linear way, and that a command-and-control approach focused on efficiency and optimization for human benefit, especially for those with power, is the primary, if not only, goal.

A different mindset is needed, one that recognizes our impact on nature and the planet as well as other societal evolutions that are upon us—increasing interconnectedness, significant and growing levels of inequity, greater complexity of systems, and ever-present and changing technology. This mindset must include the interdependence of values; be one that recognizes the importance of others, including other species; and recognizes the natural planetary boundaries within which we must work. The mindset additionally recognizes that we need the wisdom, innovative capacity, humility, and compassion that comes from explicit attention to the intersections of sciences, humanities, arts, cultures, and nature.

We need approaches that move toward flexibility in and learning from both social and ecological systems to give us the ability to deal with the turbulence of global changes. We need to be persistent in shifting toward a world that becomes more robust and resilient with the shocks and allows us to support one another for our mutual well-being and health. We must think and act innovatively to rise above crises while also adapting to inevitable change. We must rediscover, maintain, and unearth old ways that have worked, and invent new systems that use boundaries, interrelationships, and perspectives that are a better fit for the future we want than those that have dominated, and desecrated, much of the world today.

We believe that the challenges of the times in which we live require a new and rapid evolution in evaluation. We believe we all must work together in order to find ways to allow us to sustain humans and nature. We propose a new evolution—the Visionary Evaluative.

VISIONARY EVALUATIVES

Visionary Evaluatives are people who recognize the shifting state of the world and believe that they have a personal and professional responsibility to contribute to creating a sustainable, equitable future through the use of evaluative inquiry. We are using the term *visionary* to emphasize our respect for the needs of both current and future generations, with special consideration for the social and natural environments in which future generations will live. Visionary also emphasizes the need for innovative and creative thinking to give an aspirational direction, a vision, of where we are seeking to go.

Anyone can become a VE. This way of being is available to anyone who wants to use the processes of evaluative thinking and inquiry to study and constructively address important social-ecological systems utilizing the Visionary Evaluative Principles (VEPs). It is an integrated way of living that connects people, communities, organizations, disciplines, and sectors. It is a way of living during a time when the very existence of our planet and people is threatened. It goes beyond moving in the world in an isolated state, or just with our family, friends, culture, workgroup, or other personal or professional circles. This way of being recognizes that all in the world are bound together and that the more deeply we move in a VE way, the more we will all have a sustainable, equitable future.

The VE recognizes that evaluative inquiry is not the sole domain or responsibility of one group (i.e., evaluators), but rather an active, co-creative process involving those conducting evaluative inquiries and those using the results of those inquiries. Users are inclusively conceptualized to include all evaluation stakeholders. Visionary Evaluatives co-create useful evaluative knowledge, facilitating and ensuring both the usefulness of the evaluative inquiry and its action-ability throughout the process. Evaluators still play a unique and important role in a VE world. They are deeply immersed in the evaluation field, having expertise in methods, values, and use, that allows them to provide relevant evaluative perspectives, experience, and techniques.[11]

Evaluators and evaluation users differentially engage in roles in the back and forth between action and inquiry. The evaluation user is more focused on carrying out actions and the evaluator is more focused on the inquiry process itself. They support one another in their shared purpose of, and active involvement in, contributing to a sustainable, equitable future. In sharing their perspectives and experiences, they use the evaluative inquiry process to push one another's thinking, and they keep one another on the VE path.

Being a VE is a way of intentionally, mindfully, rigorously, emotionally, and creatively moving through life guided by the intentional exploration and application of values that support a sustainable, equitable future. It is about integrating these values in VEs' personal and professional lives. The complexities of a sustainable, equitable future are ever present. Visionary Evaluatives are actively, consciously, and transparently aligning their lives to their work and their work to their lives so that all of their actions support an evolution toward a future that is sustainable and equitable for all living beings and for our planet.

Visionary Evaluative Principles

Visionary Evaluatives are guided by certain principles that we refer to as fundamental Visionary Evaluative Principles (VEPs).[12] Visionary Evaluatives integrate these principles in their daily personal and work lives as they use evaluative inquiry to co-create a sustainable, equitable future:

1. Commit humbly and compassionately to a sustainable, equitable future.
2. Recognize the world as composed of living, entangled systems.

3. Discover, reveal, and respect intersectionalities.
4. Facilitate the transparency and understanding of human values.
5. Learn through iterative action and inquiry.
6. Engage in deep praxis.

Many people currently use one or more of these principles to different degrees, in different ways and combinations, and at different times. We present them to be used together, with intentionality, in the evaluative inquiry process, as a powerful personal and professional approach to creating a future that serves humanity and nature.

Visionary Evaluative Principle 1: Commit Humbly and Compassionately to a Sustainable, Equitable Future

Visionary Evaluatives have a commitment to the values of sustainability and equity. They prioritize these values in every situation with humility and compassion, recognizing that their own knowledge is inevitably limited and that situations are dynamic. That is, VEs know that in prioritizing these values, the relationship with other values are impacted, often unpredictably, lifting some and subordinating others. Visionary Evaluatives further recognize the depth of complexity of these values, and know that their and others' understanding of equity and sustainability may differ depending on how communities experience inequity and a lack of sustainability.

First, let's look at equity. Equity means many things to different people. In this book, we employ the concept of equity to mean aligning a belief in equality with mindful actions that lead to equitable outcomes. Equity entails, therefore, considering both if people are provided with access and opportunity to participate fully in society, while carrying with them the beautfy of their differences, and also considering if the results of their participation and inclusion reflect outcomes that are fair. Visionary Evaluatives regularly and honestly consider their roles in equitable outcomes—in how they treat and interact with others, in their actions and inactions, and the resulting impact on increasing or decreasing equity. Visionary Evaluatives make space for these differences and find ways to be inclusive that may feel unfamiliar and uncomfortable, and which may require unanticipated and challenging changes in their own actions.

Aligning actions with a commitment to the value of equity takes a considerable amount of reflection, open-mindedness, cultural competence, learning, resources, and, at times, creativity. For example, a university, in aspiring to equity in college admissions, may convene a diverse group of stakeholders to consider if all applicants have equal access to apply (e.g., waiving application fees when unaffordable, recruiting in underrepresented communities); if the university is utilizing application criteria that are fair (e.g., culturally inclusive testing); if they are allowing people from diverse backgrounds to provide insight on the application process and are integrating that input (e.g., regarding gender identity questions); if they are reaching out to communities that are underrepresented (e.g., rural communities); if they are allowing people to apply in creative ways (e.g., artists); and, finally, determining if the results of their collective admissions processes are an equitable reflection of our nation's vast, diverse communities. In evaluating whether the outcomes are equitable, the university may want to look at whether the efforts have actually resulted in better representation; it may undertake efforts to find out how applicants experienced the process and what encouraged or discouraged application; and, in being true to its value of equity, the university may also consider factors seemingly outside of the admission processes such as course offerings, student organization leadership, and retention of a diverse student body. Equity is considered every step of the way—from intent to action (or inaction) to outcome—and it is a complex series of value assessments along that path. Visionary Evaluatives believe in the investment necessary for equity and believe that in supporting equity, they give all of us the opportunity to live life as our full, best selves.

Similar to equity, the process of defining, describing, and supporting sustainability can be a challenge. In referring to sustainability in this book, we are referring to it in the context of and relationship with nature and the environment rather than the sustainability of a program, practice, organization, or a type of development. Early attempts to define sustainability assumed that stakeholders had a shared view of an acceptable standard of living and that capitalism and free markets were the systems within which sustainability initiatives should be defined and deployed.[13] They assumed that it was possible to determine and predict acceptable rates of natural resource depletion that would maintain or improve standards of living for humans for both present and future generations.

We now know that these assumptions underpinning descriptions of sustainability are a poor match for the current conditions of the world. For example, capitalism as currently practiced creates a mandate for perpetual growth that requires incessant, and at times, irreverent consumption of nature through systematic physical degradation of nature, introduction of synthetic materials, and extensive extraction of substances from the earth's crust. It also creates and strengthens structural obstacles to many people's health, influence, and expression of values. To thrive and survive, humans and other living beings require natural resources such as air, water, and land that humanity and its dominant economic systems are destroying.[14] Further, we cannot predict much about future generations and the world within which they will live, and our past focus on an economically based definition of sustainability may not be the currency in a future in which preserving the wonder of nature and its life-giving role may become infinitely more valuable. The Rights of Nature movement, which has been gaining prominence in the 2000s, recognizes that the well-being of human society and the human economy is interdependent with, if not ultimately wholly dependent upon, the well-being of nature. If nature fails, so do we.

In this book, we present and position sustainability and equity as complex human values that emerge from the nexus of relationships between values, actions, outcomes, and visions. Both equity and sustainability are values that cannot be untangled, isolated, and set apart from these relationships, but instead necessarily draw in all life, humans, technology, and all else that humans have created.

The combined values of equity and sustainability are an organizing force and a process, not a condition or state, that look different from all angles, for each person, at each moment and cannot be predetermined or measured against predictions. They are values that must be collectively sensed, described, and assessed in the present and used to organize and instruct for the well-being of all life. Although all of these definitions can help us understand and take action that supports equity and sustainability, at the core, it's not the definitions themselves that matter but rather the recognition that equity and sustainability are values that we individually and collectively can choose and intentionally apply in our lives. Equity and sustainability are values, not rules.

Visionary Evaluatives, in embracing the values of equity and sustainability, recognize that a commitment to both is not just for a certain situation, time, context, or circle. Values, all values, will change over time, in different situations and contexts, and with different circles. Additionally, the ways in which values interplay with one another create even more complexity. Visionary Evaluatives in their commitment to values, especially those of equity and sustainability, realize this, and in their recognition, they nevertheless work mindfully to use evaluative inquiry to understand their values and those of others and to ensure that their values permeate their daily lives—in their work, in their social life, in their buying and investing choices, in what they read, in their friendships, in their community involvement, in the policies and candidates that they support, and in every aspect of how they move in the world. Visionary Evaluatives, therefore, are always considering the intersection of their values, actions, and impact. They also consider the long term and systemic impacts rather than just the impacts that are immediately discernible. Further, VEs look not only at the impacts that are intended but also investigate unintended and difficult-to-see consequences.

Visionary Evaluative Principle 2: Recognize the World as Composed of Living, Entangled Systems

Visionary Evaluatives recognize that every issue is part of entangled, living systems. They recognize that the systems are plentiful, nuanced, networked, messy, beautiful, and most especially, living. Visionary Evaluatives move from looking at a particular issue in linear, isolated, and static ways toward seeing that issue in the larger, interdependent, and constantly shifting and evolving systems in which it exists. Visionary Evaluatives also know that an evolving issue often forms discernible patterns within an entangled, living system. Issues emerge and may mature, thrive, flourish, be threatened, rebalance, adapt, evolve, die, and/or re-emerge. The goal is not to sustain the intervention, organization, and/or system, but to allow for the transformation of the social and ecological patterns in which an issue exists toward a more sustainable, equitable future.

Similarly, VEs recognize that people and nature are all linked; we are an entangled web of life that relies on one another with increasing frequency and need. Indeed, issues do not relate to or reside in solely one social unit of life, for example, a social sector such as business or education. Rather, units intersect as do we with each other, and with other communities, other organizations, nature, and technology.

Visionary Evaluative Principle 3: Discover, Reveal, and Respect Intersectionalities

The recognition of entangled, living systems leads naturally into seeing the intersections of choices, evidence, actions, information, values, and biases. Visionary Evaluatives realize that actions affect multiple sectors, power, and cultures, none of which operates in a vacuum, but are interconnected and often deeply entrenched. Visionary Evaluatives search for those intersectional points, reveal their existence, and share their impact. When possible, and through collaboration with others, they unearth ways to release the oppressive forces that may lock them into place while still appreciating and respecting the hold they have on systems and the impact they have on people and nature. Rethinking the traditional boundaries of sectors, power, and cultures opens up new ways of thinking and acting to address the pressing issues the Anthropocene triggers. It also allows new opportunities for change as we continue to address our longtime social and environmental issues.

Visionary Evaluative Principle 4: Facilitate Transparency and Understanding of Human Values

Visionary Evaluatives realize that people will have differing understandings of and commitment to sustainability and equity and that the role of VEs, in part, is to hold that tension and facilitate conversation and joint collaboration toward increasing the transparency and understanding of human values.

Visionary Evaluatives are both attuned to values (their own and those of others) and actively increase awareness and conversation about them. Visionary Evaluatives also recognize that multiple values will be present and that many will intersect and some will conflict. They know that choices may need to be made regarding which values are most vital to the work at a given point in time and in a particular situation. Visionary Evaluatives participate in processes to determine the values that are to be prioritized and engage stakeholders in dialogue about the implications of various actions. They ensure that the prioritized values are integrated and reflected.

Visionary Evaluative Principle 5: Learn Through Iterative Action and Inquiry

Visionary Evaluatives move through their evaluative inquiry knowing that their purpose is beyond undertaking a study of the facts, an intellectual exercise, or a well-articulated report. Rather, VEs are continually engaged in iterative learning. Visionary Evaluatives utilize the evaluative process as the basis for action that, like a living, flourishing evolving system, can benefit from ongoing feedback, learning, iteration, and adaptation. Visionary Evaluatives—throughout the process of considering an issue, engaging in study and fact-gathering, analyzing and making meaning of what they find, and sharing their learning throughout this process—ask themselves how their work and way of being can help lead to strategic action.

Visionary Evaluative Principle 6: Engage in Deep Praxis

Visionary Evaluatives go beyond the basic form of praxis—where theory informs practice and practice informs theory—to a deeper praxis in which they seek to integrate creative actions, inquiry, theory, and learning, with all anchored to their guiding values and the future. Deep praxis, similar to concepts of deep ecology,[15] does not see the world as a collection of isolated events or objects but rather a network of fundamentally interconnected, intertwined phenomena. Visionary Evaluatives are actively and communally engaged in deep praxis, iteratively learning and evolving theory, practice, and evaluative inquiry to fit the situation in which they are participating. Visionary Evaluatives, reflecting different perspectives, values, and sectors, come together and also engage with others in ongoing conversation and reflection, all the while synthesizing learning and applying that learning and wisdom to the next action. Visionary Evaluatives bring together the other five VEPs in their praxis. They continuously consider how the values of equity and sustainability relate to other values. Visionary Evaluatives weave these principles together in all phases of their work and life.

Being and Becoming Visionary Evaluatives

This book was written with a belief in these VEPs. Indeed, through the process of writing and rewriting this book, we evolved in our own journeys toward understanding, trying out, and embracing the depth of what these principles mean and what it means to live as VEs.

We believe that there is no greater time in which VEs are needed than now. As current and potential evaluation practitioners and users evolve into VEs, they become a community that prioritizes equity and sustainability; uses an entangled, living systems lens; discovers and navigates intersectionality; believes in engaging with and being transparent about values; learns through iterative action and inquiry; and embraces deep praxis. Through embracing the VEPs, VEs will be an active part of co-creating a future that is sustainable and equitable for humanity and nature.

BOOK FORMAT

This book is divided into 15 chapters with the Introduction and Conclusion set in current time, and the intervening chapters presented as a story that takes place in 2030. This format and storyline provide a creative opportunity for considering possible trajectories of our current paths and for delving into design and visionary thinking for the creation of a sustainable, equitable future. While written as a story, the chapters in the "Sector Visioning" portion (Chapters 4–12) can be accessed in any order and combination. This book is written in a manner that allows readers to access the book for entry points that meet the readers' styles and interests. Taken together, this book will, ideally, provide the reader with theoretical and concrete pathways for understanding how VEs would move in the world and utilize the VEPs to address societal and ecological issues.

Chapter 1. Introduction: Visionary Evaluatives Co-Creating a Sustainable, Equitable Future

This introduction, focusing on the Anthropocene and emphasizing a shift toward equity and sustainability, provides the temporal context into which VEs arise. It reviews key information about evaluation and evaluative inquiry, introduces the concept of "Visionary Evaluatives" and the principles they follow, and provides a roadmap for the book.

Chapter 2. Visionary Evaluatives' Perspectives Part 1: A Conversation About Humans, Nature, and Technology

In Chapter 2, written as a screenplay set in 2030, our story begins. Eight highly influential and well-regarded VEs have been charged by a congressional committee to present a VE perspective at an upcoming United Nations Global Forum on ASI. The chapter consists of excerpts from conversations about their upcoming contribution to the Global Forum. They grapple with perspectives that are diverse, open, nuanced, and challenging. They begin by considering the world into which ASI may arrive, emphasizing patterns and trends that are impacting the health of social-ecological systems. However, as they endeavor to understand the potential for a future of well-being, the VEs are forced to turn inward to examine humanity's and their own capacity to understand the relationships between values, actions, outcomes, and a vision of a sustainable, equitable future. Verbal and visual exchanges set off explorations of the infinitely diverse collections of intersections shaping the Anthropocene, created by worldviews, social movements, governance, economic systems, genetics, art, memory, and more. As they sense more blind spots in their conversations, they look to include the perspectives of other VEs.

At the end of Chapter 2, the group prepares to spend the next day and a half reviewing deep praxis materials (Chapters 3–13) curated by Zindzi, the lead librarian of the Deep Praxis Library.

Chapter 3. Visionary Evaluative Principles: Deepening Understanding

Chapter 3, also set in 2030, is the transcript of a conversation between Zindzi and Omar. Zindzi had spent most of her career prior to 2020 conducting evaluative inquiries for government, nonprofit organizations, and private foundations before being introduced to the concept of VEs. For over 10 years now, Zindzi has served as the lead librarian of the Deep Praxis Library. For VEs, deep praxis is the process of integrating creative actions, evaluative inquiry, theory, and learning into one's work and life with a humble and compassionate commitment to a sustainable, equitable future.

Omar, a former evaluator who left the evaluation field in the late 2010s, is considering rejoining the field, and is intrigued by the VE approach which aligns with his own values. In the conversation, Zindzi and Omar delve into the VEPs with an emphasis on the perspective of an evaluation practitioner.

At the end of Chapter 3, Zindzi asks Omar to review the "Sector Visioning" materials (Chapters 4–12) that she has put together for the VEs described in Chapter 2. She and Omar will reference these materials in their subsequent conversation, captured in Chapter 13.

Chapters 4 Through 12: Sector Visioning

Chapters 4 through 12 are framed as "Sector Visioning" chapters which are curated materials from the Deep Praxis Library. They are written by people who are part of "praxis quests" in a variety of sectors and provide insight and information as to how these sectors have been evolving from

2020 to 2030 to address changes in the world, especially in consideration of the values of equity and sustainability.

The "Sector Visioning" chapters focus on: Social Protection, Nature, Law, Business, Health, Financial Investing, Transportation, Education, and Design. These sectors have not been chosen to signify those as the most important but rather serve to exemplify how VEs can transform sectors to intentionally change the trajectory of human history toward a more sustainable, equitable future. The authors of these chapters position themselves in 2030, and discuss some important actions, perspectives, and inquiries of VEs in their sector.

As the "Sector Visioning" authors project into 2030, they consider the ways in which their sectors are learning, adapting, transitioning, and transforming toward better situations for people, place, and planet. These chapters provide the reader an opportunity to think about how what they are learning from the sectors plays into their own VE approach.

In engaging with multiple disciplines, we hope to stimulate new conversations, learn from other sectors, and share expertise from our varied fields, experiences, and perspectives.

Chapter 13. Visionary Evaluative Inquiry: Moving From Theory to Practice

Chapter 13 is a transcript of a second conversation between our two characters, Zindzi and Omar, introduced in Chapter 3. In this conversation, Zindzi and Omar discuss how a particular approach to deep praxis, referred to as "Praxis Quests," is used to deepen any and all aspects of the evaluative inquiry process. In the term *praxis quest*, the word "quest" captures the notion of praxis being an ongoing search, exploration, and discovery. It involves engaging in praxis, refining a praxis, finding fit-for-purpose behaviors, adaptations, states of being, and more. It engages VEs across sectors and disciplines in a process of continually "becoming" both in one's life and work through a focus on evaluative inquiry. Being and becoming a VE is a journey of reflection and supportive engagement with others.

In their conversation, Zindzi and Omar frame their conversation around four basic phases of evaluative inquiry: (a) positioning and designing the evaluative inquiry; (b) data collection, compilation, and credibility; (c) meaning-making (e.g., illuminating the link between data and strategic action); and (d) shaping action and practice. They consider how each phase (or as they say, "arena") of evaluative inquiry can be thought of as encompassing the whole of the evaluative inquiry process and the whole of the VEPs.

Chapter 14. Visionary Evaluatives' Perspectives Part II: A Conversation About Creating a Future of Well-Being

Chapter 14 returns to the eight VE leaders from Chapter 2 who are preparing for the ASI Global Forum. They have now reviewed the "Sector Visioning" materials and the transcripts of the conversations between Zindzi and Omar. In Chapter 14, they reconvene to reflect upon what they have learned. Here, they discuss the roles, competencies, and responsibilities of VEs; threats to evaluation and evaluators; the relationship between the VE and evaluation; the origins and properties of values; and notions of a truly effective humanity. Finally, just as they seem to be honing some of their most critical contributions to the forum, they are blindsided by a crisis of understanding and opportunity and forced to question their fitness for the task they've been given.

Chapter 15: Living as a Visionary Evaluative

The conclusion of this book moves back to where we began—the present day—with a practical call to action for those who want to move in the direction of being VEs in order to create a sustainable, equitable future. The conclusion provides a checklist-style framework for testing the use of the VEPs as you consider what it is like to be a VE in the Anthropocene.

CONSIDERATIONS FOR THE READER

This book reflects our own values, especially those of equity and sustainability, and a belief that values, evaluative inquiry, visioning, interconnectedness, collaboration, action-ability, and praxis can be a source of hope for the future. In writing this book, we worked closely with our "Sector Visioning" chapter authors and with each other. We facilitated a series of webinars,[16] which provided an opportunity for creative cross-sector discussion and collaboration and, as co-editors, we engaged in conversation nearly every week for over four years in an effort to evolve the book into one that captured the myriad of changing impacts on our world and potential approaches that VEs can use to influence those impacts toward a more sustainable, equitable future. It was a challenging and enjoyable process that deepened our thinking, gave us a renewed sense of the potential of evaluative inquiry for the times in which we live, and, we hope, enhanced the book's value for the reader.

There are a few things the reader may want to consider. This book has a United States focus given our deep knowledge of this community. However, we view the United States as an integral part of the world whose actions, cultures, and perspectives affect the world, and vice versa. We, as well as our "Sector Visioning" chapter authors, have incorporated this orientation in our thinking and writing. We suggest that readers read through the United Nations Sustainable Development Goals (United Nations, 2018) which provide a complement to the values and perspectives reflected in this book. We further believe that the opportunities for being and moving in the world as a VE extend beyond our borders, and that the implications and call to action we provide to U.S.-based evaluators may be adapted by evaluators in other nations with careful attention to their particular context.

Our goal in writing and curating this book is to provide pathways for moving through the Anthropocene that recognizes our interconnectedness and interdependence across sectors, organizations, communities, and cultures. Evaluative thinking and inquiry are essential means by which all can consider the ways that we play a part in impacting people, place, and planet through the actions of our organizations, our institutions, our communities, our families, and—most importantly—ourselves. Evaluation practitioners and users cannot stay on the sidelines but rather must be an active, engaged, and self-reflective part of bringing to life the vision of an equitable, sustainable future for the well-being of all.

We hope that this book can be used as a resource that not only provides information and ideas for action and evaluative inquiry but one that also provides readers with ways that they can consider, learn, and iterate as they read through the book.

This book was a challenge for the three of us as we explored and challenged our own values and as we integrated our thinking, experience, and backgrounds personally and professionally. We evolved as we wrote this book. We became more deeply aware of the issues of each of our sectors, cultures, communities, identities, and histories. We also learned to not just consider our values of equity and sustainability remotely but to integrate both deeply into our daily work and lives.

Evolving is never easy—personally, organizationally, as a community, nation, species, or even planet. It is often scary as it can feel that something of us is being lost, perhaps our very selves. Evolution, however, is not only inevitable and necessary for all life but it is also a beautiful form of growth. We hope you enjoy the journey.

NOTES

1. We use digital technology (also referred to as digital and/or online media/platforms) to refer to technology publicly introduced around the mid-1900s that creates, stores, processes, and/or communicates data such as computers, social media, artificial intelligence, and so forth. Hereinafter referred to as "technology."

2. See the Subcommission on Quaternary Stratigraphy Working Group, a constituent body of the International Commission on Stratigraphy, the largest scientific organisation within the International Union of Geological Sciences. See http://quaternary.stratigraphy.org/working-groups/anthropocene/
3. See https://www.nature.com/articles/415023a
4. We are using the term "humanity-focused approach" to mean emphasizing compassion, kindness, love, and other life-enhancing ways of being.
5. See http://therightsofnature.org/what-is-rights-of-nature/
6. We use the term "field" when referring to evaluation as a disciplinary subject and evaluation as a "profession" when referring to its practice as part of an industry.
7. A social intervention is something that is intended to improve the human condition.
8. See www.eval.org
9. See The Center for Culturally Responsive Evaluation and Assessment (CREA), a highly collaborative and well known evaluation organization that brings together evaluation practitioners, users, academics, and others to continually enrich understanding of the meaning and practice of equity in evaluation. Other sources for deepening an understanding of equity and evaluation include the Equitable Evaluation Initiative and the AEA statement on Cultural Competence in Evaluation.
10. The application of the value of nature-focused sustainability in the evaluation field does not have as long a history as equity. Historically, it has been heavily intertwined with sustainable development and international issues. To understand more about this history, see the Environmental Evaluators Network, *Blue Marble Evaluation* by Michael Quinn Patton, United Nations Development Programme, Global Environmental Facility, and *Evaluating Environment in International Development*, edited by Juha Uitto (2014).
11. These are explored more fully in Chapters 3 and 13 of this book.
12. The VEPs are discussed further in Chapters 3 and 15 of this book.
13. See, for example, the 1969 National Environmental Policy Act and the 1987 Brundtland Report, *Our Common Future.*
14. See https://thenaturalstep.org/approach/
15. The term "deep praxis" parallels the term "deep ecology" that "recognizes the fundamental interdependence of all phenomena and the fact that, as individuals and societies, we are all embedded in (and ultimately dependent on) the cyclical process of nature" (Capra & Luigi Luisi, 2014, p. 12).
16. The webinars, as well as other aspects of this book's development, were supported by a generous grant from the Faster Forward Fund which strives to advance the practice and profession of evaluation.

REFERENCES

Capra, F., & Luigi Luisi, P. (2014). *The systems view of life: A unifying vision.* Cambridge, England: Cambridge University Press.

National Environmental Policy Act of 1969. (2006). 42 U.S.C. § 4331(a). For information see https://www.epa.gov/nepa

Schwartz, S. (2011). Values: Cultural and individual. In F. J. R. van de Vijver, A. Chasiotis, & S. M. Breugelmans (Eds.), *Fundamental questions in cross-cultural psychology* (pp. 463–493). Cambridge, England: Cambridge University Press.

Scriven, M. (2016). Roadblocks to recognition and revolution. In S. Rallis (Ed.), *American Journal of Evaluation, 37*(1), pp. 27–44.

United Nations. (2018). *Sustainable development goals.* New York, NY: United Nations. Retrieved from https://www.un.org/sustainabledevelopment/sustainable-development-goals/

United Nations General Assembly. (1948). *Universal declaration of human rights* (217[III]A). Paris. Retrieved from http://www.un.org/en/universal-declaration-human-rights/

CHAPTER 2

VISIONARY EVALUATIVES' PERSPECTIVES PART 1

A Conversation About Humans, Nature, and Technology

Matt Keene, Beverly Parsons, and Lovely Dhillon

SETTING THE STAGE

Background

In early 2030, the United States Congress asked a group of eight Visionary Evaluatives (VEs) to participate in a UN sponsored global forum on artificial superintelligence (ASI). They were asked to facilitate conversations about creating a sustainable and equitable future. In preparation for the approaching global forum and in the context of the potential emergence of an ASI, the VEs gathered together for a week to discuss the relationships that connect human values, actions, outcomes, patterns, and a sustainable and equitable future. The following includes excerpts from those conversations.

Visionary Evaluation for a Sustainable, Equitable Future, pages 23–53
Copyright © 2020 by Information Age Publishing

Setting

Circular room with warm lighting and rich acoustics, walls and ceiling of glass. Eight comfortable, formal chairs circle the room with a small circular, slightly raised platform in the center. The meeting room is equipped with holography presentation technology and located on a spacecraft in low Earth orbit.

Characters

Ezekiel (Zeke) Tizoc, 66. Aztec ancestry, Mexican American, humble, direct, master strategist, Marine Corps four-star general. Development and health strategist.

Gretchen Locke, 69. Northern European descent, incisive, concise, high energy, controlled, adaptive pragmatist. Impact ecologist.

Hula Lovelace, 32. Osage Native American, brilliant, fearless, patient power. Technology entrepreneur.

Jackie Mandela, 9. South African-Cuban. Family fled apartheid. Loved by all, adored, selfless, famous. Mechanically, biologically enhanced.

Lovett Williams, 55. African American, confident, humble, deliberate. Neuroscientist, attorney.

Philip Churchill, 80. British descent, dogmatic, provocative. Industrialist, politician, philanthropist.

Sōhō Miyamoto, 48. Family interned in California in WWII, genius, uses both hands to illustrate her thoughts using holographic living illustration technology. Impact artist.

Sophia Biruni, 44. Family exiled from Iran in the 1970s, positive, passionate, intensely progressive, recently more cynical and conflicted. Educator.

Note:

Presentation (P) indicates that dialogue is accompanied by visual presentation content, for example, images, graphics, video, holography, audio.

Illustration (I) indicates that Sōhō is creating holographic and other visual art to accompany dialogue.

Gretchen, 69	**Hula**, 32	**Jackie**, 9	**Lovett**, 55	**Philip**, 80	**Sōhō**, 48	**Sophia**, 44	**Zeke**, 66
Northern European	Osage American Indian	South African Cuban	African American	British descent	Japanese American	Family exiled from Iran	Mexican American
Impact Ecologist	Technology Entrepreneur	Famous Artificially Enhanced	Neuroscientist Attorney	Industrialist Politician Philanthropist	Impact Artist	Educator	General Development Strategist

HOW WILL WE LEARN?
Monday Morning 8:56 a.m. GMT

Sophia standing at a window looking toward Earth. Others sitting or standing in groups of two or three, conversations pause to watch breaking news.

P: *News reports on the devastating desertification in Southeast Europe, inhabitants migrating North; enormous camps of climate and conflict refugees from Northern Africa repopulating SE Europe; catastrophic snows blanketing the region, cutting off supply lines and communications...*

Jackie: (*joining Sophia*) We'll be beginning soon. (*News continues in the background, reflected in the window they are looking out.*)

P: *News reports on a recent spate of nuclear tests and provocative exercises by rising military powers.*)

(*Sophia's eyes are wet, Earth reflected in her pupils.*)

Sophia: How and when are we going to learn? We don't even know what questions to ask. Over and over we create horror and let hope convince us we have learned. But we haven't. We don't. We forget. We've forgotten.

Jackie: Forgotten what?

Sophia: (*looking out*) I can't even see it anymore. It's too far away to remember.

Jackie: (*quietly, reaching out and squeezing Sophia's hand*) Maybe if we all look, together.

(*Jackie turns to the room, indicating the time and all begin moving to chairs.*)

WELCOME TO THE QUESTIONS
Monday Morning 9:15 a.m. GMT

(*all seated, attentive*)

Jackie: About a year ago we began this Quest. As a brief refresher and to set the tone for the week ahead.... We are a group of Visionary Evaluatives (VEs) and we have been asked to spend this year preparing to share VE perspectives at the Global Forum.

Myriad other points of view will also be shared at the forum, now just a month away—medicine, law, transportation, space industries, education, climate, and just about any sector or field imaginable. We've touched on all of this in one way or another in this last year, but as VEs everything we will bring to this conversation stems from our interest in the relationships that connect human values, actions, and outcomes to a sustainable and equitable future. We are known for this. And under this banner you've led your own unique revolutions. Billions of lives are better off for it.

This week, we're going to narrow our inquiry to the context of the United States and revisit some of the big questions the forum has specifically asked us to address, questions like: If an ASI—an intellect superior to humans in all facets of intelligence—comes to be, how can we ensure its compatibility with humanity, and, more to the point, its compatibility with human values?

At the forum, we want to be sure we can share examples of how VEs think, live, and work. Later this week, we'll break and take some time to dig into a curated collection of VE conversations from the last 10 years or so. We'll be looking back at examples of how VEs from a variety of sectors have been using the principles to vision a future they want to create.

Throughout the week, I'll occasionally note and momentarily display (*indicating the center of the room*) points of synthesis and insight to help us keep track of the meeting.

How's that? Enough to get us started this morning?

Zeke: I like it. And as for mixing a few more perspectives from other VEs into our evolving work, that insight and guidance is badly needed.

Jackie: (*P*)

PRINCIPLES OF THE VISIONARY EVALUATIVE

1. Commit humbly and compassionately to a sustainable, equitable future.
2. Recognize the world as composed of living, entangled systems.
3. Discover, reveal, and respect intersectionalities.
4. Facilitate the transparency and understanding of human values.
5. Learn through iterative action and inquiry.
6. Engage in deep praxis.

Gretchen, 69	Hula, 32	Jackie, 9	Lovett, 55	Philip, 80	Sōhō, 48	Sophia, 44	Zeke, 66
Northern European	Osage American Indian	South African Cuban	African American	British descent	Japanese American	Family exiled from Iran	Mexican American
Impact Ecologist	Technology Entrepreneur	Famous Artificially Enhanced	Neuroscientist Attorney	Industrialist Politician Philanthropist	Impact Artist	Educator	General Development Strategist

Lovett: Zeke, let's not beat ourselves up too much *this* morning. The values in this room, like most rooms, vary. In some ways, radically. We're always bringing some of our own unique moralities and ethical understandings. No surprises there.

Philip: No indeed. But we cannot ignore that *we* have struggled for a year now to communicate about values. So how do we do this at the forum? With machines? Which values are most important? How do we know? Says who? How do our moralities and ethics change, emerge, or disappear with the evolution of humans and machines? And can *that* be a healthy co-evolution?

Hula: These are the sorts of questions that agitate my conscience and my consciousness. After these months, together, even more.

Jackie: (*P*)

SYNTHESIS AND INSIGHT

- Highly accomplished, well known VEs have been asked to contribute their perspective on creating a sustainable and equitable future at the global forum on artificial superintelligence.
- The purpose of the forum is, in part, to ensure the compatibility of humans and ASI.
- At the forum, the VEs will share their work at the intersection of human values, actions, outcomes, and visions as well as the VE perspective on, for example, evaluative inquiry, evaluative thinking, and VE principles.

PRISONS OF ASSUMPTION
Monday Morning 10:45 a.m. GMT

Jackie: We've used the question "Into what would ASI arrive?" as a way to explore our views on what has made Earth and humans what we are today. Though surprising us in many ways and with numerous caveats, we generally agree that humanity is nurturing pockets of powerful and enabling patterns that favor a present and future that is more sustainable and equitable than memories and histories of, say, 30 to 50 years ago.

Sophia: I'll be curious to find out if the sector VEs see it this way.

Jackie: For now, I wonder, Philip, as we discussed . . . would you mind?

Philip: . . . Sharing some "pockets and patterns" from my story? Of course. A privilege.

P: *simultaneous interrelated scenes of oil fields; coal and gemstone mining; chemical plants; industrial fisheries, agriculture and food production; water, air, soil pollution.*

It was the early 1970s when I began building my influence. All of it, in one way or another, solved someone's problem. I got fuel to nations, pesticides to farmers, cleaning products to the household, and diamonds to brides.... I was proud of what I was doing and it drove me. I was so motivated and so convinced of my rightness, it was not possible for me to imagine I was creating crises that we'd be left to deal with for generations, at least. To build global industrial empires, I nurtured the corruption of politicians and governments, mutilated the public trust, and actively taught humanity to become addicted to its own destruction. Today, if it was proven I was doing any of what I have done, I'd be swiftly and rightly convicted of crimes against humanity and the international crime of ecocide. But then we were all just following the rules of the day, playing in the same paradigms, doing what was needed to grow, the only imperative, the only measure of success. That was our truth.

In the late '90s, Mehala and I met. Through her and her friends and family, I came to know the ancient peoples of Aceh and Northern Sumatra. My heart had to be broken a few times before I could see the horrors I'd forced on them. They'd lost—I'd taken—their forests, waters, and traditions to sate my indefatigable ambitions.

P: *scenes and stories of the history, evolution, beauty, and destruction of people, ecosystems, wildlife, and ways of life in Aceh, Sumatra, Mentawai.*

After we married, I continued learning from Mehala's family and friends. They showed me, I learned, that owning and controlling everything was less about the autonomy and freedom I was so proud of and more about playing children's games inside a prison I'd been building for myself and everyone. When I finally looked up, sick and weak from the years of struggling against humanity and nature, I saw the walls,

Gretchen, 69	Hula, 32	Jackie, 9	Lovett, 55	Philip, 80	Sōhō, 48	Sophia, 44	Zeke, 66
Northern European	Osage American Indian	South African Cuban	African American	British descent	Japanese American	Family exiled from Iran	Mexican American
Impact Ecologist	Technology Entrepreneur	Famous Artificially Enhanced	Neuroscientist Attorney	Industrialist Politician Philanthropist	Impact Artist	Educator	General Development Strategist

stood up, and dedicated the rest of my existence to tearing them down, letting the humanness back in, and creating a more generative future.

P: *All branches of Philip's global conglomerate are legally required to generate social and ecological well-being and doing so by leading the world's transformations to total supply chain transparency, renewable energy, green chemistry, agro ecology, generative cities, and worker empowerment and protections.*

Gretchen: Your stance is jarring loose bedrock assumptions about competition, labor, and property. For one, you're showing that ignorance of relationships between energy, health, security, transportation, education, policy, culture, nature (breath)—decreases corporate life expectancy.

Jackie: (*P*)

SYNTHESIS AND INSIGHT

- In many ways, the present and future are more sustainable and equitable than the recent past.
- Always, we may be wrong and, always, we may evolve to better align with the well being of others, the world, and ourselves.
- Search out and dismantle rigid, destructive, power-dominant worldviews that fuel inequity in favor of perspectives that are a better match for a world of well-being for life and living.

REASON FOR HOPE
Monday Afternoon 2:10 p.m. GMT

Zeke: I've been facilitating the creation, development, and management of three independent States of Sudan over the last decade. The refugee camps are gone and we see meaningful improvements in all measures of social and natural sustainability. And yes, we've rolled out similar initiatives in other regions that have also abruptly interrupted cycles of ethnic violence and bigotry.

Jackie: Zeke, it's a nice break to hear about successes and wellness. It feels good. Would you, and others, mind sharing a few more portraits of positive change?

Zeke: A good idea. These are tough times but it is also easy to find reason for hope. We've altered mosquito genetics so they can't transmit disease. Robotics and atmospheric water collection technologies are freeing hundreds of millions, mostly women and children, from the work of transporting and purifying water. The Dr. Drone Initiative can access nearly anyone on Earth.

Sophia: When people no longer use most of their time and energy for basic survival and rehabilitation from illness, most turn some part of their time toward education. Whether for themselves or their families, millions more every month, children and adults, are connecting to the learning they need via platforms offering free and fit-for-purpose socio-virtual curricula. Democratized access to education has accelerated the worldwide reconceptualization of gender relations.

Lovett: With this educational renaissance, more people understand more about relationships between nutrition, behaviors, physical and mental health, and how all of that affects their performance in life and work. As parents have more freedom to take action on that new understanding, they're better able to care for their children who are learning more and faster than any children before them. As local education levels rise, so too does the prosperity of the community.

Gretchen: Universal incomes are rolling out into some of these communities when policy goals prioritize well-being over employment. When this happens, ecological and social pressures often ease and opportunities open up enabling positive network effects to take over. Small, seemingly insignificant actions often surprise us and end up triggering a contagion of localized health, security, and economic benefits.

Philip: When threats are removed, conditions stabilize. People, even entire societies, are becoming more confident that they can improve their lives and that they know how to do it. All of which makes healthy democracies more likely. People are still flowing toward the cities, but more heavily in the direction of cities being designed to enhance rather than conquer their progenitors—nature and people.

Gretchen: The Generative Movement (*indicating the example Philip has just given*) has traction because a city immediately becomes more resilient, productive, and healthful when the only

Gretchen, 69	Hula, 32	Jackie, 9	Lovett, 55	Philip, 80	Sōhō, 48	Sophia, 44	Zeke, 66
Northern European	Osage American Indian	South African Cuban	African American	British descent	Japanese American	Family exiled from Iran	Mexican American
Impact Ecologist	Technology Entrepreneur	Famous Artificially Enhanced	Neuroscientist Attorney	Industrialist Politician Philanthropist	Impact Artist	Educator	General Development Strategist

allowable impacts—whether building bridges, streets, roads, homes, offices, or factories—are those that create net social and ecological benefits.

Philip: More "waste" is repurposed, recycled, reused, and avoided altogether every day, in every city. More healthful food is grown in and around those cities, for those people. Roofs, walls, roads, and windows are sending energy to the buses, cars, and trains of mobility systems that look less and less like the hard infrastructure of traditional transportation systems and more and more like biological circulatory systems.

Sōhō: (*Sōhō, standing, creating holographic drawings*) Our ability to perform on Earth has given our ambitions the confidence to spread.

I: Scenes of off-world mining, manufacturing, food production, colonization, expansion of religions, and growth of designer and previously extinct species

Sophia: (*watching, slowly*) And that (*indicating Sōhō's illustrations*) *could* relieve on-world pressures.

Lovett: That's one way to avoid being convicted of crimes against nature by the International Criminal Court, but will our descendants be more impressed by our cleverness or our morality?

Jackie: (*P*)

SYNTHESIS AND INSIGHT

▪ Diverse social and technological transformations are setting conditions for a very different future, one that may be more sustainable and equitable.
▪ Living systems are highly interdependent and unpredictable and our understanding is inevitably partial.
▪ Challenge assumptions about the relationships between outcomes and diverse and divergent human values.

THE HUMAN–AI RELATIONSHIP
Monday Afternoon 4:45 p.m. GMT

Jackie: We've been peering out at the accelerating change caused by our species—the world we are creating and the one into which an artificial superintelligence, an ASI, would arrive. Hula, as VEs, we've worked to sustain and balance our inquiry, action, and reflection over the last year. How have you experienced this?

Hula: Hmm, we (*looking around the room*), like many others in the past, were called together around what has been assumed to be a technological problem, following lines of thinking like "What's the tech solution to aligning machine intelligence with human values?"; "How do we upload values?"; or, say, "How can we engineer a machine's ability to learn or adopt values?"

Probably owing to our evaluative perspective, we didn't spend much time on those questions and quickly reached consensus that tech isn't the primary threat or the challenge. Caring and understanding too little about human values is. We've focused on that gap between where we are and where we need to be in our understanding of values.

Lovett: Concerns about ASI have forced the recognition of that gap. We evidently didn't have a powerful enough incentive to care before now. Difference now is that we're having to look for answers right here (*gesturing to self*) rather than out there (*gesturing out*). Not really our strength.

Hula: True. We don't know enough to craft comprehensive values-action alignment in machines. Values of humanity should shape the future we want for ourselves or for society. But where do values originate, how do they evolve, what are they? And can we even describe relationships among values or between values, actions, outcomes, and visions of what we want to create?

Sophia: Not well enough. Physics, biology, engineering, finance . . . we've built deep expertise on countless fronts, enthralled with creations of our cleverness, which has been a good distraction from devoting the same level—it should be much more—of investigative energy to values, the primordial and contemporary thrust behind all human exploration, invention, and mastery.

Lovett: With that misdirected fascination, we applied physical sciences to human and natural systems and, apparently comfortable with the notion of a Newtonian social science, engineered a seriously flawed existence for ourselves.

Gretchen, 69	Hula, 32	Jackie, 9	Lovett, 55	Philip, 80	Sōhō, 48	Sophia, 44	Zeke, 66
Northern European	Osage American Indian	South African Cuban	African American	British descent	Japanese American	Family exiled from Iran	Mexican American
Impact Ecologist	Technology Entrepreneur	Famous Artificially Enhanced	Neuroscientist Attorney	Industrialist Politician Philanthropist	Impact Artist	Educator	General Development Strategist

Jackie: (*P*)

SYNTHESIS AND INSIGHT

- Attend to the gap between what we understand about human values and what we could understand.
- ASI is perceived as an unprecedented and existential threat that is forcing all of humanity to become more aware of the gap.
- Building knowledge and understanding of human values is first a human challenge, not a technological one.
- Human intellect is advancing quickly but, partly, in destructive and misguided directions.

AI ABILITY
Tuesday Morning 9:40 a.m. GMT

Sophia: AIs are tools, facilitators that VEs need and even depend on, but some things—where we govern, inquire, make meaning and judgments in the context of human values—should, must, remain primarily human functions.

Hula: Those boundaries become more fuzzy each day. Narrow AIs have been exploding in numbers and applications for a few decades now. The total quantity of existing data is still growing exponentially. Machines are in a perpetual state of analysis and synthesis to produce the articles we read, personalize our medicine, transform the legal and healthcare systems, drive us around, design our clothes, run financial markets, manage businesses and employees, build cities, and make this perfect espresso. They are replacing soldiers on the battlefield, doctors in the emergency room, artists in the studio, and organs in our body.

Sophia: All the types of machine intelligence—whether for language, prediction, evidence, or recommendations—are examples of narrow AI. General AI, one that's more like a human, able to flexibly synthesize cognitive processes and new knowledge to make values-oriented decisions . . . basically human level intelligence . . . that's still somewhere beyond the horizon.

Hula: Most think a superintelligent AI will arrive in somewhere between five years and never.

Jackie: (*P*)

SYNTHESIS AND INSIGHT

- Machine intelligence is ubiquitous and continues to rapidly extend human ability.
- The boundaries that distinguish the responsibility and authority of both humans and machines will evolve quickly and must be constantly questioned.
- Timelines and characteristics of the human-nature-technology co-evolution are uncertain.

MEASURING THE IMPACT OF THE INVISIBLES
Tuesday Morning 10:07 a.m. GMT

Hula: Point taken. Yes, recent breakthroughs in applied nanotechnologies, mechanical and biological, and secure distributed peer to peer networks, will bring the entire lifecycle of quantum supercomputing to the world, and at room temperature.

Sophia: (*head bowed*) Our affair with our cleverness has been passionate and enduring and we can remember a lot of good that's come from it. But now, our egos are obese, lusting after "the answer," and precision is distracting us from an examination of the question. We've been so slow to turn away from our busyness (*lifting head*) we were blind to the change, the decay, surrounding us.

(*Shaking it off*) But we are beginning to let go, let go, and look around.

(*Jackie looks toward Sōhō and she stands and begins illustrating scenes that come alive.*)

Sōhō: I work with the financial industry. Some of those who once took, made, and destroyed now work to protect, conserve, and save. The competition to prove who can do the most good is fierce. Trillions in investment. Claims are impressive.

Gretchen, 69	Hula, 32	Jackie, 9	Lovett, 55	Philip, 80	Sōhō, 48	Sophia, 44	Zeke, 66
Northern European	Osage American Indian	South African Cuban	African American	British descent	Japanese American	Family exiled from Iran	Mexican American
Impact Ecologist	Technology Entrepreneur	Famous Artificially Enhanced	Neuroscientist Attorney	Industrialist Politician Philanthropist	Impact Artist	Educator	General Development Strategist

I: *Past growth and collapse of equity, commodity, bond, and housing markets. National financial crises, ballooning debt with GDP, and other traditional measures indicating progress. Increasing sustainability impact investment aimed at improving human health; soil, water, and air quality; climate resilience and adaptation; safety and security; economic well-being. Audacious claims of the success and triumph of impact investments seen on TV, magazine covers, international awards.*

Sophia: Proof of actual positive impact has been less impressive, and there are plenty of laggards who even today have not yet joined that competition.

Sōhō: (*illustrating while she speaks*) Nevertheless the impact investment industry has grown quickly and its traditions immediately demanded proof of impact, high-quality measurement, and evidence to substantiate claims. First measurement attempts were enthusiastic.

I: *A college chemistry class following a simple stepwise, highly-controlled process. A second grade art class, high energy, students running around, no discernable process or significant products, class ends. Kids, teacher and parents are happy to have made it through the day—no one is better off.*

Gretchen: (*reflecting on the illustrations*) The good intentions of many were and are genuine. But reductionism alone isn't going to produce the knowledge we need when life and living is mostly the fuzziness, the in-betweenness. We can't keep ignoring it.

Sōhō: It was often hard to know if investment was more helpful than harmful. In the confusion, most defaulted to traditional measures of progress that revealed little about well-being. On a whim I asked if I could surround a few investments, from conceptualization to final assessment, with artists.

I: *Networks of thousands of painters, musicians, poets, sculptors converging on hundreds of investments, creating art describing social and environmental systems, baselines, and changes in relation to investments.*

Sophia: Millions of our students participate. As viewers, their perceptions of and interactions with processes, products, and outcomes—all completely open access—they are sources of information for impact measurement and improvement. It's been fascinating to see, through the artists and the viewers alike, how and which interacting, interdependent values underpin enormously diverse descriptions and expectations for "sustainable" and "equitable" outcomes. This is a demonstration of how the arts will once again become a preeminent force for transformation.

Zeke: In our work, we've also made many attempts to combine networked creativity and evaluative thinking to better account for multiple truths and facilitate a natural evolution toward fit-for-purpose investment.

Philip: I support the arts and always have and this is certainly creating lots of jobs for artists and improving public appreciation for the arts and artists. But, where's the proof that an arts-based approach to measurement provides better evidence of impact than anything else?

Sophia: That question represents a systemic problem. It is the invisibles, our values, the inherent complexity of life and the world about which we lack information and understanding. Our ignorance of these things and their significance relative to stuff that has price tags, limits our interest in meaningful assessment of the invisibles and so the arts and humanities, which are the disciplines and professions best equipped to describe them, are overlooked and marginalized.

Jackie: (*P*)

SYNTHESIS AND INSIGHT

- Technological advances disconnected from the invisibles will feed destructive hubris and distract from the most cherished and necessary facets of our humanness.
- Awakening to the need for required transformations is slow, obstructed by pervasive worldviews that are mismatched to our reality.
- There are many approaches to assessment and most have not yet been tried.
- The arts are a lifting force for humanity, helping to describe and understand life, living, and identity.

Gretchen, 69	Hula, 32	Jackie, 9	Lovett, 55	Philip, 80	Sōhō, 48	Sophia, 44	Zeke, 66
Northern European	Osage American Indian	South African Cuban	African American	British descent	Japanese American	Family exiled from Iran	Mexican American
Impact Ecologist	Technology Entrepreneur	Famous Artificially Enhanced	Neuroscientist Attorney	Industrialist Politician Philanthropist	Impact Artist	Educator	General Development Strategist

EQUITY: CHOOSING A REALITY AND A DREAM
Tuesday Morning 11:28 a.m. GMT

Sophia: Not symmetrical, no. So not equal. But in a given context with the right forces in play, asymmetrical parts may be in dynamic equilibrium, balanced.

Jackie: Our journey toward that balance is the pursuit of equity, the process we've been talking about. Our working definition this year, so far, has been: Equity is the process of aligning a belief in equality with actions that lead to equitable outcomes. To guide our conversations we often ask: "Is there access and opportunity for people to participate fully in society while maintaining and nurturing their own identity?" So how are VEs facilitating greater equity?

Lovett: Evaluatives are shining a light on the view that we, each of us, sees the world not as it is, but as we are. For one, Jackie, going back to that definition of equity, the VE perspective can, and has I believe, enriched our understanding of each other's views of "equality," whether the views be utilitarian, intrinsic, and/or relational.

Gretchen: And show us that a better understanding of an infinitely complex universe of relational values, like equity, is limited only by the questions we are compelled to ask about ourselves.

Sōhō: It is a choice to search out, find, and understand inequality. A choice to then facilitate increased equity. And a choice to judge unequal conditions as equitable. The Evaluative has taken on the responsibility for facilitating the inquiry, judgments, and actions necessary to make these choices.

Lovett: Health offers some clear opportunities. Turns out the dentists, doing their best to keep us healthy, always had it right. The beginnings of a shift from "sick" care systems—designed to heal—toward "health" care systems—designed to maintain and generate wellness and avoid illness—is monumental in adjusting incentives for research and our overall views of mental and physical well-being. Understanding our health as a high-dimension and dynamic space versus a sick–well dualism brings us a lot closer to an equitable world.

Sophia: Even so, the choice and tradition to draw bright lines between disorder and order, ability and disability, has set up more than our fair share of obstacles between where we are today and more equitable care tomorrow. We're still recovering from the artifacts of race-based medicine that reduced efficacy of treatments for hundreds of years. Though we've known of the differences right down to the molecular level for a long time, modern medical research discounted gender and totally ignored transgender. The Evaluative has been helpful and will be crucial in facilitating progress toward more equitable health care.

Zeke: We're comfortable enough meeting the quality and worth standards of the provider, but the patient is still an afterthought. Most will find it hard to understand how these things are possible today, myself included. But leaving assumptions about the significance of differences unquestioned is a tradition all its own that Evaluatives need to fiercely challenge.

Sophia: "If we give this to them, then they will have what they need" is one of those framing assumptions that perennially reseeds our shared histories and divergent memories of what was oppression and what was opportunity.

Zeke: What about better ways to identify these types of assumptions that cause inequity and other imbalances? To be clear, my question here is not to be confused with equality of human rights as a prima facie condition. No, no, my question is as we have more values-action-outcome information and it becomes more accessible and useful, at what point can we, or even should we, use that empirical evidence to make judgments about the merit, worth and significance of a person and their actions in terms of, for instance, that person's values and the values surrounding them?

Lovett: Would it depend on the specificity of what's being judged and who's doing the judging? As you all are well aware by now, I wonder at the meaning of equality in our description of equity. I still can't help but think it's a problematic starting point.

Hula: I know that you are referring primarily to genetic and biological or neurological developmental diversity. You've often said, "we are not born as a blank slate." I've come to agree with you but my problem with this starting point is different. . . . Is *saying* that all are equal, granted equal rights, whether in law or in principle—is that rhetoric, amidst everything that obviously contradicts and prevents its reality, is that the most helpful framing?

Gretchen, 69	Hula, 32	Jackie, 9	Lovett, 55	Philip, 80	Sōhō, 48	Sophia, 44	Zeke, 66
Northern European	Osage American Indian	South African Cuban	African American	British descent	Japanese American	Family exiled from Iran	Mexican American
Impact Ecologist	Technology Entrepreneur	Famous Artificially Enhanced	Neuroscientist Attorney	Industrialist Politician Philanthropist	Impact Artist	Educator	General Development Strategist

Sophia: How could it not be?

Hula: In my experience, the more people view their situation in society as equitable, the more likely it is that they are the ones with the power. And the more likely they perceive too few relevant perspectives and assume that those should converge around their own. Even worse, that false sense of understanding the problem nurtured by the reassurance in one's rightness that follows making a decision and taking action, even if the action is misguided, engenders complacency in the people whose transformation is most critical to our ability to realize a future we want. Meanwhile suffering continues and the message that things are getting better, delivered by those with the power to do such things, is known to be absurd by those with the least power to prove it or change it. A revisiting of the assumptions underpinning our framing, tactics, and strategies is in order. Evaluatives will be useful here.

Gretchen: These interactions are as confusing and contorted as any conversation can be.

Lovett: Gretchen, we've worked through this a few times together haven't we?

Gretchen: Right. My team is in a perpetual cycle of discovering and addressing inequities. It was the source of significant inefficiency in our work. We needed ways to better systematize the process, the conversation.

Lovett: That's it. The peaceful, healthful reorganization, reconceptualization, and evolution of values that must underpin all equity processes requires conversation. It's not the most efficient way to identify inequity but it is mandatory for navigating it.

Gretchen: But these conversations are so fragile and break down so fast. This is something we've (*gesturing to Lovett*) been working on. Thinking we should know better and that we were mature enough to handle it, we'd repeatedly trap ourselves somewhere in the middle of the debate, wanting our voices to be heard, allowing tension to build up.

Lovett: While trapped, we knew the stress was caused by the difference between our perception of what is and our perception of what should be.

Gretchen: But where to go from there? Lovett, let's try to recreate the line of inquiry we used in one of those early attempts to sidestep the trap. You first.

Lovett: (*nodding, smiling*) Okay, I hope I said it more politely but it probably went something like this (*leaning forward, speaking* *directly to Gretchen*): "Gretchen, you do not understand this situation or the implications of your actions."

Gretchen: "What do you think I don't understand?"

Lovett: (*sitting back*) I asked myself, "What do I think, specifically, that she doesn't know or understand about this?" and then asked, "What do you know about it?"

Gretchen: "What do you know about it?"

Lovett: "Why do you think you do understand?"

Gretchen: "Why do you think I don't?"

Lovett: And as we respond to each other's inquiry, I start thinking, "To what degree do I believe I know more about this than I actually do?"

Gretchen: And I, "To what degree am I filtering for evidence that supports my view?"

Lovett: That back and forth could go on forever. The final question, that we started asking at the beginning, is when to stop? Maybe never.

Gretchen: Maybe never, but we must assess progress, the evolution of the conversation. When should we be satisfied that we have adequately dealt with one issue so we can move to the next? To both search out better questions and keep making progress while we do, we are building technologies that leverage proven tools and constructs to facilitate these sorts of conversations at pace and scale.

Jackie: (*P*)

SYNTHESIS AND INSIGHT

- Equity is a process of seeking balance, fairness, justice; characteristics of equity are dependent upon context.
- Equity is a value that emerges from the relationships at the nexus of values, actions, outcomes, and visions in a given situation.
- Challenge superficial either/or dualisms in favor of ways that are a better match for a complex living world.
- Design and facilitate processes of creativity, action, learning, and reflection that actively pursue and lift up equity and sustainability.

Gretchen, 69	Hula, 32	Jackie, 9	Lovett, 55	Philip, 80	Sōhō, 48	Sophia, 44	Zeke, 66
Northern European	Osage American Indian	South African Cuban	African American	British descent	Japanese American	Family exiled from Iran	Mexican American
Impact Ecologist	Technology Entrepreneur	Famous Artificially Enhanced	Neuroscientist Attorney	Industrialist Politician Philanthropist	Impact Artist	Educator	General Development Strategist

DEMOCRACY, CAPITALISM, AND VALUES
Tuesday Afternoon 1:11 p.m. GMT

Lovett: If we are going to start a conversation about the relationship between the common and private good, or gain, why
not put up some guardrails? For instance, what is the goal of
democracy?

Philip: To attend to and honor the well-being of each person as a
distinct and significant part of humanity.

(Heads nod as good enough to continue.)

Lovett: Okay. How about capitalism?

Sophia: Accumulation of wealth.

Jackie: Can the two—capitalism and democracy—healthfully
co-exist?

Sophia: One person one vote versus one dollar one vote? I'd say a
world littered with broken and warped democracies is answer
enough.

Zeke: Quizás. The ways both are practiced change, evolve, over time
and place, with context. As needs of a people change, so does
the shape of their governance. Co-exist? As they are? No. Co-
evolve to something more healthy? Maybe.

Philip: And if I may...going back to the goals of each. Capitalism
has characteristics, yes, but goals? I don't think so. Capital is
like the universe, it hasn't purpose until we give it one. And so
purposes of capital are dependent on each of the distinct and
significant persons within a given democracy. Capital exerts
that warping and destructive force upon democracies because
it can be used to create and anchor conversations and notions
of well-being, a cornerstone of democracy, that prioritize the
accumulation of more capital. And so, entanglement and
conflict are activated.

Zeke: First, I believe the universe does have intrinsic purpose.
Second, capitalism may undermine democracy, but I'm also
convinced that democracy is not the solution to every problem. Third, those notions about well-being are not necessarily
wrong, but they do indicate the need for more transparency
around who and what is influencing values, and how.

Philip: More information is undoubtedly the right direction. But
without the ability to use it to facilitate that more healthful
co-evolution? Well, in this, talented Evaluatives will be instrumental. But I wonder if we haven't already passed the point
of no return. As a CEO and as a politician, I see democracies
enabling the existence of free'ish markets and creation of the

public sector, which is, by the way, also the first blamed for market inefficiencies and typically the first held responsible for repairing them.

Sophia: And so here we are, waking from the insanity of encouraging corporations to dominate culture and the global economy and regaining consciousness just as we take our last steps toward the edge of collapse.

Gretchen: Mismatches in purpose, power, and incentives between democracy and capitalism make meaningful "reparations" an unlikely outcome. Energy, agriculture, fisheries, healthcare, finance—the world's imbalanced by perverse incentives underpinning the sectors the world depends on. Under these conditions, suffering—poverty, illness, extinction, conflict— flourishes and becomes codified in structures difficult to disrupt. Every day the United States becomes less a democracy and more an oligarchy, a plutocracy.

Philip: . . . And will be so, as long as money is an effective tool to manipulate values that advance the well-being of the few and the deprivation of the many.

Gretchen: This is key. An economic system that encourages manipulations of values favoring a small cohort within the whole undermines the potential efficacy of a democratic governance system . . . so, a mutually beneficial co-evolution of capitalism and democracy? Doubtful, one will likely dominate the other.

Hula: Injustice that reduces social well-being opens the door wide for non-democratic governance—the military, groups of experts, self-interested individuals—to take over, perpetuate inequity, and further diminish social well-being.

Philip: Look, capitalism is just an approach, not inherently good or bad. I've come to think of it as the best of bad options and that it is what we make of it. Its faults are our faults. It all depends on who the "we" is. That we know less about that than we need to is the problem at hand.

Lovett: I'm afraid the hook's not so easy to jump. It's got a few barbs. Capitalism, the good and the bad, is not something external to us. It is in us. Americans accumulate. That's what we do. Knowledge, friends, stuff, square feet, land, jokes, degrees,

Gretchen, 69	Hula, 32	Jackie, 9	Lovett, 55	Philip, 80	Sōhō, 48	Sophia, 44	Zeke, 66
Northern European	Osage American Indian	South African Cuban	African American	British descent	Japanese American	Family exiled from Iran	Mexican American
Impact Ecologist	Technology Entrepreneur	Famous Artificially Enhanced	Neuroscientist Attorney	Industrialist Politician Philanthropist	Impact Artist	Educator	General Development Strategist

frequent flyer miles, and cash. It's an integral part of us, our culture, our values. Then this funny thing happens. Once we believe ourselves to be "comfortable," we believe we have made something of ourselves. And the things we've accumulated? We then feel good about giving them away.

Hula: Bill and Melinda Gates and the Walton family alleviated the suffering of hundreds of millions by living that life.

Lovett: What I'm saying is "we" have set our world up in a certain way. And it's that way that needs attention. Because that way, it is of us. It becomes us. It changes us and so changes the world. And by and by, if from birth we lived generously rather than trying to die that way, the problems that cause most of humanity's suffering might never have existed at all.

Jackie: (*P*)

SYNTHESIS AND INSIGHT

- Facilitate understanding of the relationships among dominant structures influencing, creating, and obstructing relevant values.
- Power may be used to change values and/or to change how and the degree to which values are honored.
- Facilitate the transparency, accessibility, and use of information about values.
- Point evaluative inquiry at beliefs about who or what is responsible for actions and outcomes related to the challenge at hand.

COMPETE TO COOPERATE
Tuesday Afternoon 2:18 p.m. GMT

Gretchen: The people—"we"—have created the public sector through votes, taxes, donations, and advocacy for the public good. The charge, in theory, is to embody and honor the values of the public that created this public sector. But markets are picking up more and stronger signals that traditional approaches to delivering public goods and services are inefficient and ineffective.

Zeke: These are the opportunities our group looks for. The gap has been widening between what is and what is possible. If those working for the public good don't fill the gap and enough value is being left on the table, others will snatch up the opportunities. They'll monetize and quickly, absolutely privatize what have traditionally been equity-enabling, non-rivalrous, non-excludable goods and services by bringing the reality of what is and the possibility of what could be closer together. Because most governments are too rigid and linear in structure and thinking to keep pace with accelerating change, almost all public goods are at risk.

Philip: And then it's about the strategy used to close the gap. By either changing the "what is"—adjusting, for instance, the current rules and values in your favor—or working toward the "what could be"—taking on the responsibility to improve the delivery of the public good.

Gretchen: We see the private sector closing the gap and taking over responsibility for public goods like transportation, education, diplomacy, restoration, and delivery of ecological services . . . everywhere.

Zeke: Transformative advances are coming out of that transition. Is that a problem?

Sophia: Maybe not now but it will be. Your group is beholden to ecological and social bottom lines but that's still a rarity. The problem isn't improvement, it's the transfer of ownership, authority, and responsibility. Look, combine convincing evidence of public sector waste with inevitable future economic and ecological crises, the realization that the private sector has no mandate to perform for the public good and, well, right there's the wellspring of human rights violations and, then, justified social rebellion.

Gretchen: Competition—for funding, expertise, reputation, and to own and solve the problem—is an assumed condition of growth and integral in implicit theories of change of any given system targeted for transformation.

Sōhō: It permeates our existence and shapes and instructs our identity from birth.

Gretchen: The merit, significance, and worth of the notion of competition in the context of a world advocating for liberalism and capitalism needs to be challenged, especially in systems where full accounting and transparency of social and ecological outcomes are rarely accurate, possible, or attributable to cause or source.

Gretchen, 69	Hula, 32	Jackie, 9	Lovett, 55	Philip, 80	Sōhō, 48	Sophia, 44	Zeke, 66
Northern European	Osage American Indian	South African Cuban	African American	British descent	Japanese American	Family exiled from Iran	Mexican American
Impact Ecologist	Technology Entrepreneur	Famous Artificially Enhanced	Neuroscientist Attorney	Industrialist Politician Philanthropist	Impact Artist	Educator	General Development Strategist

Philip: I am in complete agreement. Rather than competition around "who can do how much good for whom the fastest," which is at best reducing our values to some falsely commendable set decided by a few, we need to incentivize something different: competition to cooperate as one civilization with an absolute monopoly on realizing the well-being of, not shareholders or a nation, but all life.

Hula: I have a lot of questions about that. But I can see your point in some settings, like education, where Sophia and her colleagues have set multi-sided platforms and distributed secure networks to the task. But, again, we have systems laden with invisibles and little capacity to assess their importance.

Gretchen: And without that, it is not possible to accurately measure and diagnose the health of the whole.

Lovett: In our world, what matters is what's measured and the things necessary to do the measuring. As far as the things we give our attention to, we've abandoned arts, humanities, culture, language, history, and a systems view of life about a hundred years ago. These are the tools necessary to describe and understand humanity, life, and living. Without them, we'll forget and lose our human identity before we even knew what it was.

Gretchen: (*nodding*) Dropping parts of the whole in ignorance—like allowing species or discipines to go extinct because they don't seem that important and short term requirements obscure long term value—decreases our resilience and ability to adapt. Proceed with caution.

Zeke: A more liberal use of the precautionary principle might be valid in this instance. But it's been abused often enough too. What we need more of at a time when we are more ignorant than ever? The courage to move into uncertainty with wise actions that create the learning we need.

Jackie: (*P*)

SYNTHESIS AND INSIGHT

- The public sector is intended to serve the values of society or some segment therein.
- Competition is a dominant and unquestioned mindset and its force can be generative and constructive or wasteful and destructive.
- Any assessment involving humans and nature is replete with unknowns, always partial.
- The arts, humanities, and other disciplines for description and understanding are a good fit for grappling with living, entangled systems.

THE NUANCE OF IDENTITY
Tuesday Afternoon 4:52 p.m. GMT

Jackie: Facilitating humanity's and each individual's ability to craft and realize identity? Identity that will lead to a more sustainable and equitable future? Whether that's possible will depend on how much we, some of us especially, are willing to let go.

Sōhō: (*standing, illustrating living scenes in the center of the room*) It is our nature to create and take sides, split and honor those allegiances, gather up and hold on to our power.

I: *U.S. stereotypes of Republican–Democrat, American–immigrant, success–failure, White–Black–Brown, young–old, rich–poor, blue–white–pink collar, male–female*

Sophia: (*referring to the scenes*) Choosing from these options is easier than starting from scratch.

Zeke: Competing to be a new choice or removing traditional ones is difficult.

Philip: (*sarcastic and genuine*) Allowing people to choose their own, original, unique identity? Who benefits from that?

Sōhō: The choice may be made easier but the dualisms we create are not suited to the nuance of reality. They breed conflict and confusion.

I: *Science vs religion, environment vs economy, native vs foreign, life vs choice*

Zeke: Our food, the stuff that makes us and that sets the course of our lives, was transformed to maximize profits for private gain. No one asked our permission to use synthetics, GMOs, petrochemicals, or to strip the nutrition from our soils and feed us chemicals and disease.

Lovett: Hardly anyone noticed it was happening until it was already done.

Zeke: It's true. And so a false baseline was set and we are unable to get back to where we began.

Lovett: It's happening all over again today but on many fronts and it's more targeted and intentional. Human health and identity is still what's at stake, but instead of food and transforming our bodies, which remains a crisis and a threat to our future, the new threat is the race to acquire cognitive territory. In the last

Gretchen, 69	Hula, 32	Jackie, 9	Lovett, 55	Philip, 80	Sōhō, 48	Sophia, 44	Zeke, 66
Northern European	Osage American Indian	South African Cuban	African American	British descent	Japanese American	Family exiled from Iran	Mexican American
Impact Ecologist	Technology Entrepreneur	Famous Artificially Enhanced	Neuroscientist Attorney	Industrialist Politician Philanthropist	Impact Artist	Educator	General Development Strategist

15 years, neuroscience coupled with ever more sophisticated machine intelligences have changed a game few knew they were playing.

Hula: Absolutely. Our attentions were focused on concerns about political regimes, governments, and national security. All the while a few tech companies were opening connections to billions of people and, without our consent, rewiring and using our brains as labor for their ends.

Gretchen: Like with our food systems, not enough of us knew the transformation was happening. Effects on humans, beyond just a few years, were totally unknown so the social energy to keep it in check was inadequate. With no serious repercussions in sight, all of the financial incentives fell on the side of "How do we manipulate the brain faster?"

Hula: The maturing cryptocosm now provides the foundation to secure many facets of our identity. Even so, while we were requiring permissions to access personal information and contact lists, we needed to be requiring permission to access and change the person.

Lovett: We have been giving away our right to our own lives and person. There is no higher kind of ownership.

Hula: Entire societies perceived their agency increasing even while it was being taken by black box marketing, political campaigns, and financial markets.

Lovett: The social contract is being amended. The act of an individual or business accessing and using information does not, ipso facto, grant permission to another party to access and change that individual's brain. This is today's most pressing privacy and security issue.

Hula: The effectiveness of passive and active cognitive rewiring is accelerating. The battleground is the human brain. The kingdom to be won? Our mind. Thought. Beliefs. Our values. This is an unprecedented existential threat to free thought, free action, and free exchange of ideas . . . the threat is the genesis and motivating force of the Hidden Mind movement.

Sophia: It's pushing millions to the Universal Party's adaptive and pluralist platform that ignores political boundaries created by governments that no longer protect them, while validating and advocating for all members' values. The consent of the ancestors does not bind the descendants.

Philip: An alternative to the traditions of the parochial prescriptive platform is long overdue. But these folks? A little more harm than good, eh?

Gretchen: Disruption and upheaval? Usually necessary to find a new beginning.

Jackie: (*P*)

SYNTHESIS AND INSIGHT

- Prioritize values related to self awareness and wisdom as a path to increased transparency and understanding of values.
- Those with power have the option to design and present choices of identity that confirm and edify their values.
- Be skeptical of actions that reduce and manipulate nature and ignore evolutionary evidence in favor of meeting short-term human measures of success.
- As change accelerates on many fronts, tipping points or phase shifts become more common and remain unpredictable.
- Offloading human social relationships to technology undermines human commitment and capacity for respectful and compassionate relationships.

ACCELERATING EVOLUTION:
STRESS, TOLERANCE, AND WELL-BEING
Wednesday Morning 11:01 a.m. GMT

Gretchen: Human augmentation is evolving at a speed that is difficult to . . . well, the potential for rapid divarication of our species increases each day. But (*pause*), the issue has been so politicized, healthy discussion is impossible.

(A few look toward Jackie, shifting in chairs.)

Jackie: The potential for the divergent evolution of our species certainly makes this conversation both natural and necessary (*tension eases*). When I was four, Shaquita was my best friend. We liked to play in the grass in the shade of a sprawling oak tree. My mom watched from our porch swing. One day I looked up and saw something unfamiliar in my Mom's face. "You and Shaquita have fun don't you?" she asked that evening. I asked if Shaquita could stay for dinner next time. "We'll see," she said. A few months later we moved to New

Gretchen, 69	Hula, 32	Jackie, 9	Lovett, 55	Philip, 80	Sōhō, 48	Sophia, 44	Zeke, 66
Northern European	Osage American Indian	South African Cuban	African American	British descent	Japanese American	Family exiled from Iran	Mexican American
Impact Ecologist	Technology Entrepreneur	Famous Artificially Enhanced	Neuroscientist Attorney	Industrialist Politician Philanthropist	Impact Artist	Educator	General Development Strategist

York so that I could attend a school for "designer" kids. Before I was born, doctors detected and corrected severe mental and physical disabilities with significant mechanical and biological enhancement. My parents, always very poor, had already lost two children. I was offered to them, they accepted, and I am grateful. And they're over the moon.

(all smile, pause)

Zeke: Thank you, Jackie. Perhaps this is just where we need to be right now, talking about where our values come from, what they are, and what we do and create because of them.

I was born in Monterrey, Mexico. When I was little, my family followed the maquiladora economy across the border to McAllen, Texas where many Mexican immigrants worked in textile and machining factories. We stayed poor.

I ended up a four-star general and now I direct a consortium of firms that has the sole purpose of improving humanity's well-being. We prioritize the rights of nature and humans above corporations. We see no need for more billionaires on Earth and we will not be them or create them. We partner with mature and startup development cooperatives aligned with our values to transform cities, regions, and nations that are severely disabled by conflict, natural disaster, disease, poverty, corruption, and compromised water and food systems.

Sophia: Some say your publicized good works are a veil that shrouds your true intentions—delivering massive returns to a few investors.

Zeke: Yes. And thankfully our investors care for all sorts of returns. We live in the same world as everyone else. We aren't trying to create a new one in a day. We are building many small partial worlds. Ones that are connected, healthy, resilient, anti-fragile, and designed to affect the trajectories and conditions of the whole.

Philip: Seeing what you are doing gives us all an idea of what a sustainable and equitable future might actually look like.

Zeke: For some, maybe. Everywhere sustainability and equity look different. Expectations and perceptions vary enormously. And it all depends upon how people feel about what they see shaping up around them. The more we know about that, the more we know about requirements for sustainable and equitable processes and outcomes. Once we start a project, we are always explicitly designing the work to reveal, first, how actions and subsequent outcomes are perceived in terms of the values relevant to the initiative, and second, the effect of those actions and outcomes on the evolution of those values.

Lovett: Zeke, if you don't mind my pointing it out, you are, in many ways, accelerating evolution. I have to wonder, is what you are doing out of bounds?

Zeke: (*to Philip and Lovett*) Possibly. We perceive boundaries through what we call "humanity mapping." Like any other kind of mapping perhaps but here, rather than geography or politics, human values are the organizing force. And to your point, yes, naturally, oppressed peoples want an advantage—education, health, security, development. Biological and mechanical enhancements can transform the oppressed into the oppressors easily enough. And in that, we have the power to inadvertently create new intransigent inequities.

Sōhō: Whatever you do, take action or wait and see, the world is watching you.

Zeke: Yes ma'am.

Philip: Standing by won't help anyone.

Zeke: No sir.

(pause)

Gretchen: Everyone is looking to enhancement for the quick fix. Some have access, some don't. The same results could usually be achieved through diet, diplomacy, cooperation, policy reform, or better management and leadership.

Sōhō: (*seated, begins illustrating*) The bifurcation—natural versus enhanced—will continue to magnify inequities in every way imaginable.

I: *Widening disparities in human intelligence, physique, health, exposure to impacts of climate change, environmental quality, worker rights. Increasing breaks between and within cultures, religions, nations, families. Unequal access to and benefits from education, work, recreation.*

Hula: (*watching Sōhō illustrate*) These leaps in performance result in more haves and more have nots ... the next leaps will be higher, faster, and farther.

Lovett: Can we ... no, should we design ourselves for these accelerating evolutions?

Hula: Still an open question.

Gretchen, 69	Hula, 32	Jackie, 9	Lovett, 55	Philip, 80	Sōhō, 48	Sophia, 44	Zeke, 66
Northern European	Osage American Indian	South African Cuban	African American	British descent	Japanese American	Family exiled from Iran	Mexican American
Impact Ecologist	Technology Entrepreneur	Famous Artificially Enhanced	Neuroscientist Attorney	Industrialist Politician Philanthropist	Impact Artist	Educator	General Development Strategist

Philip: My grandchildren are "naturals," learning to know themselves, others, the value of autonomy, and how to create themselves to be fit for their lives' purposes. But in the blink of an eye, they will be labeled "disabled." Just because they have chosen to grow and develop unengineered. Obviously there are circumstances that must be navigated (*directly and compassionately acknowledging Jackie*), but we must reign in this so-called improvement!

Hula: Today we are enhancing our abilities with machines and other technologies at unprecedented scale and speed. But this has always been so.

Gretchen: Humans learned to hunt, cook, defend, take, build, all in the name of improvement. It's contagious. We value our lives and longevity. A child born today is likely to live well into her 100s. We've designed all of it to improve something or remove some impediment. Medicine, food, governments, business, mobility, education, security, everything.

Philip: If nothing on Earth is untouched by humans, is everything in the Anthropocene, by definition, artificial?

Gretchen: Certainly not natural.

Sophia: So, something natural that is changed by humans becomes artificial. At what point? It is our values that drive us to change what is natural, our intent to make "what is" something better? Improvement-related values are what's led to the separation of humans from nature.

Gretchen: Maximization is an improvement-related value held high by many. It seems to mandate that we create technologies to maximize for profit, speed, power, size, access, intelligence, beauty, even the longevity and influence of our species in the universe. Nature improves too, but only to the point of doing whatever it is just well enough.

Lovett: That human tendency toward maximization has been a, if not the, cause of the stress and trauma to life and Earth. But our brains, bodies, and technologies, they are all adapting to the trauma, sustaining us and keeping us and everything alive longer. Look, we can clearly create a less healthy world and increase our tolerance for it. Perhaps there is no limit to our ability to do this. The question is: Is that the change we want to make?

Jackie: (*P*)

SYNTHESIS AND INSIGHT

- To increase transparency and understanding of values, spend lots of time in conversation about life and living.
- Revealing intersectionalities may be a discrete event but more often a process of searching out and observing co-evolutions and interdependencies.
- Sources, perceptions, and experiences of inequity are changing and expanding quickly; approaches to addressing inequity will need to match this pace of change.
- Values evolve and the change may be influenced by forces that are internal and external, passive and active, anticipated and not.

INTRODUCING VE SECTOR VISIONING
Wednesday Afternoon 12:00 p.m. GMT

Jackie: Alexander the Great was busy conquering the world, when he saw, on the banks of a river, a yogi, looking down at the dirt. "What are you doing?" asked Alexander. "Experiencing nothingness," answered the yogi. "What are you doing?" "Conquering the world," said Alexander. Both laughed at the other as a fool. "Conquering the world is pointless," thought the yogi. "What a waste of a life, to sit around and do nothing," thought Alexander.[1]

As required by our Congressional Representatives, it is our responsibility to lead informative and meaningful conversations at the Global Forum. As we know through her support of our work this last year, Zindzi, through the collaborative for which she serves as librarian, has spent the last decade creating spaces for VEs to come together in the search, discovery, and exploration of integrated creativity, inquiry, action, and learning. The documentation from those "Praxis Quests" has connected us with many VEs and powerful examples of how they work. She and I have pulled and curated another collection of Praxis Quest materials that will help us

Gretchen, 69	Hula, 32	Jackie, 9	Lovett, 55	Philip, 80	Sōhō, 48	Sophia, 44	Zeke, 66
Northern European	Osage American Indian	South African Cuban	African American	British descent	Japanese American	Family exiled from Iran	Mexican American
Impact Ecologist	Technology Entrepreneur	Famous Artificially Enhanced	Neuroscientist Attorney	Industrialist Politician Philanthropist	Impact Artist	Educator	General Development Strategist

to discuss the work of VEs at the global forum with people and sectors that have perspectives as different as Alexander and the Yogi.

Gretchen: I've started reviewing them. The sectors are diverse, but I take it our emphasis is not on the sector but how the VE navigates it?

Zeke: I had that thought too. The forum is explicitly about assessing various futures, what we can do to navigate away from some and toward others. What Zindzi has put together are examples of VEs in exactly that position. They are facilitating the visioning of futures in a variety of conditions and showing how VEs use evaluative thinking and evaluative thinking and evaluative inquiry and co-evolve with the VE principles.

Jackie: I'm glad you can see how this collection of Praxis Quests will help us to present the perspective and work of the VE at the global forum. Now we're going to take a break from this discussion format until Friday morning and spend our time revising the collection. Oh, and to spark some memories of how you started down the VE path, I'd encourage you all to start with the conversation between Zindzi and Omar, where they are discussing the VE principles.

NOTE

1. See https://www.ted.com/talks/devdutt_pattanaik

CHAPTER 3

VISIONARY EVALUATIVE PRINCIPLES

Deepening Understanding

Beverly Parsons, Lovely Dhillon, and Matt Keene

SETTING

Listen in on a conversation between Zindzi and Omar about the concept of Visionary Evaluatives (VEs) and the six Visionary Evaluative Principles (VEPs) that guide VEs' way of moving in the world both personally and professionally. The conversation occurred in 2030. The concepts of VEs and VEPs were developed in 2019.

> Zindzi is a VE. She spent most of her career conducting evaluative inquiries for government, nonprofit organizations, and private foundations before being introduced to the concept of VEs. For over ten years now, Zindzi has served as the lead librarian of the Visionary Evaluative Praxis Library. For VEs, deep praxis is the process of integrating creative actions, evaluative inquiry, theory, and learning into one's work and life with a humble and compassionate commitment to a sustainable, equitable future.

Visionary Evaluation for a Sustainable, Equitable Future, pages 55–76
Copyright © 2020 by Information Age Publishing

VEs use various deep praxis formats. In this conversation, Zindzi is talking about a recent popular format called Praxis Quests. As librarian, Zindzi plays the complex role of archiving, organizing, and curating materials used in, and produced through, Praxis Quests. Zindzi's librarian role and mastery of complex AI tools positions her to be a major broker of learning. Toward the end of this conversation and in a subsequent conversation (see Chapter 13), Zindzi explains the format for Praxis Quests.

Omar left the evaluation field a decade ago when he started an organic farm with his partner and their children. He reconnected with Zindzi, whom he had known through their shared involvement in the American Evaluation Association (AEA).

Through his farming experience, Omar has developed a deep sense of connection with nature. Omar, a systems thinker, also is involved in the broader network of food-related businesses and community organizations, bringing his evaluation perspective and skills to the network. Now that their farm is operating fairly smoothly as an environmentally sustainable and socially responsible enterprise with a number of employees and their children are into their adulthood, Omar is considering getting involved in the evaluation field again.

Zindzi and Omar are sitting on the front porch of his house with a view of the farm with forested hillsides in the background.

> **Omar:** Welcome to our farm, Zindzi. I'm very pleased that we have reconnected. Based on what I've heard recently about VEs and the VEPs, I'm realizing that there is an orientation to evaluative inquiry that I could be using to leverage my evaluation skills and background to support equity and sustainability. I'm eager to do this in relation to the food systems of our community. And, of course, our community systems are tied to county, state, and global systems.
>
> **Zindzi:** Your focus on food systems is very important; it is at the heart of human survival. In these times of transformation in social sectors, we desperately need to understand and address the complexity of our multiple cultures, the impact humans have on nature, and the technological advances—from AI, genetic modifications, robotics, synthetic biology, social networks, and more. These are all influencing our food systems and our communities.

A VISIONARY EVALUATIVE

> **Omar:** From various sources, I have a piecemeal understanding of the idea of a VE. Could you give me your take on what a VE is

and elaborate on the set of principles that guide a VE vis-à-vis evaluation?

When I left the evaluation field a decade ago, there was an ever-growing number of evaluation approaches. However, in nearly all of those approaches there seemed to be a clear distinction between practitioners of evaluation—evaluators—and users of evaluation. I'm excited to see that the VE approach acknowledges and openly advocates for a close connection between "doers" and "users" of evaluation. I like having a term that encompasses both evaluation practitioners and users of evaluation results to emphasize their shared desire for high-quality evidence and action.

Zindzi: Yes, this shift in thinking helps VEs, whatever their roles in the process, walk side-by-side and support one another toward a desired future rather than assuming that the evaluators have the answers from their inquiries and just need to deliver those answers to the users for their action. Instead, I think of it as looking at one of those optical illusions. Remember that one where you look at it one way and you see a young woman? You look at it another way and you see an old woman? In both cases, it is the same picture. We are emphasizing one pattern one time and another the other time. One time we are creating one "whole," one pattern, one image. The next time it is a different pattern that creates a whole with the rest of the visual being the context.

Omar: That's a good reminder of how we all have different perspectives on a situation.

Zindzi: Let's step back and consider a couple points about the field of evaluation in the United States, while not forgetting that the field of evaluation spans the globe. I'll emphasize what I've seen through involvement in the American Evaluation Association, since we've both been involved in the organization, albeit over different time periods.

The field of evaluation emerged in the United States in the 1960s out of a desire to know the effect of large federal investments targeting improvements in education, labor, healthcare, and other key sectors. Today, evaluation is co-evolving with demands for changes in society and also with accelerating technological and ecological change.

The VE concept reminds us that evaluation is grounded in values and performed for the purpose of *use*, specifically, the use of evaluative findings to influence actions. As strange as it may seem given the term "eVALUation," past evaluation practices all too often insufficiently acknowledged the importance of values. As evaluators—and I include myself—we often jumped too quickly to the technicalities of generating credible evidence. But both clarity of values and technical quality are essential to a well-designed evaluative inquiry.

Part of the problem back then was that evaluation, in its efforts to be viewed as scientifically and technically credible, used the then-prevalent research paradigm that was assumed to be objective. Many evaluators and evaluation users prioritized "objectivity," assuming evaluation and science generally are and should be value-less. Today, we understand how deeply values are incorporated throughout science and inquiry whether we realize it or not. A VE's focus is on making the presence of values explicit as a means of establishing credibility of data through honesty, integrity, and transparency. Ignoring values completely, or thinking their influence is insignificant, is naïve, and in some instances disingenous. We are learning in evaluation practice to acknowledge and make those values transparent and explicit so we can better recognize and address the influence of values rather than assuming evaluators are "objective."

Omar: You've touched a nerve when you bring up the lack of attention to values in evaluation. This is at the core of why I left the field of evaluation. I just couldn't see myself getting roped into another evaluation defined by boundaries I didn't believe in, defined by people least affected by program and policy outcomes—except in relation to their political power. I was often required to check my values at the door given the strict guidelines for what could and could not be part of the evaluation methods, tools, deliverables, or methods of delivery—a terrible mismatch between the approaches to evaluation of systems and the complexity of the systems themselves.

Also I couldn't reconcile, in a profession focused on evidence for decision making, the lack of evidence at the very beginning of an evaluation to support my engagement as an evaluator with one program over another. For example, why was one literacy program in a school being evaluated when another one was not. I often thought that other programs would benefit much more from evaluation but for various reasons the evaluation resources were directed in ways that didn't work for me. Was it someone's fear of what would be learned? Was I part of creating that fear by the methods I was trained to use or choose to use? I could rarely say that the evaluations I conducted resulted in the program and people being better off than if no evaluation had been done. Often, this was because the findings weren't tied to any change in action.

The VE idea of practitioners of evaluation and users of evaluation focusing jointly on equity and sustainability gives me a new sense of possibility. My love of the evaluative inquiry process is reignited when I think about the possibilities of evaluation practitioners and users engaging in an evaluative inquiry process that goes deeply into understanding and attending to the complexity of social and ecological systems. Maybe it's all wishful thinking, but I'm ready to give it a try. Given the lack of equity and attention to environmental sustainability still too prevalent in our world today, there is too much of a mismatch with my values for me to simply focus on my own well-being. I must step up to the challenge, make a commitment to re-engage, and use my evaluation skills and experience in conjunction with others who share these values.

PRINCIPLES OF A VISIONARY EVALUATIVE

Zindzi: Being a VE involves functioning in line with a set of six principles. As you know, we call these the Visionary Evaluative Principles, the VEPs. Let's get into those. From having worked with guiding principles in your past evaluation work, I am sure you recognize that principles are not step-by-step rules.[1] They are general ways of approaching situations in our professional and personal lives. The VE has to determine how the VEPs interact with one another and how they apply to a specific situation. While you apply all the VEPs, you're looking for "fit for purpose," that is, how do the VEPs apply in the situation and for what purpose, for whose purpose?

As you know, the six VEPs that guide a VE are:

1. Commit humbly and compassionately to a sustainable, equitable future.
2. Recognize the world as composed of living, entangled systems.
3. Discover, reveal, and respect intersectionalities.
4. Facilitate the transparency and understanding of human values.
5. Learn through iterative action and inquiry.
6. Engage in deep praxis.

Omar: It would be helpful to look at each VEP individually, but, of course, keeping in mind that they are interconnected and are part of an overall, powerful approach. As I look at them, I think about how we do our planning and work on the farm. We think about the water, nutrients in the soil and air, the weather, the quality of the seeds, the different requirements of the plants, changes in the market, and more. The attention we give each of these conditions varies from one situation to another, from one year to another.

Zindzi: Indeed. The VE has the intention of using all of the VEPs but in a given situation the VEPs may not all need to be addressed in equal measure or even to the same depth. Rather, certain situations may require more attention to one VEP and less to another. For example, one evaluative inquiry may require more attention to the values that are shaping the innovation, the values of equity and sustainability, whereas another inquiry that already is clearly addressing those values and is focused on a long-term seemingly intractable situation might emphasize the VEP that addresses intersectionalities of deeply-rooted power structures and cultures.

Visionary Evaluatives consider all of the VEPs as they fit the reality of the situation at hand. Visionary Evaluatives test them. They play with them. They creatively apply and use them. They listen to the wisdom of others in the VE community and beyond. They are steadfast in their learning and in their dedication to bringing about a better world. Visionary Evaluatives know there is not one solution, no magic bullet, and no one way to address the challenges of the Anthropocene and of our humanity. And the VE also has a constant dedication to others—people, living beings, and our planet—and matches this dedication with a commitment to engaging the VEPs. Visionary Evaluatives believe this will lead not only to the world's best chances but also to their own.

Omar: One of the challenges I've found in working with principles in general is determining if some action actually fits the principle. I've found that one of the best ways is to explore what it is *not*. For example, I'd say that working within one sector, like say, transportation, without paying attention to its long term impact on the natural environment or how it affects the economic opportunities for people in certain neighborhoods would be an example of *not* following the third VEP, that is, it would *not* be discovering, revealing, and respecting intersectionalities.

Zindzi: Yes, these are the kinds of discussions we have in the Praxis Quests—more on those later. Let's look more closely at the first VEP.

Visionary Evaluative Principle 1: Commit Humbly and Compassionately to a Sustainable, Equitable Future

Zindzi: The first VEP, "Commit humbly and compassionately to a sustainable, equitable future," focuses squarely on the heart of being a VE. It's about being committed to a future where equity and environmental sustainability are prioritized in all we do and in how we see the world. I especially like the way in which we make this commitment—with humility and compassion. We all bring our past with its wisdom, foolishness, pain, joy, and more to making this commitment. We want to avoid forcing a convergence on universal definitions of equity and sustainability, knowing there are many, and that these mean different things to different people.

However, it's important to remember that equity and sustainability are not historically the foundational values of social systems in the United States, nor are they, for that matter, the values of Homo sapiens throughout civilization. The lack of true equity and sustainability values exists within key declarations such as the U.S. Constitution itself. The values that permeate the dominant culture of the United States are, in many ways, not necessarily moral, so the highly evolved future-oriented values of sustainability and equity must be truly recognized and understood as challenges to the status quo that may conflict with our predispositions.

Our nation's history, along with the histories of most nations in this world, are laden with oppression, genocide, and colonization. Our histories are also laden with disrespect and lack of caring for the lives of the plants, animals, nutrients, and all else that constitutes the ecological space in which we live and on which the future of humanity and all life forms on earth depend. Though some say that technological developments in energy production, as well as carbon capture and storage, have put us on track to hit net zero emissions by 2050, our ignorance of values and culture, along with rigid policy and governance structures, leave that goal uncertain or simply too late. Even if we have gotten our arms around the climate change challenge for the long term, we are still left to suffer through the coming decades of disease, diaspora, and conflict caused by climate change that we could have prevented nearly completely had we acted earlier. This suffering also results from pharmaceutical, plastic, and agricultural pollution; reduced function of air, water, and soil systems; species extinction and loss of genetic diversity; and systemic harm to health and well-being.

We've made important progress in the last few decades but we've still got quite a ways to go. We are getting better at seeing that the values of equity and sustainability are the flip sides of the same coin, but even with that, there are many other values on which people differ considerably.

We all struggle with finding that sweet spot of the combination of both equity and sustainability and holding both values in mind and action. In fact, historically, they have far too rarely been considered together. Now we are much more attentive to their connection such as when hazardous waste dumps are located closest to poor communities. Now we are paying attention to environmental justice. There's no perfect answer. The main thing we can do is continually, intentionally, and with as much transparency and understanding as we can generate, hold these values up for ourselves and others. Every little and every big step we take needs to be informed by these values if we are to create a positive world for people, nature, and planet. Visionary Evaluatives attend to these values not only at the beginning of an evaluative inquiry, and indeed when they wake up in the morning, but keep checking in throughout their day in their work and social interactions to maintain, humbly and compassionately, their focus on these as priority values. This is part of "fit for purpose."

Omar: This is such an important issue. All too often I have experienced the mismatch between evaluators saying that they believe in equality for all but they don't focus on what the results of their evaluation actually revealed about that program's equity-related successes and limitations. Are the results actually illuminating issues related to equity?

Zindzi: Yes. For example, a program may intend that all community members have access to an organic food kitchen. As VEs engage in evaluative inquiry with the community, they look at not only whether the efforts to reach diverse members of the community were made, but also at whether the diverse communities did in fact have access to the organic food. They may unearth, perhaps, that the pamphlet-outreach in diverse neighborhoods did provide notification of the effort but that it excluded sightless and non-English reading individuals from participation because it was not in braille nor translated into other languages.

Another important point to keep in mind in the application of the first VEP is that VEs do not just prioritize equity and sustainability in their work but also consider how those values affect how they move through their daily lives. They consider, for example, how they can increase equity as it relates to their family, workplace, children's schools, neighborhood, friendships, local government, and judiciary as well as purchasing and investment choices. As we recognize the magnitude and ubiquitous nature of the inequities in our society as VEs, we daily commit to working through the challenges to help generate equitable outcomes. We consider how our actions not only intend for equity to exist but also whether the results are such that more equitable outcomes actually *do* result. Visionary Evaluatives consider their own privilege—the advantages that they receive, often unknowingly, that derive from immutable characteristics (e.g., ethnicity, gender, able-bodiedness) and otherwise (e.g., income level, education, urban residences). They do not hold those as places for shame and regret but rather for honesty about the gifts that those characteristics and history provide them while acknowledging the challenges that exist for others from not having such privileges. And VEs move further, thinking about how to increase equity in providing access to centers of power as well as how they individually can contribute to ensuring there is the opportunity for others to participate fully as a part of that power.

Similarly, the VE is challenged by, but deeply committed to, sustainability. We're not talking here about sustainability of a program. No. Here we're talking about environmental sustainability, the sustainability of our natural environment for generations to come. I recall hearing someone boil this down to a very simple phrase: "Enough, for all, forever." That's pretty much it—as long as the "all" includes people *and* nature. And by nature we include not only species living on the planet but also the planet itself.

Omar: Yes, sustainability goes well beyond just thinking about what to recycle and how quickly to turn off your water tap. Sustainability means a dedication to and intentionality about the survival of the planet, its species, and ecosystems. As I work with others related to the food systems in our community, we are regularly looking at the impact of a variety of organizations— ranging from transportation to education to health care and more—on natural resources, climate, and the environment, whether or not that impact was intended. As farmers, though, we remind ourselves to not shift our attention to blaming others and calling out their problems but rather keep focused on our responsibility to care for the earth. For some of us, it becomes a sacred duty.

Zindzi: Yes, human and planet well-being are intimately connected and interdependent. In fact, that leads right into the next VEP.

Visionary Evaluative Principle 2: Recognize the World as Composed of Living, Entangled Systems

Zindzi: The second principle of a VE is recognizing that we exist within dynamic living systems. How we envision the world shapes our approach to inquiry and action. A living systems' view is a shift from reductionism and linear thinking and a shift from separating the natural world from the socioeconomic-political world constructed by humans. Visionary Evaluatives connect their own personhood with the society and ecological systems in which they live. Visionary Evaluatives are in a dynamic interplay between who they are as people and how they are interacting with the world around them. Visionary Evaluatives approach situations as part of them and vice-versa. The challenges faced are not on a page in a book or a screen in a classroom or passed along by someone else. They are the lives we are living, internal and external, in here and out there. Systems are not stationary nor are their elements. Indeed, human-created systems follow the many patterns of natural systems—emerging, forming, growing, adapting, evolving, dying, and re-emerging. Those systems are in both society and nature.

Take, for example, the basic pattern of the life of a forest—or any life for that matter. It is an infinite loop rather than a linear pattern or an S-shaped curve. The infinite loop reminds us of the recursive pattern of four situations in life: birth, maturity, release, and reconfiguring to new conditions. There's no beginning or end in living systems. I think you've seen that visual of the forest analogy on our website. Here, let me pull it up (see Figure 3.1).

The typical S curve talked about as the growth curve in the business world is similar to the movement from birth to maturity. By not including the release and reconfiguring phases of the cycle, an organization or other system can fall in the trap of thinking the system can continually grow or at least

Figure 3.1 Phases of the ecocycle of a forest. Adapted from Zimmerman, Lindberg, & Plsek (2001).

stay long-term in a mature state. It doesn't acknowledge the inevitable release part of the infinity loop and the need for reconfiguring of resources for new conditions. So much of life in the Anthropocene involves the dismantling—the release—part of the loop. The release phase will come. It can be a sustainable renewing release or a highly destructive release that is harmful to many living beings. We are seeing it all around us where governments, corporations, and individuals have tried to stay in the maturation stage built on assumptions and processes that fit conditions when they were developed but do not fit current and future conditions. Contrast this with the sustainable forestry practices used by indigenous cultures over many generations where small scale releases through careful use of fire led to renewing forests over many generations.

Evaluation for too long has focused only on moving from birth of, say, a program into its maturity. But evaluation is also needed in the release and reconfiguring phases. Some structures and systems have to die and be rebuilt for the next situations and conditions. Those living systems and structures are also deeply influenced by the technological capacities that we have today that were not there when the systems were initially built.

Using a nature-based analogy to understand social systems can help us see that different dynamics, resources, and structures fit different locations and times. Within our organization, we regularly use nature-based analogies to help people think about their systemic theories of change. It keeps a focus on a broad orientation to living systems, thinking about not only people but also the rest of nature. The analogies help us express our understanding of complex systems in images that engage people's emotions and visual senses as well as their rational thinking. They help us see patterns and gain new insights that inform evaluative inquiry and strategic action in our daily lives. Visionary Evaluatives also see change as a natural part of life's ever-moving cycles, often freeing themselves up from being too attached to any one part of a cycle.

Omar: As you might guess, I'm a strong believer in ecological analogies for understanding social systems. But where does the role of technology fit?

Zindzi: The entanglements and liveliness of systems is mushrooming with the expanding technologies of our day. In fact, we now think in terms of three streams of entanglements—human, nature, and technology.

Omar: As I've been involved in farming, I've been continually applying my knowledge of complex living systems but I've tended to think in terms of human and nature. I appreciate your emphasis on technology as a major system in its own right. It is so powerful today. For example, artificial intelligence has certainly found its way into nearly every aspect of what we do here on the farm from planning to testing to harvest to marketing and sales. Technologies are expanding the capacities of human and natural systems although whether it is a good thing or a bad thing is not a simple determination.

Zindzi: Yes, Omar, it is indeed everywhere and every day it is becoming more integrated into our world with more and more discussion of the possibility of artificial superintelligence. We need to consider it as part of our living systems.

Another aspect of living systems is thinking of the world as having moved more fully into a sort of societal net. Movement in one part of that net impacts and is impacted by all else to which it is connected. The net is an entangled, sometimes gnarled, web of systems. And, further, the net is always undulating. The VE understands that success (or failure) of the problem or intervention being evaluated does not occur in a motionless, static world.

Omar: In addition to nature's systems, Zindzi, what other types of systems do you consider in this systemic net?

Zindzi: Systems are varied and profuse. Examples include social systems such as family, friendships, and social media; professional systems such as the workplace and professional associations; systems of power such as government and social class; culturally-determined systems based on shared values and behaviors; and, of course, sector-focused systems such as an education system or health system.

Omar: This reminds me of a quote I have on my office wall by Chief Seattle of the Suquamish Tribe: "Humankind has not woven the web of life. We are but one thread within it. Whatever we do to the web, we do to ourselves. All things are bound together. All things connect."

Zindzi: Yes, that is a very wise statement about the interconnectedness of all systems on our little planet.

Visionary Evaluatives look at patterns that form a system and also the patterns that are within the system(s). Are there behavioral patterns? Cultural patterns? Political patterns? What are the other existing social patterns? Are there ways in which people, issues, or ideas are organized? What are the patterns that emerge from one organization, social class, community, or geographic area that may be different from another? What are the macro-patterns that cross many areas or the ones that exist only in one arena?

Omar: I can see how VEs would need to consider the networks and structures and the ways in which they shift, what shifts them, and what *could* shift them. Visionary Evaluatives, I imagine, might even consider why networks, structures, or patterns didn't form, or did but then fell away. Visionary Evaluatives would learn about the systems at play when they listen to the people within those systems as they talk about the breadth of the issues they deal with and the people, nature, and technology with which they connect. I would imagine that a VE needs to ask not only about the obvious and surfaced connections but also needs to inquire and facilitate conversations about the ones that may be hidden or unintended.

Zindzi: Yes, indeed.

Visionary Evaluative Principle 3: Discover, Reveal, and Respect Intersectionalities

Zindzi: This leads nicely into the third VEP—discover, reveal, and respect intersectionalities. It draws our attention to how to *change* social, natural, and technological systems. It focuses on intersectionalities that hold promise as worthwhile system leverage points. Essentially all sectors are being transformed as they intersect with one another. Those transformations all involve changes in the traditional implicit or explicit boundaries of sectors, power, and cultures. Looking for and loosening these boundaries—creating and conceiving of them as more pervious, adaptive, and temporary while at the same time respecting them—invites creativity to discover new pathways for VEs to facilitate transformation. People who are prioritizing equity and sustainability as they live and work at these intersections are creating ideas—big and small—that are transforming our movement into the future. Our society is making hard-won progress on untangling and reconfiguring those intersectionalities that created structural racialization, oppression, and colonization in the past. We're learning to use the intersectionalities to create a different structural foundation—one built on the intersection of equity and sustainability.

Omar: Indeed. The intersectionality of equity and sustainability is the foundation.

This reminds me that one of the beauties of being part of the AEA and the field of evaluation generally is its interdisciplinary, actually, transdisciplinary nature. Because people involved in evaluation come from all types of disciplines and are interacting with one another, evaluation is a natural playground for discovering and navigating intersectionalities. Even with that, though, I didn't mind a lot of models for exploring intersectionality when I was an evaluation practitioner. It is good to see more of that happening now.

Zindzi: Yes, and one key part of this VEP, these intersectionalities, involves looking closely at who is holding what types of power and what are the broader shared values—cultures— that are present. Through attention to the intersectionalities of sectors, power, and cultures, we are using evaluative inquiry to discover small but strategic actions that have large influence to move toward equity and sustainability for future generations. By addressing these intersections, we are changing boundaries that had been implicitly or explicitly set.

VEs see the deeply embedded structures of power and culture that span generations and sectors, institutions and communities. They grasp the potentials of different sectors, institutions, cultures, communities, people, ideas, perspectives, and more to create new approaches to shifting the energy of those cross-cutting social forces toward a desired future. This requires honest, humble, compassionate inquiry and thinking about those structures and contexts.

VEs look for effective actions that allow the structures and systems to co-evolve for the benefit of humankind and nature. They seek to unlock forces from their historical, oppressive, and negative consequences for so many people, and create overall progress toward equity.

Omar: A few examples come to mind for me: How does a history of farming influence the local views on immigration policy? Or what are the ways in which the local schools and communities are dealing with a legacy of segregation in a formerly-farming community? I can see how VEs must not only think about what they observe and recognize, but also ask questions and listen to find out more about the cultural considerations, broadly defined, in the situation. There are often times that important cultural issues are moving like ghosts among some of us because we have not lived in that culture, experienced those cultural forces, or been impacted by those cultural issues. These cultures can intersect, segregate, hide, hold power, and generate feelings of powerlessness for some and feelings of influence by others. We must honestly, fearlessly, and respectfully go into those conversations and experiences to learn and unearth the realities of others.

Zindzi: And another example: there will be a different culture within a Fortune 500 company than a 20-person operation. Even within an organization, there will be many different cultures—one for the company executives, another for those working in the call center, and another for those on the front line producing the products. And the reality of someone who is a first in their family college graduate from a rural, midwest town will be different than that of one who comes from a long line of corporate leaders. Listening and engaging in ways that allow those cultural forces to be seen, unearthed, and heard is a key aspect of the VE's way of becoming culturally engaged.

Omar: My partner and I live in a faith-based community with a culture that is sometimes challenged by our union. I grew up in the Methodist church, much of it about as "liberal" as it gets in formal Christian denominations. The denomination is beginning another round of dialogue about human sexuality. It is very challenging but Methodism has a history of dialogues. And they have had policies regarding sustainability and other social issues in place for many years now with more in development. My husband has no formal faith tradition but we have raised our children who are as diverse as they are beautiful in a faith tradition that has actively chosen to grapple with the most challenging social issues for many faiths, including making it absolutely clear that all are loved equally.

Zindzi: Yes, the VE way is not to dictate a way of being or reacting but to walk the path of understanding and compassion. Visionary Evaluatives reflect upon how they engage with knowledge and understanding of the cultural issues of a person, organization, or community.

A VE understands that this isn't just about bringing diverse groups together but that it is about honest, analytical, systematic inquiry into how issues have become embedded, the people who are deeply impacted by intesectionality, and the ways in which to uproot those forces that have a choking grip on the ability to make progress.

Omar: There is so much to this principle of intersectionality. We could spend all day talking about it.

Zindzi: Yes! Improving our ability to search out, discover, explore, unentangle, navigate, and respect cultural, power, sectoral, and other intersectionalities, in many ways, depends upon our ability to make information about human values both transparent and useful. And when it comes to values, we have a lot left to learn. This leads nicely into the fourth principle, "facilitate the transparency and understanding of values."

Visionary Evaluative Principle 4: Facilitate the Transparency and Understanding of Human Values

Omar: I remember that, several years ago, the AEA membership approved an updated set of guiding ethical principles. I recall that the updated version put greater emphasis on transparency.[2]

Zindzi: Yes, that principle focused on evaluators behaving with honesty and transparency to ensure the integrity of an evaluation. One of the specific areas of emphasis within that broad principle was on assessing and making explicit the values, perspectives, and interests of stakeholders, clients, and evaluators concerning the conduct and outcome of the evaluation. Visionary Evaluatives have built upon that AEA principle and taken it further by emphasizing transparency of values in particular. It's not only about making our own values transparent to others but also engaging in honest and deep introspection of our values to make them visible to ourselves. In fact, that is the critical starting point. So often I act without realizing which of the many values I hold is driving my action. I have to surface those values, reflect on my actions and their results, and see if those values are really the ones that are most important to me and to others who will be effected by my actions. It involves peeling off deeper and deeper layers of assumptions that I scarcely realize I have. It involves being vision-oriented, not assuming the past works for the future. What do we want, what is our vision? That's a guiding question for supporting transparency in our values.

So many of our actions are simply habitual ways of thinking and acting that we don't even think to question. Then when you add the proliferation and manipulation of data in today's world and the discrepancies between social media and reality, not to mention the echo-chamber created by social media, it can be crazy-making. That's why this principle calls on VEs to facilitate both the transparency and understanding of our own and others' values to create a desired future for all.

Omar: I like the emphasis on facilitation, be it with my own family or with the many stakeholders involved in an organization, community, or other setting. We're helping one another surface our values and understand the connection of those values to our actions or potential actions. It requires deep self-reflection as well as respect and compassion for both ourselves and other people.

Zindzi: Yes, VEs identify and raise questions about the alignment of values with actions and outcomes. Often times, there is an assumption that the belief in certain values, even strong and deep beliefs, will naturally lead to actions and outcomes that reflect those values. For example, many sectors have asserted a value of equity, such as the corporate and government sectors, and much progress has indeed been made, but it requires ongoing vigilance to ensure the translation of values into action. It is not enough to only uncover and state what the values are. There must be an intentional effort to use evaluative inquiry to help ensure that outcomes reflect the values of equity and sustainability at deeper and deeper levels of our social structures and collective consciousness.

Omar: And we have to remember that when an organization or sector asserts a value, it still takes each individual member of that group to enact those values. Actually, that leads nicely into the fifth VEP—learning.

Visionary Evaluative Principle 5: Learn Through Iterative Action and Inquiry

Zindzi: Yes, the fifth principle, "learn through iterative action and inquiry," moves us from values to the most visible aspect of bringing about change grounded in values. This VEP explicitly addresses the positioning and purpose of evaluative inquiry—learning. It acknowledges the iterative nature of action and inquiry and the purpose being to learn our way into a new way of social functioning. All too often we segregate action from inquiry and design, with different people being engaged in each with little contact one with the other. Or we engage in action and inquiry for a particular length of time, but don't recognize the ongoing, iterative nature of action and inquiry in complex systems.

    We also tend to forget how long it takes humans to change their behaviors. I would argue that we all have our own expressions of inequitable and ecologically unsustainable behaviors and values. It may be a more radical change for some than others but we are all participating in some way or another. We need to progressively learn our way out of our individual and collective patterns of the past, a past and culture heavily influenced by values other than equity and sustainability. We need to learn our way into creating a future that includes honoring the place and purpose of each living thing, independent of its instrumental use for humans. We are very fortunate to have made substantial progress on achieving the legal recognition of nature's rights.

Omar: Say more about what you mean by nature's rights.

Zindzi: From the time of the early colonization of the United States, colonizers treated nature as property under the law in the United States. The term "rights of nature" recognizes and honors the right of our ecosystems including plants, animals, rivers, oceans, and mountains to exist and maintain their regenerative cycles. Recognizing the rights of nature is consistent with the traditions of indigenous cultures in the United States and around the world. They have long understood what it means to live in harmony with nature. Ecuador was the first country to recognize the rights of nature in its constitution. The Ecuadorian Constitution ratified by the people of Ecuador in 2008 includes a chapter specific to Rights of Nature. The people of Ecuador have the legal authority to enforce these rights on behalf of ecosystems. A growing number of communities in the United States are moving in this direction. Contrast this with the way the U.S. Constitution and laws have been created or interpreted to give rights to corporations to own and subjugate nature.

Omar: I view this as an excellent example of how deeply rooted values of environmental unsustainability are present in today's society, while at the same time bringing forth the even longer tradition of values of sustainability in this country through indigenous cultures. I wish we more wisely used the lessons of our indigenous cultures. Iterative action and inquiry helps us all learn our way into the redistribution of power toward environmental sustainability.

Zindzi: Yes, we must use the iterative process of aligning action with data derived from evaluative inquiry to learn our way back to equity and sustainability. As evaluation practitioners and evaluation users work closely together as VEs, they see what happens when a particular action is taken and then use the inquiry to help determine the next wise action.

Omar: Speaking of learning, that makes me think about the sixth VEP, about praxis. As I understand the term, praxis refers to theory informing practice and practice informing theory.

Visionary Evaluative Principle 6: Engage in Deep Praxis

Zindzi: Yes, the sixth VEP, "engage in deep praxis," is about learning but it goes beyond the basic definition of praxis that you mentioned. We use the term "deep praxis" in a way similar to "deep ecology" which means seeing the world not as a collection of isolated events or objects but rather a network of interconnected, intertwined phenomena. So deep praxis refers to a way of learning that brings together iterative action and inquiry with theory, creativity, and the broader patterns of practice and theory. How we engage in this process—this praxis—is critical to adjusting living systems. It is through deep praxis that, for example, we avoid getting overly focused on a few indicators of progress that could cause us to lose sight of the longer journey and its patterns. Evaluators' tradition of focusing on outcomes is both a strength and a weakness. Having an outcome can be a very helpful way for moving in a desired direction, but not if the outcome becomes the destination rather than a step in a longer term and dynamic journey of systemic change. Focusing on the dynamic journey is necessary to restructure the entangled living systems of people, nature, and technologies to uproot the values that contradict equity and sustainability. Here too is where creativity and technological advances come to the fore.

When we meet next week, Omar, we will talk about Praxis Quests but let me talk generally about those quests to illustrate deep praxis. Praxis Quests are one form of deep praxis that VEs use. Praxis Quests can be structured in many different ways. In the particular approach that I'll be discussing, a Praxis Quest consists of a group of people who intentionally—and with commitment—come together virtually and/or in-person to openly and honestly share their values and their struggles with acting on those values in real time, in real life, and in their work. A key feature is that each participant brings a current situation related to an evaluative inquiry that is challenging personally and professionally. The Praxis Quests involve VEs and potential VEs. Remember, anyone, can be a VE. It's an individual's choice and based on their utilization of the VEPs. If someone has made the choice to explore the approach, they are welcome. Some people may be at very early stages of moving to the VE way of being—a way of moving in the world that is based on creating a future based on values of equity and sustainability. Those in our Praxis Quests want to, and are expected to, build relationships with others who desire to be on this journey.

We're bringing together action, inquiry, theory, reflection, innovation, listening, research, and learning in this mix. It's the combination that results in deep praxis that affects the next step for those involved in a Praxis Quest. We all need each other; we still sometimes forget that.

Omar: That is quite a different way of engaging with one another from what I tended to use when I was in the evaluation field before. But it's very much like the form of permaculture we've been living and advocating for at the farm. That is, it's a system of agricultural design principles that simulate or directly utilize the patterns and features observed in natural ecosystems rather than fighting against them. It also reminds me of my jujitsu practice. Jujutsu involves an artful technique of turning an opponent's own force against him rather than confronting the force with one's own. It's a different way of bringing about change.

Zindzi: Yes, it is a shift. It's a way of using the energy that is already in a system and its environment to change direction, change purposes or goals, and thus change the system. It's easy to say but not easy to build into one's very way of being, of living, given the many generations of a dominant culture in the United States of reductionism. By reductionism, I mean the tendency to break things into parts and just look at the parts instead of attending to the larger whole created through the interconnections of those parts. The whole is different than the sum of the parts.

Omar: This is helping me create an image of myself as shaping and being shaped by my own situation. I'm envisioning this process as part of a larger movement—an individual and joint way of moving in the world with keen attention to how I am interconnected to social, natural, and technological environments that are especially influencing me and that I am also influencing. They are both proximal and distant.

I'm also seeing how we as VEs can create small patches of new ways of human–nature–technology interchange in scattered locations. Have you ever watched a lake freeze over as winter approaches? Small patches of ice tend to form scattered across the lake. Then in a very short time, in the matter of a few short hours, you can see that lake freeze over, creating a solid covering of the lake. A lot of that redefining is not very visible or stable. There are many changes happening in the lake just before the visible freezing of the lake. That's my image of us as VEs engaged in praxis and moving in our various cultures and sectors and in our cross-cultural and cross-sector work. We can be catalysts for creating the defining look of our society and planet—one of equity and sustainability for nature and for generations to come. It's a thriving, flourishing place. Being engaged in our own praxis is often an invisible aspect of that change.

Zindzi: You have a great advantage in moving into this type of work given your experience of years of farming. I suspect you have developed a deep sense of connection to nature and its cycles, its patterns, its uncertainties as well as its stabilities. All of those variations are going on at once in different life forms in a given location and time.

Omar: It took me several years to feel that connection to nature, that place where I accept the simultaneous interplay of growth and decay as characteristic of health. I've also learned so much about how plants in a forest communicate with and support one another. I also have spent a lot of time with my indigenous friends whose deep connection to the earth brings a calmness to my being. I can tell from what I've learned so far about VEs, this kind of personal connection is critical.

Zindzi: Yes, that is so important. . . . I see that the sun is setting. I need to get home for our weekly community dinner with neighbors and friends.

Omar: Thanks for coming here. I'll see you at your office next week to discuss Praxis Quests.

NOTES

1. See Patton (2018).
2. See https://www.eval.org/p/cm/ld/fid=51 for the AEA Guiding Principles for Evaluators.

REFERENCE

Patton, M. (2018). *Principles-focused evaluation: The GUIDE.* New York, NY: Guildford Press.

Zimmerman, B., Lindberg, C., & Plsek, P. (2001). *Edgware: Insights from complexity science for health care leaders.* Irving, TX: VHA Inc.

SECTOR VISIONING

CHAPTER 4

SOCIAL PROTECTION

Reframing Toward Individual, Community, and National Well-Being

Lateefah Simon, Charlyn Harper Browne, Ryan Eller, Bo Pryor, and Justin Speegle

ZINDZI'S ABSTRACT[1]

The first perspective presented here is a first-hand description of the life of a young woman of color in harrowing situations several decades ago. She shows the shift to life today in 2030 with advancements in social protection as women such as herself enter policymaking positions at every level of community and government. The next contributor brings attention to strength-based and systems thinking with an emphasis on protective factors among parents, children, and youth living in adverse conditions. Today, people focus as much on building protective factors as reducing risk factors. Thereafter, our attention is drawn to immigrant and refugee families as the next contributor shares the realities of U.S. history of injustice and possibilities for reparations. The final contribution focuses on the changing role of the military from lethal force to cooperation and collaboration with other countries and cultures.

The perspectives, at different scales, illustrate what it means for the United States to shift away from its history of colonization, genocide, and slavery to one that genuinely attends to equity and well-being.

Visionary Evaluation for a Sustainable, Equitable Future, pages 79–94
Copyright © 2020 by Information Age Publishing
79

The contributions provide a window into how Visionary Evaluatives (VEs) can use any and all phases of evaluative inquiry to deconstruct old world views and construct new ones that are grounded in equity and sustainability.

OUR DAUGHTERS' DAUGHTERS: THE UNAPOLOGETIC FOURTH WAVE
by Lateefah Simon

I began working with low-income, young women on the streets of San Francisco when I was a child. I was 17, failing high school, and 2 years short of giving birth to my first child. Living in low-income housing with the world caving in on me, I found my breath in organizing girls—girls who, like me, had been failed by systems developed to protect them.

As a street outreach worker charged with building community with girls who were out of sight to most and, later as the executive director of a small grassroots nonprofit, I bore witness to a thousand ways that community and government turned their backs on girls of color, girls with babies. I remember the consistent vitriol that law enforcement spewed on girls who were bought and sold on the streets. I remember the disregard for girls who were acting out—rightfully so—in response to years of being raped, being ripped from their families, and battling the many demons of racism and urban poverty. No one wanted us.

In broad daylight, I saw police perform illegal cavity searches on girls who peddled crack cocaine—and held babies after detained women gave birth while chained to their beds. These young women, the thousands that I got to know, are now adults. We are in our fifties—and the lives of our children's children hold this historical trauma of mass incarceration and the failed drug war.

But now, these girls are fighting the war on women. It's 2030 and the fourth wave of feminism has birthed voices of resilience. We never found the missing girls in DC. We never closed down women's prisons. Women still must travel across the pond to receive a safe abortion—and girls, black and brown girls, are still being bought and sold on the streets and through the intrawebs. In reflection, the gallant fights for racial justice, for Black Lives, for Queer liberation—for health care and a livable minimum wage—have shifted the nation's language to describe what oppression feels and tastes like. But our republic still incarcerates and throws away its girls.

The daughters of the millions of women who laid their lives on the line for Black Lives and those who marched in the Women's March of 2017, the women whose mothers died in prisons after serving lifetime sentences for nonviolent drug crimes, and the sisters of trans women who were murdered in mass—these women have developed into more than a branch of the

1960's feminist movement. They are more like their own political party. Organized by regional chapters and funded by chapter members, this fourth wave force is aligned to expose and heal the dirty and profound wounds that are stained on the skin of the United States. The millions of women of the fourth wave are intersectional savants who come from turn-of-the-century radical promise.

The fourth wave's agenda will make this country free. From gender parity in government to free health care and free education—the conversation about race is central and has acquired relevance. In the last 5 years, we have witnessed over 25 state legislatures pass legislation to make community and state college free. This movement is training poor women of color to run for office and govern with dignity and fierceness. Never before have we seen the demography of the local electorates shift the gender scale.

I may not see prisons fall in my lifetime, but my daughters' daughters are moving the pendulum sharply towards justice.

PROTECTIVE FACTORS AND SOCIAL SERVICES
by Charlyn Harper Browne

Based on numerous studies and evaluations, in 2030 the scales are tipping toward a new view of the health, well-being, successes, and challenges of children and their parents. This perspective in 2030 builds on research and practice over several decades with much of it growing out of work in the field of social services.

In the past, social services work primarily was deficit-based. That is, social service approaches with "at risk" individuals, families, and communities singularly focused on perceived needs, problems, or weaknesses and on addressing risk factors. Preventing, mitigating, coping with, or eliminating risk factors is necessary to decrease the likelihood of poor outcomes, but only addressing risk factors is not sufficient to increase the likelihood that families are on a trajectory of healthy, productive child, adult, and family outcomes. Research has shown that deficit-based approaches implicitly communicate low expectations of individuals, families, and communities and do not sustain positive change (Abrams & Ceballos, 2012).

Numerous studies provided the basis for 2030's view that better outcomes are achieved by using strengths-based approaches that build or enhance protective factors (Centers for Disease Control and Prevention, 2015). Strengths-based approaches assume that, even though there may be problems, individuals, families, and communities have untapped potential, competencies, and resources that can be employed to improve conditions and outcomes. Effective social services in 2030 focus on identifying and mobilizing family strengths, promoting protective factors, and reducing realistically modifiable risk factors. This trend has been building over several decades now. For example, in 2013 researchers stated:

> In a strengths-based intervention approach that focuses on building protective factors, parents themselves can identify and build on their own strengths to help enhance their parenting capacity. Promoting protective factors may also help professionals working with families to build more positive relationships with clients. (Smart, 2017, para. 12)

Two Protective Factors Frameworks

To move from theory to practice, the Center for the Study of Social Policy (CSSP) developed two evidence-informed frameworks about protective factors that can be integrated seamlessly into the day-to-day work of social service agencies, educational settings, and other child, youth, and family-focused organizations. Called the Strengthening Families Protective Factors Framework™ (SF) and the Youth Thrive Framework™ (YT), respectively, these frameworks apply to families of young children birth to 8 years old and to youth and young adults ages nine and older. Although the SF and YT frameworks may be implemented in contexts that serve individuals and families experiencing adversity, CSSP emphasizes that the protective factors are attributes and conditions that help to keep all children, youth, and parents strong and on a pathway of healthy development and well-being. This emphasis is continuing in 2030.

At the foundation of both frameworks are five interrelated protective factors. Protective factors are defined in the frameworks as attributes or conditions that simultaneously (a) prevent or mitigate the effect of exposure to risk factors and stressful life events, and (b) build family strengths and a family environment that promotes healthy development and well-being (Harper Browne, 2014a, 2014b). The components of both frameworks are listed in Table 4.1; a brief description of the SF and YT protective factors follows.

TABLE 4.1 The Strengthening Families and Youth Thrive Protective Factors	
The Strengthening Families Protective Factors	**The Youth Thrive Protective Factors**
Parental Resilience	Youth Resilience
Social Connections	Social Connections
Knowledge of Parenting and Child Development	Knowledge of Adolescent Development
Social and Emotional Competence of Children	Cognitive & Social-Emotional Competence
Concrete Support in Times of Need	Concrete Support in Times of Need

Parental Resilience and Youth Resilience

Within the SF and YT frameworks, resilience is conceived as the process of managing stress and functioning well in a particular context when faced with adversity (Luthar & Cicchetti, 2000). Resilience is learned through exposure to challenging life events facilitated by supportive relationships and environments; the outcome of demonstrating resilience is positive change and growth (Walsh, 2006). Through these means of building resilience, individuals are increasing their sense of self-efficacy because they are able to see evidence of their ability to face challenges competently, be accountable for their actions and the consequences of their actions, make wise choices about addressing challenges, and feel more in control of what happens to them (Harper Browne, 2014a, 2014b). We are seeing that demonstrating resilience helps individuals to internalize the belief that their lives are important and meaningful. Thus, they can envision and conscientiously work with purpose and optimism toward future possibilities for themselves.

Social Connections

As a protective factor in both frameworks, social connections refers to having healthy, sustained relationships with people, institutions, a community, or a higher power that promote a sense of connectedness (Harper Browne, 2014a, 2014b). "Connectedness" is used in the literature to describe the protective relationship between individuals and their social contexts that promotes a sense of belonging, attachment, and well-being and decreases vulnerability to negative outcomes (Bernat & Resnick, 2009). High-quality social connections enable individuals to experience meaningful interactions that help buffer them from, or mediate the impact of, life's challenges.

Knowledge of Parenting, Child Development, and/or Adolescent Development

The SF and YT frameworks emphasize that all parents, and those who work with children and youth, can benefit from increasing their knowledge and understanding of the science of early childhood and adolescent development. Increased knowledge enables adults to develop and apply strategies that emerge from current research into their day-to-day interactions with children and youth, and to develop programs and policies that are designed to help children and youth flourish in all developmental domains—physical, cognitive, language, social, and emotional. The YT framework also emphasizes that young people themselves can benefit from increasing their understanding about adolescent development because this helps to "normalize" their individual experiences as developmentally typical, and even healthy, as they prepare for adulthood.

Social-Emotional and Cognitive Competence

Within the SF and YT frameworks, building social-emotional competence involves providing an environment and experiences that promote and enhance self-regulation and executive function skills in parents, children, or youth. Self-regulation incorporates two components: (a) the control and coordination of thoughts, emotions, and behaviors, and (b) the ability to adapt behavior in order to achieve a goal. Executive functions are interrelated processes (e.g., persistence, personal agency, ignoring distractions, controlling impulses, inhibition) that contribute to self-regulation and influence cognitive processes and social-emotional behaviors (Center on the Developing Child at Harvard University, 2011). Over many years, a growing body of research has demonstrated the positive relationship between social-emotional competence and cognitive and language skills, mental health, identity development, communication skills, social skills, school readiness and academic achievement, occupational success, and the ability to persevere despite circumstances and conditions that threaten healthy development and well-being (The Annie E. Casey Foundation, 2013). This orientation in research and practice continues to grow even now in 2030.

Concrete Support in Times of Need

Within the SF and YT frameworks, concrete support in times of need includes a person component and a service component. First, this protective factor affirms that it is essential for adults and youth who are faced with adversity to have experiences that enable them to identify, seek, access, advocate for, navigate through, and receive needed social services and supports. In this context, seeking appropriate help is regarded as a step toward improving one's circumstances, learning to better manage stress and function well, and developing self-advocacy skills. When individuals have self-advocacy skills they are able to identify and describe their strengths and needs, as well as the desired concrete supports that address their needs. Second, this protective factor stresses the importance of providing children, youth, and adults with a quality of service that is respectful, culturally responsive, strengths-based, trauma-informed, and designed to preserve individuals' dignity and to promote healthy development and well-being.

A Systems View

Family systems are embedded in community, cultural, and societal systems that have a profound impact on the health, well-being, and functioning of children, parents, and families as a unit. Research and evaluative inquiry is continuing to show, here in 2030, that in order to affect the best outcomes for children, parents, and families, it is essential to address both risk factors and protective factors in multiple domains of the social ecology including community factors (e.g., access to quality education), social factors (e.g., economic conditions), or structural factors (e.g., institutional racism). Targeting only one domain reduces the chances of successful outcomes (National Research Council and Institute of Medicine, 2009). For example, implementing family-centered maternity and paternity leave policies is helping to relieve some of the stressors associated with parenting, as well as strengthen a secure parent–child emotional attachment.

It is critical that evaluators and researchers continue to actively focus on protective factors in their work. The SF and YT protective factors frameworks serve as useful and effective guides for improving outcomes for all children, youth, and families. Given the increase in racial, ethnic/cultural, and linguistic diversity of the population in the United States and the recognition that children of color are still disproportionately represented and receive differential treatment in social protective systems, in 2030 intentional efforts are being made to understand how protective factors are manifest in culturally and gender-specific ways.

CREATING A WELCOMING CULTURE
by Ryan Eller

In 2030, America is more racially diverse than at any time in its history. The continuation of this trend seems inevitable because the population growth has come mainly from immigrants, particularly Asian and Latinx immigrants, and the percentage of children being born to multiracial parents has increased.[2] As America has become more diverse, more people are showing an openness to exploring the country's diverse roots. More communities have realized that insularity is a false safety, opting instead for a sense of American identity and access to citizenship centered on one's bondedness to values and the pursuit of inclusivity (Gest, 2016; 2018).

Media (the news, popular-culture, and digitally created content) are reconciling the two prevailing, yet competing, narratives embedded in the American experience: (a) the welcoming nation of opportunity for all people and (b) the divisive nation of resistance to diversity and equity. Both narratives have always been present in America but the importance of reconciling them is more important as the country becomes more diverse. The authentic story has led to policies that reflect the modern challenges to protect all Americans, including Americans who are undocumented or happen to have been born elsewhere.

In an era of dystopian TV and film where negative news rules, all to promote a fear-based narrative (and thousands of kids sit, some dying, in jails), we are also seeing hope-filled visioning. To me, it's a vision of our borders as national, protected parks where instead of money being spent towards imprisonment and death, it's spent helping families move from one place to another in order to live safely, set up roots, and pursue a newly renewed American dream.

In 2030, evaluators no longer see only challenges or look for deficiencies in tactics that mitigate those challenges. They no longer lose sight of what's possible or risk devaluing workers whose hands are on the plow of a more inclusive future. They now focus on informing and helping to shape those hopeful visions of the future.

Strengthening Immigrant and Refugee Families

People in the world were on the move in 2015. A record number of people had been forcibly migrated from their homes—over 65 million people became immigrants; in all, there were 244 million immigrants across the globe.[3] People migrated in response to violence, to global climate shifts, to a reduction in resources, and to conflicts over limited resources. Despite the desire of some folks to draw inward and wall themselves off from the world, these global events were being felt locally, especially as technology produced more interconnections.

In the United States, record numbers of people were being deported. The majority of those deported had never committed any type of crime in the United States. Some communities saw a clear and urgent need for protection strategies. The strategies went by different names: "sanctuaries,"[4] "solidarity movements," and "efforts of compassion and welcome."

These communities began to move towards an emphasis on family resilience. Most immigrants had a broad sense of the nuclear family because, at some point in their lives, they had been cared for by an aunt, an uncle, or a grandparent. In response to the deportations, some community groups set up workshops to help documented family members get powers of attorney so that children would not be sent into foster care.

In the United States, social connections provided critical protection. Those with social connections might find help from churches that let them claim sanctuary. Community groups used technology to connect rapidly and build power rapidly. Technology did not start change movements, but it was used as a tool to grow change. For example, there were online campaigns that opposed deportations and separations of families. People with social connections could gather enough signatures on online petitions to bring their case to the attention of the director of the local office of Immigration and Customs Enforcement (ICE).

Social connections also helped undocumented people get assistance in finding an attorney (they had no guaranteed-by-law right to an attorney).

The social systems that affected immigrants and refugees were incredibly complex and confusing. Legal counsel could be crucial. Without an attorney representing them, defendants in asylum cases were seldom granted asylum. Hundreds of those deported were killed when they were returned to their nation of origin.

Community groups also advised immigrants of their rights in the system. For example, they explained that people didn't have to open the door for an ICE agent unless the agent had a warrant signed by a judge. If an ICE agent stopped them on the street in a random search, they didn't have to speak to the agent. They also didn't have to speak to an ICE agent who was conducting a raid. The law permitted them to remain silent. They could also choose to hand the agent the card of their attorney. This knowledge helped prevent families from being separated and deported.

In one community, nine interfaith communities joined in a covenant of solidarity that provided support for sanctuaries. In another, concrete support came in the form of phone trees that helped those affected by ICE raids. The members of the response team ensured that children were picked up from school or home so that they weren't caught up in the system when their family members were detained. Attorneys were notified so that they could intervene before those detained were sent to a private prison and processed for deportation.

Other communities set up support systems that enabled refugees to make the transition into American society. They provided direct services to families such as helping them navigate the grocery store or helping them learn to ride on the bus system. Although these types of concrete support might only be needed at specific times, they were critically important to helping refugees join and contribute to society in ways that benefited everybody.

Those involved in this work recognize that they need long-term solutions. For example, now in 2030, conversations are occurring in the public space about population growth and factors with a stabilizing effect on birth rates such as women's access to education. Media stories explain how both social and natural resources intersected with immigration. Sustainability requires that they could no longer silo conversations about the environment, immigration, and shifts in population.

Shifting Conversations to Change the Politics of Immigration

The work of Define American is an example of how one activist media and culture organization used the power of story to shift conversations about race and immigration. Define American viewed immigration as an issue of racial justice. To change the politics of immigration, they set out to change the way the culture viewed the country's 43 million immigrants, over 11 million of whom were undocumented.

The work at Define American honored the examples set by predecessors such as Harvey Milk who had led modern historical movements for justice and equality. Taking inspiration from Milk, they made "coming out of the shadows" one of the key components of their early campaigns that focused on encouraging undocumented Americans to make their undocumented status visible. They explored new ways to integrate stories that recognized immigrants as a critical, positive part of the American identity.

Data suggested that the most determinative factor in people deciding whom to vote for was not their voting history or other demographics, but which television shows they watched for entertainment (Katz, 2016; Gauthier, 2016). Define American assessed key outputs like the number of people who were engaged in media that featured an immigrant character (e.g., online conversations, participation in an artistic presentation, or attendance at a film screening or lecture). They assessed changes in perception among those who experienced their work over time by comparing the data on changed perceptions to polling data in the larger population.

Americans needed to reconcile their whole history—the sanitized version they were used to hearing with the fact that their ancestors had committed mass genocide on indigenous people and enslaved other groups of people. Also rarely heard were the stories about the bloody battles between successive waves of white immigrants.

Stories about family history encouraged Americans to come to terms with their own family heritage. Research into family history could reveal, for instance, that a "White guy from the south" had Native American, Dutch, English, German, and Puerto Rican ancestors. That, in turn, could lead to reflections on what it meant to be a privileged White person.

In many ways, the community of Dayton, Ohio served as the example that led Americans towards the welcoming view of immigrants that predominates in 2030. In 2011, the Dayton community had lost its manufacturing base and was hemorrhaging its population. This out-migration meant tax revenues were drying up. Many neighborhoods fell into disrepair. Those who stayed in their homes saw their home values plummet. But, a radical idea was proposed: Open Dayton's doors as a welcoming city to immigrants, encouraging people—no matter where they were from—to relocate in Dayton. As chronicled in the *New York Times* (Preston, 2013), the success of this initiative was undeniable. New businesses began to pop up. Boarded-up homes were repaired. Local classrooms refilled. Although the immigrants sometimes had little more than the clothes on their backs and a dream in their minds, they rebuilt Dayton.

Their efforts mirrored what had been done centuries earlier by newcomers. Other small towns picked up on the successes in Dayton and saw that they could replicate those outcomes by welcoming immigrants. In an age when the belief in the American dream had waned, (Cooper, 2015) new hope was found. As the culture moved, people used digital tools to bring about even more change.

Reconciliation and Welcoming

The forces of global migration and the interconnectedness of the global economy brought many changes to America. But even during divided times, progress can and has been made. Now in 2030, patches of America have started to reconcile with their whole story and to discover that fears of one another need not be the basis of relationships. There is an increase in the strengthening of protective factors for all people, an increased engagement in stories about diversity, and a shift in policies towards equity and sustainability. Welcoming has become a part of everyday life.

A BALANCING STABILITY[5]
by Bo Pryor and Justin Speegle

Learning From Our Past Military Thinking

Until recently the focus of military institutional thinking was on defeating the military of another country. In World War II, that type of thinking allowed the United States to be successful. Our later conflicts were incompatible with that model. Conflicts in Vietnam, Iraq, and Afghanistan demonstrated that military and technological "superiority" might result in fewer battlefield casualties yet not ensure victory. Fewer battlefield casualties ("losing less") did not mean success, particularly when prolonged conflict resulted in impact on the civilian population in terrible ways.

"Losing less" goals became often-cited examples of false measures of improvement and success. Increasingly, we recognized that using narrowly defined notions of "effectiveness" was an inadequate approach in highly dynamic and uncertain situations with accelerating change on many fronts (e.g., information access, the capacity for people anywhere to efficiently organize and mobilize). We began systematic reexaminations of long-standing assumptions and policies.

The 2007–2008 global financial crisis pushed a lot of nations and societies off balance. The events of the 2010s further exposed vulnerabilities. Unexpected and unfamiliar conflicts were fueled by radical changes in climate, migration, economic inequity, energy use, and material use. We witnessed new relationships coming out of these increasingly complex scenarios. All of these affected the availability of financial, social, and natural resources and impacted the security of individual nations and the world.

In this dire worldwide security situation, there were multiple national and international military initiatives set up to revisit assumptions and policies related to conflicts over resources. A new world required new kinds of questions. How did we fight with something that wasn't a country? How did we combat rising seas? Too little drinkable water? Changing climates? Pandemic disease? Diaspora?

In the early 2020s, the senior civilian and military leadership from our country and many of our allies and partners shifted their focus from expending resources on conflict and deterrence to investing in protection and conflict prevention. The investment aimed at identifying and promoting values relevant to protection that were shared among nations, cultures, communities, and other dimensions of society.

An Evolving Approach to Protecting a Nation

In 2030, we defend the United States by promoting our national values through cooperation, collaboration, and co-evolution. We avoid using lethal force if at all possible. This position evolved from our past experiences and the experiences of others in conflicts and emergencies. We shifted to valuing stability as it relates to security and embracing complexity rather than simplification. These adaptive shifts allowed us to better navigate rapidly changing environments. Success is now defined as preventing conflict, tragedy, and deprivation. Period. We achieved this change by helping the global community reduce conflict and chaos.

Think of a forest. When someone conjures a mental picture of a forest, it will probably be incomplete. If we modeled the mental construct, our model forest would probably fail fast because it lacked some parts and relationships. We might have forgotten to include species, habitat, or community that held the secrets to the forest's capacity for adaptation and resilience.

A healthy forest persists and generates because of the flows of energy, the buffers to rapid change, and the communications and interactions between a multitude of organisms, many invisible to the naked eye. The interrelationships keep the forest in a fluid, dynamic, and balanced state, somewhere between stability and chaos.

The aim of our long-term national defense in 2030 is to achieve a similarly stable level of instability that can be "naturally" maintained rather than imposed. It is inappropriate, for example, to remove a hostile dictator or impose a military occupation on an unstable region because those actions may provoke resistance that increases the probability of chaos and conflict. Our enemies are not the militaries and peoples of other nations or groups.

Our true enemy is the destabilization that upsets the balance in the forest and moves it toward chaos. This perspective means that we provide both humanitarian aid and military deterrence—they are equal in priority.

We don't want a crisis situation to be the first time we work together with allies or other countries. Thus, in 2029 a MEU (Marine Expeditionary Unit) participated in a combined training exercise along with African Union and NATO partners. It was a win/win/win because we trained and practiced together. We trained by doing. Some training was tactical (e.g., applying effective close air support with both local and allied aircraft; practicing the tactics of fighting in close-quartered urban areas with an emphasis on re-ducing civilian casualties and disruptions to their way of life). Much of the training emphasized developing our partnerships and efficient delivery of civil-affairs missions (e.g., the rapid deployment of field hospitals).

Values Adaptation, Connectedness, and a Systems Approach to National Security

One mistake we made around the turn of the century was "mirror imag-ing," that is, assuming that our values were universal. Who wouldn't want truth, justice, and the American way? We found that our values were not universal at all. When using a systems approach to national security, we saw clearly that our tactical, operational, and theater objectives had to be nested in our strategic objectives.

Transparency of values played a part in building some collaborative part-nerships. We learned not to be so quick to assume that the world shared our values. We learned about the consequences of letting that assumption go unquestioned. We strove to understand others' values and adapted our policies and objectives. We improved our ability to tailor our engagements to match specific regions, groups, and nations. Heightened sensitivity to the importance of that match enabled us to keep the support missions as the focal point, rather than U.S. military involvement. Instead, we worked in the background, promoting the legitimacy of local governments, demonstrating to our partners how we worked, as well as showing how our values drove what we did. Our goal was to support the host nation in dealing with a regional crisis because that built legitimacy among the local population and helped us achieve our strategic objective—a state of dynamic, balancing stability.

We learned the hard way that actions in one part of the system often had unanticipated, sometimes negative, effects on other parts of the system. In 2022, we thought we had a win/win when we set up a way for one Caribbean nation to supply potatoes to a country in Africa. What we failed to antici-pate was the destabilizing shift in the balance of power in the Caribbean as only one nation profited from the potato sales. We also didn't account for the tension and fighting between different groups in Africa as the much-needed potatoes were distributed. We learned that easy wins were not always the best course of action if overall system stability was the goal. We had to think and evaluate our actions with a broader lens.

We understand that the military cannot achieve security alone. Our missions are getting more diverse. We still plan and prepare for major theater warfare but our goal is to avoid it if at all possible. Today, we also plan and prepare for collaborative action. An explicit policy priority is designing, developing, and nurturing collaborative relationships with other countries and U.S. government agencies. To that end, our military participates in hundreds of combined training exercises.

We perform a variety of roles from combat to civil affairs to medical engagement. Thus, our teams work with our public health corps and the public health departments of host countries and international nongovernmental organizations (NGOs) to identify and prevent future epidemics. We work with investigators from the Department of Treasury to follow the trails left by the black-market money that is used to fund insurgent groups. When we want to help another country with their infrastructure or agriculture programs, we work with the U.S. Agency for International Development (USAID) folks who oversee those projects. During those projects, our civil affairs officers show our USAID colleagues how we move people and equipment in different environments.

Learning for the Present

We live in a more secure and stable world today because the military has benefited from prioritizing an understanding of how our nation's military values and our connectedness affect national security. Many of our lessons about the need for this shift were learned the hard way. The military has a long tradition of learning from its failures as well as its successes. The After Action Review (AAR) is a lessons-learned process ingrained in all leaders from the time they enter the military. AAR takes on different forms in different branches of the military but they always involve (a) gathering the participants involved in a situation, (b) discussing what each saw from their perspective, and (c) identifying ways to improve. Recently, AAR has become more systematic, making use of advances in a range of social sciences, from management to psychology to evaluation, to make the most of this opportunity to learn.

Information technology has made it possible to pull learning out of the small groups where it originates, integrate other relevant information sources, and get synthesized learning quickly out to the people and teams who need it to make better decisions. Today AAR information is a primary source of information supporting the Before Action Review (BAR) where teams discuss and rapidly analyze intentions, challenges, and risks prior to taking action.

Advanced AAR and BAR have been instrumental in both anticipating and avoiding more unintended negative impacts of actions as well as prioritizing connectedness and human values in the pursuit of our strategic objective: A balanced stability. A healthy forest.

NOTES

1. Each "Sector Visioning" chapter begins with an abstract prepared by the book's editors and attributed to Zindzi in keeping with the storyline of the book. Zindzi is introduced in Chapter 2.
2. http://www.pewhispanic.org/2015/09/28/modern-immigration-wave -brings-59-million-to-u-s-driving-population-growth-and-change-through -2065/
3. https://www.unhcr.org/5b27be547
4. According to *Groundswell* (Auburn Seminary), sanctuary is when faith communities offer safe havens. They have been doing that from the beginning of the Old Testament, to the times of slavery and the Underground Railroad, to housing Jews during WWII, to the draft during the Vietnam War.
5. Although not specifically quoted, some of the ideas about the future of security come from *A National Strategic Narrative* by Mr. Y (2011), Woodrow Wilson International Center for Scholars. Available online at www.wilsoncenter.org/ sites/default/files/A%20National%20Strategic%20Narrative.pdf

REFERENCES

Abrams, L., & Ceballos, P. L. (2012). Exploring classism and internalized classism. In D. C. Sturm & D. M. Gibson (Eds.), *Social class and the helping professions: A clinician's guide to navigating the landscape of class in America* (pp. 142–154). New York, NY: Taylor & Francis.

Bernat, D. H., & Resnick, M. D. (2009). Connectedness in the lives of adolescents. In R. J. DiClemente, J. S. Santelli, & R. A. Crosby (Eds.), *Adolescent health: Understanding and preventing risk behaviors* (pp. 375–399). San Francisco, CA: Jossey-Bass.

Center on the Developing Child at Harvard University. (2011). *Building the brain's "air traffic control" system: How early experiences shape the development of executive function* (Working Paper No. 11). Retrieved from https://developingchild .harvard.edu/resources/building-the-brains-air-traffic-control-system-how -early-experiences-shape-the-development-of-executive-function/

Centers for Disease Control and Prevention, Division of Adolescent and School Health, National Center for HIV/AIDS, Viral Hepatitis, STD, and TB Prevention. (2015, September). *Protective factors*. Retrieved from https://www.cdc.gov/healthyyouth/protective/

Cooper, M. (2015, October 2). *The downsizing of the American dream*. Retreived from https://www.theatlantic.com/business/archive/2015/10/american-dreams/408535/

Gauthier, B. (2016, December 28). Your favorite TV show says a lot about where you live and whom you voted for. Retrieved from http://www.salon.com/2016/12/28/your-favorite-tv-show-says-a-lot-about-where-you-live-and-whom-you-voted-for/

Gest, J. (2016). *The new minority: White working class politics in an age of immigration and inequity*. New York, NY: Oxford University Press.

Gest, J. (2018). *The white working class: What everyone needs to know*. New York, NY: Oxford University Press.

Harper Browne, C. (2014a, September). *The strengthening families approach and protective factors framework: Branching out and reaching deeper*. Washington, DC: Center for the Study of Social Policy. Retrieved from https://cssp.org/wp-content/uploads/2018/11/Branching-Out-and-Reaching-Deeper.pdf

Harper Browne, C. (2014b, July). *Youth Thrive: Advancing healthy adolescent development and well-being*. Washington, DC: Center for the Study of Social Policy.

Katz, J. (2016, December 27). "Duck Dynasty" vs. "Modern Family": 50 maps of the U.S. cultural divide. *New York Times*. Retrieved at https://www.nytimes.com/interactive/2016/12/26/upshot/duck-dynasty-vs-modern-family-television-maps.html

Luthar, S. S., & Cicchetti, D. (2000). The construct of resilience: Implications for interventions and social policies. *Developmental Psychopathology, 12*(4), 857–885. Retrieved from www.ncbi.nlm.nih.gov/pmc/articles/PMC1903337/

National Research Council and Institute of Medicine. (2009). *Preventing mental, emotional, and behavioral disorders among young people: Progress and possibilities*. Washington, DC: The National Academies Press.

Preston, J. (2013, October 6). Ailing midwestern cities extend a welcoming hand to immigrants. *New York Times*. Retrieved from http://www.nytimes.com/2013/10/07/us/ailing-cities-extend-hand-to-immigrants.html

Smart, J. (2017, May). Risk and protective factors for child abuse and neglect, CFCA Resource Sheet. Australian Institute for Family Studies. Retrieved at https://aifs.gov.au/cfca/publications/risk-and-protective-factors-child-abuse-and-neglect

The Annie E. Casey Foundation. (2013). *The first eight years: Giving kids a foundation for lifetime success*. Baltimore, MD: Author. Retrieved from https://www.aecf.org/resources/the-first-eight-years-giving-kids-a-foundation-for-lifetime-success/

Walsh, F. (2006). *Strengthening family resilience, 2nd ed.* New York, NY: The Guilford Press.

CHAPTER 5

NATURE

Connecting Well-Being and Conservation Praxis

Kent H. Redford, Carly Cook, Duan Biggs, and Glenda Eoyang

ZINDZI'S ABSTRACT[1]

After decades of increasingly devastating anthropogenic impacts on the biosphere and climate, the United States significantly reduced protections for human health, the environment and climate stability in the late 20-teens. The world responded by rising up in support of nature conservation. To meet the challenge, the field of nature conservation and its practitioners prioritized transparency of values, equitable solutions, systems thinking, and deliberate collaboration to co-create models of social-ecological systems. As a result, conservation evolved from being relatively insular and a primarily scientific field to become more self-aware as a politically enacted community endeavor. The conservation community committed to understanding stakeholder values and agency and to using evaluative inquiry to reveal the intersectionality that would enable sustainable and equitable solutions. From the context of ecosystem management and wildlife trade, the materials below introduce three case examples. Each case exemplifies opportunities that were taken and that were

Visionary Evaluation for a Sustainable, Equitable Future, pages 95–109
Copyright © 2020 by Information Age Publishing
All rights of reproduction in any form reserved.

missed in order to: humbly understand human values; let go of power and
expectations of certainty and control; investigate and respect intersectionality
of social-ecological systems with particular attention to cultures, politics, and
economics; discover collaborative solutions; use evaluative inquiry to shape
practice over long term processes; and develop praxis for transformation.

A worldwide groundswell in public action in favor of conservation emerged
after 4 years of rule in the United States by a government administration
led by Donald J. Trump that effectively abrogated many forms of environmental protection and action on climate change.

This worldwide shift in favor of conservation brought about positive
change in a number of key ways. First, there has been a greater willing-
ness to make the stakeholder values underlying approaches to conservation
transparent. This has led, second, to greater emphasis on equitable solutions for all stakeholders. Third, from a generally reductionist approach to
problem solving there has been a movement towards systems thinking, in
particular, framing conservation questions as germane to socio-ecological
systems and part of overall planetary health. Lastly, as part of this rise in
systems thinking, previously disconnected efforts have been integrated into
purposeful collaboration under co-developed system models—models of
how relevant systems function with each other. Together these four efforts
have led to a more effective and sustainable approach to the use and conservation of social and natural resources.

Such sustainable approaches emerge when critical factors that influence
socio-ecological systems either align or, when unaligned, are resolved transparently and equitably. These critical factors include values, politics, culture, history, and leadership. Arguably, the most important of these factors
is values, defined as trans-situational goals that serve as guiding principles
in the life of a person or group (Schwartz, 2011). A transparent exploration
of values is used to contrast the foundational goals of the diverse groups
involved in an issue, clarify the basis of conflict among stakeholders, and
more generally provide for the understanding and prediction of human behavior (Manfredo et al., 2016). Nontransparent and conflicting values have
long served as major impediments to achieving equitable and sustainable
solutions to conservation problems.

Unfortunately, these critical factors do not always align and, by 2030, sustainable approaches to nature have not emerged in all parts of the world.
This uneven success is in part due to the lack of concordant manifestation of values, politics, culture, history, and leadership. Values play a key
role in shaping the relationship between humans and the natural world
and are often not made transparent when stakeholders gather to make decisions. When left opaque, differences in values can result in heated dis-
agreement over potentially resolvable issues, or even in false solutions that
disintegrate when implemented. Politics, culture, and history interact to

create or suppress enabling conditions for sustainable solutions in the face of diverse values. Leadership is often the means by which these enabling conditions can be modified and, help resolve or overcome inevitable differences. These factors have not aligned in major regions of all continents of the world—particularly where the effects of climate change are most pronounced and where new resource frontiers have opened.

In 2030, a comprehensive equitable solution has not been developed to the complex and dynamic relationship between humans and nature. The difficulty in resolving this relationship begins with the fact that "nature" has been called the most complicated word in the English language (Williams, 1976) and there is little agreement over time or across cultures as to its meaning (Coates, 1998). Compounding this difficulty is the fact that conservation, another commonly used term, also lacks a common definition (Redford & Mace, 2016). So, though widely used in the last half of the 20th century and the first decades of the 21st, "conservation of nature" continues to mean different things to different stakeholders, creating misunderstandings and hampering equitable solutions.

The lack of a commonly-held, operational definition of nature is in part due to cultural differences in its meaning and in understanding the relationship between humans and nature. Amplified through the prior actions of colonial nations and differentiated power, these differences have created enduring conflicts over resource management and protected areas. The advent of new genetic technologies in the early 2000s led to the emergence of synthetic biology, a field that applies engineering principles to biology, creating novel life forms through alterations of the genome. Though still a young science as applied to conservation, by 2030 it shows the potential to change the relationships between humans and the natural world. We will see these effects by 2050 (Redford, Adams, Carlson, Mace, & Ceccarell, 2014).

Beginning in the early 2000s, however, in many parts of the world, relationships between protected area authorities and local peoples improved markedly as benefits came to be shared more widely. Part of the basis for this benefit sharing was the realization that nature is the source of important economically valuable goods and is a fundamental part of what allows human well-being. Nature provides four types of services: supporting services (e.g., nutrient cycling, primary production), provisioning services (e.g., food, fresh water), regulating services (e.g., climate regulation, water purification), and cultural services (e.g., spiritual, recreational). These services collectively contribute to constituents of well-being such as security, basic material for a good life, health, good social relations, and freedom of choice and action (Reid et al., 2005).

Though there is broad agreement that nature is essential for the well-being of humanity, there continues to be divergent perspectives on how humans assign value to nature, which aspects of nature are valued more than others, and who gets to decide. The conservation community has been through a variety of phases in how it views the relationship between humans and the natural world (Mace, 2014). The first phase began before the 1960s and was called "nature for itself," followed by "nature despite people," then "nature for people," and then "people and nature" which brought us up to 2025. Starting about then, we entered the current phase "people for nature" in which there is widespread recognition that the tremendously significant impacts that humans are having on the biosphere, including climate change, means that, in order to survive, nature requires ongoing management by humans. Moreover, in the conservation and ecology research communities, there is increasing recognition and acceptance of the physiological and spiritual benefits that nature provides to individuals, communities, and society. This makes conservation scientists more willing to engage with nonscientists as equals in defining, understanding, and measuring the state of wild nature, and designing actions to conserve it.

Management of the human–nature relationship has been the provenance of conservation biology, which provided the scientific foundations for conservation action. By 2020, this field had moved from being a technocratic, scientific exercise toward a more value-based, politically enacted activity. It made this change only after it recognized that conservation is politics—the public contestation of values—and, as such, that conservation is a firmly value-based endeavor that requires explicit discussion of values as well as of agency. Agency, the ability to act and achieve on the basis of what one values and has reason to value (Hicks et al., 2016), turns out to be a key concept in allowing conservation to move from its static roots in natural sciences to a broadly inclusive movement of praxis.

Conservation has traditionally advocated for caution and avoidance of all risk to nature, locating its practice in opposition to dominant capitalist social decisions. It is positioned to resist change emanating from this worldview while simultaneously promulgating change that leads to greater respect for and conservation of the nonhuman world. The world of 2030 is one where the natural world is in better shape overall than it was in the early part of the century due to the rise of evaluative thinking and praxis. However, this progress is spotty. The following three examples illustrate some of the reasons for this uneven progress in the development of equitable solutions to the problems facing both the human and nonhuman world and hopefully provide a path forward for more widespread success. Though based on fact until 2015, they move to speculation as extrapolated to 2030.

ECOSYSTEM MANAGEMENT IN 2030:
NEW ZEALAND VERSUS PUERTO RICO

For many decades, one of the key roles of conservation managers was maintaining ecosystems in a pristine state or restoring ecosystems degraded by
human activities. As a common goal, this led to a strong focus by managers
on controlling or eradicating species that were not native to the ecosystem—
exotic species. However, the decades preceding 2030 saw a divergence in
the approach to ecosystem management, creating two very different strategies. The first strategy is the traditional conservation model, whereby the
desired ecosystem condition is defined as a state that prevailed at some
previous time when the elements valued by managers, such as a diversity
of native species, were present. Management efforts are then directed at
attempting to restore the system to that historic state. The alternative approach, which emerged in the early 2010s, is based on a view that ecosystems are dynamic rather than static entities, ever evolving and changing. As
such, in this second approach, the focus of management shifts away from
a fixed view of an ecosystem towards a dynamic one in which the ecological and evolutionary processes that promote diverse ecosystems are what is
valued, regardless of the origins of species.

The two approaches to ecosystem conservation are both attempts to
manage environments in a way that achieves society's values for the environment. They create a vision for environmental managers, although the
values that underpin these visions are not always explicitly discussed. For
example, should species or ecosystems be the focus, and how important
is collaboration with stakeholders and communities in achieving these visions? The bifurcation between the two models for ecosystem management,
and the strategies adopted to achieve these visions, can be illustrated by the
approaches taken by New Zealand (traditional conservation model) and
Puerto Rico (dynamic ecosystems model). These two geographies pursued
different models of ecosystem management, and the different paths they
took in pursuing their visions reveal how evaluative thinking can influence
the outcomes of environmental management.

New Zealand and the Traditional Conservation Model

New Zealand's two main islands are located over 2,300 km from their
nearest neighbor, New Caledonia. The isolation and long separation (80
million years) led to a unique set of species, rich in bird life (Saunders
& Norton, 2001). The indigenous Maori people settled the country over
700 years ago and were responsible for the extinction of 34 land-bird species (Duncan, Blackburn, & Worthy, 2002). Their arrival was followed by

European settlement 500 years later, which resulted in the extinction of a further 11 land-bird species (Duncan et al., 2002). While both waves of human settlement led to the introduction of exotic species, Europeans introduced mammalian predators, such as rats, stoats, and weasels, which decimated the ground-nesting endemic bird species (species found nowhere else in the world) through nest predation (Towns, West, & Broome, 2012).

Contemporary New Zealanders are conservation-minded, valuing the conservation science that documented the decline of their unique native species. This evidence-base, built during the late 1990s and early 2000s, led to strong public support for a campaign to eradicate all mammalian species from New Zealand. Implicit in this campaign was the fact that the New Zealand community valued the country's unique biota and did not want to see it lost due to the impacts of exotic species. During the public consultation period for the new strategy in 2008 there was opposition from community groups who objected to the large redirection of funds from other programs; however, this opposition was drowned out as being unpatriotic. A group of evaluative thinkers approached the government at this time, concerned that important perspectives were not being heard in the debate. However, the evaluative thinkers had difficulty communicating the importance of taking a more holistic view of the challenge, and the government continued to believe that science would provide the solution. On reflection, the evaluative thinkers realized that a deeper understanding of conservation science and practice, which could have been gained by working more closely with scientists, may have improved their ability to persuade the government of the value of their approach.

The goal of the eradication program was to restore New Zealand ecosystems to the condition they were in prior to European settlement in 1840. In 2015, the New Zealand government made an unprecedented financial investment in the program, initiating intensive control programs for rats, weasels, ferrets, and stoats focusing on protecting populations of the most vulnerable endangered species. There were initial successes associated with the eradication program due to the huge injection of funds. Monitoring programs showed populations of several endangered species of particular significance to New Zealanders, such as kiwis, rebounded during the first 3 years. However, due to the need to prioritize control efforts, there were many species that continued to decline, including several species of cultural significance to Maori people. Local communities objected to the lack of transparency around the processes used to prioritize where management was focused, leading to a breakdown in communication with the government. In protest, many communities prevented government officials from accessing their land to undertake control programs. The result was areas that acted as source populations of predators and compromised broader eradication efforts.

Beginning in 2020, several studies documented adaptations in endemic bird species that reduced the impact of mammalian predators. There were also studies indicating that populations of predators were increasing in size in areas of moderate control intensity. It was suggested that control programs could have been contributing to these changes by selecting for larger individuals who could withstand sub-lethal doses of the poisons used in control programs. However, public support for the eradication program remained high during the early 2020s because of the well-publicized successes associated with protecting valued species, such as the kakapo, and the studies were largely discredited or ignored by the scientists guiding the eradication program.

The initial success of the program led to a sense of "mission accomplished" within the general population, who had little understanding that when attempting to eradicate a species, control efforts get harder as populations are reduced because more effort is involved in killing each individual. However, the impacts of rising sea levels due to climate change and a series of severe earthquakes created public pressure to redirect funds to other environmental, social, and infrastructure programs. Commencing in 2021, there was increasing pressure from politicians to reduce the investment in the eradication program. The reduction in funds during the decade that followed meant that control efforts experienced disruptions that enabled predator populations to reestablish. As resources were removed from control programs, conservation scientists lamented the unraveling of their efforts. But, as we commence the 2030s, conservation professionals take comfort in the fact that, while they were not able to eradicate predators on the mainland, several vulnerable species had been secured on offshore islands. Conservation professionals now lobby the government for enough funding to enable ongoing surveillance efforts to prevent predators recolonizing those islands.

Puerto Rico and the Dynamic Ecosystems Model

In the first half of the 19th century, Puerto Rico experienced significant conversion of its extensive native forests to agricultural land (Lugo, Carlo, & Wuderle, 2012). However, by the 1960s, agricultural land was increasingly being abandoned as farmers moved into the cities and forest cover was increasing (Brandeis, Helmer, & Oswalt, 2007). The forests that returned were significantly different in composition from those originally cleared, containing a large number of species that had been introduced for agriculture (Lugo & Helmer, 2004). In response to concerns about the impacts of exotic species, local conservation groups advocated for more resources to increase eradication efforts. During this period, social justice groups were lobbying the government to invest more resources in poverty reduction and building the Puerto Rican economy. These groups aggressively attacked one another through the media, refusing to concede ground and accusing each other of being callous and unjust.

In 2017, the Puerto Rican government was approached by a group of evaluative thinkers, containing practitioners in systems thinking and evaluation. This group convinced the government that a solution to the seemingly intractable problem of whether to invest in social or environmental issues could be found through evaluative inquiry. They proposed bringing together a diverse array of stakeholders to discuss solutions, including leaders from indigenous and nonindigenous communities, conservation biologists, evolutionary biologists, social scientists, economists, and environmental managers. They explained that this forum would provide an opportunity to hear a wide range of perspectives, and reveal critical information about the values underpinning the diverse and seemingly irreconcilable positions. In need of guidance, the government agreed to all stakeholders being given an opportunity to voice their perspectives and forums were held across the country during 2017. The evaluative thinkers helped the different groups to recognize that deeply held beliefs lay beneath all of these perspectives. The process revealed dominant worldviews that prioritized either nature or human interests. By listening to one another, stakeholders came to understand that any lasting solution must involve both humans and nature being given a central role, with compromises being made on all sides to accommodate core values.

In making their values explicit, stakeholders clarified that those who prioritized nature fundamentally valued diversity, but feared the natural environment becoming homogenous and losing much of what made Puerto Rico unique. Those who prioritized humans gained a clearer understanding of the central role of nature to human physical, cultural, and spiritual well-being. While diverting funds from conservation to social services could provide short-term benefits, they recognized that environmental management could support sustainable use of nature to benefit humans over the long term. In recognition of the central tenets of the two worldviews, and in consultation with natural and social scientists, a decision was taken to refocus environmental management. The new strategy moved away from the idea of restoring pristine environments free from exotic species toward ecosystems supported by ecological and evolutionary processes that promote diversity and build resilience that could enable ecosystems to adapt to future environmental change.

Initially, the new strategy was difficult for many conservation professionals to accept because it led to the extinction of several endemic species and some changes to the character of ecological communities (e.g., more vines and fewer understory plants in the forest). However, in 2018, both natural scientists and practitioners were asked to use their knowledge to plan management strategies that would preserve much of the diversity they valued using control efforts directed toward exotic species that disrupted natural processes critical to healthy ecosystems. Practitioners and scientists grew to value this approach because it provided an unparalleled opportunity for scientific inquiry that yielded a deeper understanding of the ecological and evolutionary processes that govern natural systems. The important ecosystem functions they valued, such as interactions between species and recovery from disturbances like hurricanes, remained intact, supporting many of the endemic species. Social research conducted during the early 2020s showed that people's experience of nature did not diminish because they enjoyed the diversity of the ecosystems regardless of the origins of the species. Now in 2030, younger generations of Puerto Ricans say that one of the things they value most about their natural environment is that it is dynamic and ever changing to adapt to environmental conditions while continuing to contribute material, cultural, and spiritual values.

During the 2020s, moving away from the traditional, highly interventionist approach to ecosystem management allowed Puerto Rico to redirect those resources to poverty reduction schemes. In the decade that followed, these additional resources materially improved the lives of many of the country's poorest peoples. Up until 2025, Puerto Rico's indigenous and mestizo communities were amongst some of the most disadvantaged within the country. During the consultation process, they expressed their deep spiritual connection with nature, and their concern that changes could sever that connection. In recognition of the importance of this connection, in 2022, the government created a program that brought local people together with biologists and social scientists to frame management programs to preserve the important character of their lands. This program created jobs for the local community and re-established their connection to the landscape through active stewardship.

Now in 2030, as the impacts of climate change are increasingly felt globally, Puerto Rico's ecosystems services have remained relatively intact. This means that the forests support a diversity of species and provide Puerto Ricans with critical resources. While natural disasters have become more frequent, the ecosystems are resilient, recovering from and adapting to these disturbances. This has made Puerto Rico a desirable tourist destination, providing additional economic benefits to the broader community.

A Process of Evaluative Thinking

The different approaches taken by New Zealand and Puerto Rico are valuable in illustrating how evaluative thinking can shape positive, equitable solutions to environmental problems. Neither model of ecosystem management is "right" or "wrong." Both are reflections of the values of these two communities. However, the differences in the approaches to implementing these models significantly influenced the outcomes achieved. In Puerto Rico, values were placed at the center of the public discourse, providing for all perspectives to be recognized and increasing the inclusiveness and transparency of decision-making. Taking a position of inquiry and mutual respect for different perspectives facilitated the ability to reach an acceptable compromise. In New Zealand, the dominant worldviews prioritized nature over humans, and the failures to promote dialogue amongst all stakeholders suppressed the less common, but equally valid, worldviews and the perspectives of other stakeholders, such as indigenous people. Considering the influence of different actors in the system from a perspective of humility and respect is a central tenet of evaluative thinking. The lack of a respectful dialogue meant barriers to the successful implementation of the control program were not recognized, compromising the conservation outcomes. Conversely, in Puerto Rico, seeking acceptable compromises between the two worldviews led to the identification of solutions that achieved positive outcomes for both the environment and society.

Another key difference between the two cases was the role of science in the process. In Puerto Rico, the focus was on the system and the processes that govern healthy ecosystems, creating space for learning and the generation of new knowledge. In New Zealand, the focus was on species rather than processes. While this led to highly targeted efforts, there was less focus on inquiry, which may have contributed to slow recognition of the changes that occurred in the system (e.g., predators adapting to control methods). As such, the failure to take a systems approach to finding solutions created barriers to recognizing problems and possible solutions. Now in 2030, we have an opportunity to learn from the increasing number of positive case studies to find the elements of evaluative thinking that can help achieve equitable and sustainable solutions to conservation problems.

EVALUATIVE THINKING AND A MORE HOLISTIC SOLUTION TO THE ILLEGAL WILDLIFE TRADE CRISIS

By 2017, the Illegal Wildlife Trade (IWT) had become one of the most contested and hotly debated areas of conservation. The challenge was most serious in Africa where the two species of African rhino and the African elephant were being poached at unprecedented levels. This surge in poaching started in the mid-2000s, driven by increasing wealth in East Asia and a resurgent cultural identity that included using rhino horn for traditional Chinese medicine and ivory in making highly valued ornaments. There were ferocious debates among African countries and the international conservation community about how to deal most effectively with the IWT problem. Kenya, supported by the international community including powerful conservation and animal welfare NGOs, strongly favored an approach based on banning all trade in wildlife products accompanied by heavy penalties and enforcement. The Kenyan approach was based on the intrinsic value of wildlife and nature—that it should be conserved because of its inherent existence value. In contrast, South Africa and its neighbors like Namibia and Zimbabwe argued that the best solution was to create highly regulated markets for wildlife products. Their argument was that the income from the sale of wildlife products could be used to fund conservation as well as rural development among some of their country's poorest communities that live around conservation areas, thereby providing economic justification for the continued conservation of elephants and rhinos. These countries had a very different utilitarian approach based on a pragmatic determination of the cost required to conserve these species.

Since 1977, international trade in endangered species had been governed by the Convention on Trade in Endangered Species (CITES). In theory, CITES allowed for nuanced policies on trade by different countries. However, the political dynamics of CITES and the power of animal welfare NGOs meant that CITES, especially with regard to iconic mammals like rhinos and elephants, had become a one-size-fits-all treaty. There was no longer room for different approaches by different countries to manage the threat from IWT. The outcome was a highly polarized debate with the South Africans, Namibians, and Zimbabweans on the one hand trying to convince the Kenyans and the rest of the world that creating a regulated market for wildlife products is the solution. On the other hand, the international conservation community was trying to convince and force South Africa, Namibia, and Zimbabwe to adopt the Kenyan model.

An unfortunate result of this polarization was that the different interpretations of what "conservation" means, and the different approaches and diverse value systems that underpinned these approaches were never discussed. Moreover, little or no attention was paid to the need for equitable solutions for different stakeholders in the approaches to tackling IWT. Nor was there an appreciation of the complex socio-ecological systems in which the IWT challenge manifested.

In the middle of 2018, a group of conservation researchers and practitioners exposed to evaluative thinking teamed up with the world's leading systemic evaluators to facilitate a dialogue between these opposing stakeholders. The objective was to try and bring the different values to the table and find the common ground about how to move forward together. These discussions took place initially behind the scenes. In the public sphere, the levels of polarization and conflict between groups appeared to still be on the increase, concomitant with increased poaching across the continent.

After numerous iterations of discussions and workshops, common ground and a shared understanding started emerging between the South Africans, Zimbabweans, Namibians, Kenyans, and key members of the international conservation community.

However, in April of 2020, social revolution broke out in South Africa leading to an unexpectedly rapid change in government. The new government vowed to address centuries of inequity between the races and between the rich and poor through a radical wealth redistribution drive. As part of this, South Africa renegotiated its relationship with the international community and, instead of focusing international investment to address poverty alleviation through the private sector, it switched to government-driven socialist policies. This upset the capitalist world and raised the expectations of rapid failure due to mismanagement and rampant corruption. As part of this, the new South African government withdrew from the CITES treaty because it was seen that through CITES, the wealthy global elite in cities like London and New York were dictating what South Africa could and could not do with its own wildlife resources.

Western countries and the South African business community were very critical of the new government. However, the success of the new South African government in growing the economy and improving the well-being of its citizens surprised its critics. A key contributor to this success was a group of leading evaluative and systems thinkers who worked with the new South African government and key stakeholders to understand the challenges facing the country from a systemic perspective and identify key risks and opportunities in an evaluative and holistic way. Although the new government had withdrawn from CITES, it saw the importance of trying to work in partnership with the international community to conserve wildlife. South Africa was home to 95% of Africa's remaining rhinos at that time, and the Kenyans, international NGOs, and other key stakeholders in CITES realized they had to come to the discussion table because of this. The conservation scientists and evaluative thinkers who facilitated earlier talks between the Kenyans, South Africans, and international NGOs were, in the mid-2020s, in an ideal position to assist and were asked to facilitate and guide these discussions and negotiations.

For the first time, the different stakeholders understood each other's very different value positions, and their different interpretations of what conservation means. This ultimately enabled the stakeholders, by 2028, to understand that a one-size-fits-all solution to the IWT problem was not possible, or even desirable. The stakeholder group was extended to involve Traditional Chinese Medicine practitioners and buyers of rhino horn and ivory. Through skilled facilitation and evaluative systems thinking, the buyers and users of wildlife products slowly stopped being perceived as criminals who should be incarcerated but, rather, as other human beings with their own value system and interpretation of how humans interact with nature. After a series of these open, systemically oriented discussions, all stakeholders came to the agreement that rhino and elephant conservation is of paramount importance. But, that the conservation of these species should allow for multiple value systems and interpretations of conservation to coexist.

After many months of discussion, in 2029, the Kenyans, South Africans, and key international NGOs and CITES decided on a plan forward based on a multiplicity of value systems. South Africa would be able to sell rhino horn and ivory under a strict regulatory framework to users in East Asia and a part of the proceeds would go to conserve rhinos and elephants throughout their African ranges including in Kenya. Kenya, in turn, would continue its nonuse approach to conservation with the management costs subsidized by transfers of wealth from the international community.

CITES and the strategies to combat IWT had accommodated the diverse value systems and the different interpretations of what conservation means. As a result, the polarization was addressed and reduced. Moreover, this shift enabled more equitable outcomes between stakeholders based on the collective understanding of IWT as a problem that needed to be addressed in a systemic fashion that accounted for social-ecological complexity.

WHAT CHANGED AND WHY?

As outlined above, political, social, and economic changes, coupled with the stress of climate change, have forced adaptation in conservation theory and practice during the first 3 decades of the 21st century. What was the fundamental cause and content of that shift? What will prepare us for more of the same in the future?

Each of these stories, New Zealand, Puerto Rico, and Southern Africa, reflects the same challenges and opportunities that emerge around the world as people deal with conservation and other complex problems. Each story tracks emerging questions and consequences (both intended and unintended). The changes in policy and practice described here are not superficial shifts in perspective, nor are they simply redistributions of power and voice. Something much more profound and fundamental was happening as visionary evaluative thinking was woven into conservation theory and practice.

The conceptual and pragmatic turning was about certainty. Individually and collectively, between 2010 and 2030, people gave up the expectation, sometimes even the hope, of predictability and control of complex, natural systems. They began to find ways to make decisions and take action when they realized that absolute and final answers were no longer possible.

In the absence of ethical certainty, institutions were forced to accept greater transparency and public accountability to values that were as diverse as they were strongly held. With the rise of complex, ambiguous system boundaries, people lost the ability to distinguish between intended and unintended consequences. Systemic, evaluative thinking supported meaning making and understanding, even when prediction and control were not possible. As the voices of class and race rose, elites could no longer be certain that they deserved or could preserve their privileged positions. They were forced to enter into dialogue and explore questions of inequity and social justice.

As challenges became more complex and systemic, people and their institutions realized that none of their answers were sufficient by themselves. They could no longer be certain of their understanding or capacity to act alone. When that certainty faded, the only option—however difficult or unimaginable—was to collaborate. The final, and probably the most critical, uncertainty related to the ability of our natural environments to persist. As that certainty was shaken, there was no choice but to explore new options for systemic and evaluative action.

These stories describe a range of options for action that offer hope in response to uncertainty. Dialogue, transparency with data and decision making, inquiry, curiosity, creativity, patience with ambiguity, respect for diversity, humility, and mutual respect are the keys to solutions that will work, when certainty is no longer an option.

As the awareness of uncertainty continues to spread, the need for inquiry-based methods will become more acute. In conservation, as in other natural and social sciences, adaptive capacity will continue to rise in importance. Individuals and institutions, scholars and practitioners, technicians and policy makers, elites and disenfranchised must develop a praxis that allows everyone to work together across differences and with the natural environment to replace the certainty of answers with the sustainability of good questions. Visionary, systemic evaluation makes this transformation possible.

NOTE

1. Each "Sector Visioning" chapter begins with an abstract prepared by the book editors and attributed to Zindzi in keeping with the storyline of the book. Zindzi is introduced in Chapter 2.

REFERENCES

Brandeis, T. J., Helmer, E. H., & Oswalt, S. N. (2007). The status of Puerto Rico's forests, 2003. *Southern Research Station Resource Bulletin SRS-119*. Asheville, NC: USDA Forest Service.

Coates, P. (1998). *Nature: Western attitudes since ancient times.* Los Angeles, CA: University of California Press.

Duncan, R. P., Blackburn, T. M., & Worthy, T. H. (2002). Prehistoric bird extinctions and human hunting. Proceedings of the Royal Society of London. *Biological Sciences, 269*(1490), 517–521.

Hicks, C. C., Levine, A., Agrawal, A., Basurto, X., Breslow, S. J., Carothers, C., . . . Levin, P. S. (2016). Engage key social concepts for sustainability. *Science, 352(6281),* 38–40.

Lugo, A. E., Carlo, T. A., & Wunderle, J. M., Jr. (2012). Natural mixing of species: Novel plant–animal communities on Caribbean Islands. *Animal Conservation, 15,* 233–241.

Lugo, A. E., & Helmer, E. (2004). Emerging forests on abandoned land: Puerto Rico's new forests. *Forest Ecology and Management, 190,* 145–161.

Mace, G. M. (2014). Whose conservation is it? *Science, 345,* 1558–1560.

Manfredo, M., Bruskotter, J. T., Teel, T. L., Fulton, D., Schwartz, S. H., Arlinghaus, R., . . . Sullivan, L. (2016). Why social values cannot be changed for the sake of conservation. In *Conservation Biology, 31(4),* 772–780. https://doi.org/10.1111/cobi.12855

Redford, K. H., Adams, W. A., Carlson, R., Mace, G. M., & Ceccarelli, B. (2014). Synthetic biology and the conservation of biodiversity. *Oryx, 48*(3), 330–336. https://doi.org/10.1017/S0030605314000040

Redford, K. H., & Mace, G. M. (2016, June). Conserving and contesting biodiversity in the homogocene. Unpublished paper presented at the Ernst Strüngmann Forum, *Rethinking Environmentalism: Justice, Sustainability, and Diversity,* Frankfurt, Germany.

Reid, W. A., Mooney, A., Cropper, D., Capistrano, D., Carpenter, S. R., Chopra, K., . . . Zurek, M. B. (2005). *Ecosystems and human well-being.* A report of the Millennium Ecosystem Assessment. Washington, DC: Island Press.

Saunders, A., & Norton, D. A. (2001). Ecological restoration at mainland islands in New Zealand. *Biological Conservation, 99,* 109–119.

Schwartz, S. (2011). Values: Cultural and individual. In F. J. R. van de Vijver, A. Chasiotis, & S. M. Breugelmans (Eds.), *Fundamental Questions in Cross-Cultural Psychology* (pp. 463–493). Cambridge, England: Cambridge University Press.

Towns, D. R., West, C. J., & Broome, K. G. (2013). Purposes, outcomes and challenges of eradicating invasive mammals from New Zealand islands: An historical perspective. *Wildlife Research, 40,* 94–107.

Williams, R. (1976). *Keywords: A vocabulary of culture and society.* Oxford, England: Oxford University Press.

CHAPTER 6

LAW

Living Values in Our Legal System

Ellen Lawton and Joe Scantlebury

ZINDZI'S ABSTRACT[1]

For many years, the legal field remained relatively fixed in the way it operated. Innovation was further stymied as leaders grappled with a sector that, especially in the early 21st century, floundered as law school graduates struggled to find legal positions that repaid loans and offered meaningful careers. The inequitable application of the law and the limited ability of most Americans to afford a lawyer further challenged the legal profession and the many lawyers, judges, and legal officers working with it. As the practice of law seemed to become more about power and money and less about justice and truth, the profession was not seen as reflective or embracing of the values embodied in the U.S. Constitution and its aspirational amendments. These fissures broke open through two events in the mid-2010s—Flint, Michigan and Ferguson, Missouri. The legal contributors take us through these events and show how they were the basis for vast change in legal practice so that now, in 2030, laws and the profession that supports them are focused on access, equity, sustainability, innovation, service, and impact.

Visionary Evaluation for a Sustainable, Equitable Future, pages 111–126
Copyright © 2020 by Information Age Publishing

It is 2030, and the legal profession is transforming into a sector that increasingly recognizes that its "objective reasonable man standard" has at times been both subjective and unreasonable. In doing so, it has become a field that is deepening its understanding of and responsibility for the contributions of the legal sector in systems change and that is building integrated approaches with other sectors toward social progress. Indeed, this transformation harkens back to the shift in the healthcare field that began at the turn of the century, when communities started to align financing and outcomes in a values-driven framework, emphasizing prevention and a population health approach. Mimicking the healthcare field's evolution, the legal profession has embraced data collection, research, and technology to improve access to legal expertise, document impact, and drive resource allocation, especially in the sectors that serve vulnerable populations.

This maturation of the legal profession was in part catalyzed by the experiences of two American communities attempting to heal from the effects of racially discriminatory laws, policies, and community dynamics. Examining and understanding the experiences of a water crisis in Flint, Michigan and police brutality in Ferguson, Missouri paved the way for a reconceptualization of the role, activities, and financing of the legal profession, allowing lawyers to diversify their problem solving approach, blend seamlessly with other sectors and professions, and access new tools and strategies to achieve long-standing goals such as (a) reducing structural discriminatory patterns (e.g., segregated poverty, racial bias in prosecutions and sentencing, and environmental justice issues), (b) increasing access to scarce legal resources, and (c) developing and deploying a prevention strategy for civil and criminal legal needs in vulnerable populations that improves access to basic needs.

THE LEGAL PROFESSION
AND SOCIETAL ROLE OF LAWYERS

BOX 6.1

The profession of law is fundamental to the flourishing of American democracy. Today, however, critics of the legal profession, both from within and without, have pointed to a great profession suffering from varying degrees of confusion and demoralization. A reawakening of professional élan must include revitalizing legal preparation.
—Carnegie Foundation, *"Preparation for the Profession of Law"*
(Sullivan Colby, Wegner, Bond, & Shulman, 2007)

The Legal Profession and Legal Education— A Saturated Market

In 2016, the legal profession was the largest professional group in the world, with the American Bar Association reporting 1.3 million registered lawyers. As lawyers continued to practice for longer periods of time, the number of opportunities for young lawyers diminished (American Bar Association, 2016), exacerbated by an explosion of growth in law schools, which saturated the market.

At the same time, this demographic trend collided with the rupturing of the law business model, in which law firms and corporations found they could make do with far fewer in-house lawyers, squeezing out those just starting their careers (Scheiber, 2016). Further, law students graduated from law school with significant debt ($88,000 for public law schools alone; Harper, 2015) and few business skills, contributing to a solo and small-firm lawyer community that felt both burdened and sometimes ill-equipped (Cohen, 2016; Lerner, 2006). This shift reverberated through to law schools, many of which had expanded or opened but without creating or cementing pathways for post-graduate employment. For example, in 2014, only 60% of graduates had found full-time, long-term jobs that required passage of the bar exam (Harper, 2015). Despite enrollment declines, the numbers of law school graduates did not fall at the pace necessary to reach equilibrium in a stagnant legal job market, resulting in too many new lawyers for too few jobs.

While there were a myriad of potential reasons for the glut and stagnancy of the legal profession, the bottom line is that there was a market imperative at that time for innovative dynamic change in the business of practicing law and in employment opportunities for professionals with a law degree (Scheiber, 2016). It is in this environment that the emerging popularity of joint or dual degree programs escalated, promising to equip the next generation of lawyers with a broader skill set that would accelerate employment opportunities. At the same time, the saturated market had lawyers increasingly looking outside the "traditional" legal employment sector, towards adjacent settings like health and technology, where the legal profession's highly analytical skills could lead to employment (Spahn, n.d.).

Houston, We Have a (Another) Problem in the Legal Profession

A 2013 Pew Study found that only 18% of the American public believed that lawyers had an important role to play in society; the study ranked lawyers dead last in "perceived contributions," just below artists (30%) and business executives (24%). Researchers in 2016 hypothesized that this reflected a dissonance between society's ethical behavioral standards and a lawyer's responsibility to be a "zealous advocate," alongside the law profession's own "myopic materialism" that led to issues such as long hours, work–life balance challenges and commercialism. Collectively these pressures and perceptions cemented a low public opinion of lawyers and the legal profession.[2] Furthermore, there was also the reality that most Americans could not personally afford to hire a lawyer, severely limiting access to justice (Cohen, 2017).

Other experts in the legal profession hypothesized that the root of the low public opinion of lawyers lay in its hyper-focus on an adversarial, litigation strategy (Zeidel, Yu, & Zerehi, 2015). Alternative strategies such as "peacemaking" lawyering, collaborative law, and unbundling representation could reduce the animosity, expense, and inefficiency of the legal system, while improving outcomes for clients and job satisfaction for lawyers (American Bar Association, 2017).

Add to all of this the fact that the legal profession took a harsher social toll than most other professions. According to a 2015 study by the American Bar Association, one in three lawyers were problem drinkers, 28% suffered from depression, and 19% showed symptoms of anxiety. By comparison, only about 6.8% of all Americans over the age of eighteen had alcohol use disorders (Cuban, 2017; Olson, 2016). Young lawyers in 2015 were more likely to suffer from problematic drinking, with studies suggesting that the private practice environment normalized problem drinking (Olson, 2016).

The Next Generation of Diverse Leaders in the Legal Profession

Perhaps most dispiritingly, law has persisted as one of the least racially diverse professions in the United States despite increases early in the century of visible, high-ranking lawyers from diverse backgrounds, such as three female Supreme Court justices, a female African-American Attorney General, and a president and first lady who were both lawyers of color. In 2015, 88% of lawyers were White. Although Latinos, African Americans, and Native Americans constituted a fifth of law school graduates, they made up fewer than 7% of law firm partners and 9% of general counsels of large corporations. While women in 2016 made up over a third of lawyers, they only represented about one fifth of law firm partners, general counsels of Fortune 500 corporations, and law school deans. Even when controlling for variables such as law school grades and time spent out of the workforce or on a part-time schedule, men were two to five times more likely than women to make partner (Rhode, 2015). These dismal demographic statistics were also a flashpoint for change in the profession during this time, led by a strong, activist coalition within both the American Bar Association and the private sector, accelerated through the advent of the Trump administration (see below) and a recognition of how quickly wins could be eroded by changes in political power. This reality was amplified by the fact that dominant political parties retain the right to appoint judges, and where there was no balance of power between political parties, they could potentially solidify a politically leaning judiciary for generations.

Effect of Legal Profession Trends on Vulnerable Populations and Communities

The effort to address inequity in the profession contributed substantially to a parallel initiative to align public interest legal work with the systemic goal of achieving societal equity, and accelerated solutions to the problem of insufficient legal professionals to tackle the civil and criminal legal needs of low income Americans, despite an overabundance of lawyers in the legal sector.

A reconceptualization of the role of a publicly funded legal sector included rethinking the financing mechanisms currently in place for legal professionals, whereby insufficient public funds are allocated towards a small public sector of legal work (Williams, Platt, & Lee, 2015). Indeed, early legal innovators in the private sector advanced models for change, which include a shift from fee-for-service towards value-based payments that mimicked changes at the time in the health care financing sector.[3] For example, in 2017, the Los Angeles County Department of Health Services included legal services as part of a California Medi-Cal demonstration program aimed at improving health and social well-being outcomes and reducing costs.[4] The ongoing change environment in the legal sector helped to bridge those learnings into the public law sectors (Cohen, 2018). Ultimately, the legal sector was in a vicious cycle: Young adults continued to be interested and motivated to train as lawyers in large numbers, and low-income Americans wanted and needed access to low cost or free criminal and civil legal assistance. But unlike the health sector, which recognized the need for every American to have access to some kind of health professional—there was no parallel recognition for lawyers. That started to change in 2020.

Gradually, influenced by key innovations like the medical-legal partnership movement that anchored public interest legal attorneys in the health setting, the legal sector appropriated the subsidized strategy that recruits, trains, and supports healthcare professionals for underserved populations. Lawyers are deployed along-side health professionals to prevent the negative impact of social determinants—such as the asthmatic child who needed legal advocacy to force the landlord to eradicate the mold at home in order to resolve his asthma (Regenstein, Trott, Williamson, & Theiss, 2018). With medical–legal partnership as a fundamental paradigm shift, the public interest legal sector began to build a more robust infrastructure and financing mechanisms with the requisite capacity (Farrington, 2014). Ultimately, the kind of transformation needed hinged on improving the public perception and perceived value of legal professionals—which was, up to this time, abysmal, as highlighted by the Pew study.

All told, the message in 2016 for the legal community was clear: To be relevant, sustainable, and impactful in a 2030 landscape, the legal profession needed to create the kind of public embrace and value that could usher in a reconceptualization of the fundamental legal infrastructure and delivery system—the kind of seismic professional shift that cannot occur without support and incentives external to the profession and rooted in our core constitutional values. Touchstone events in Flint, Michigan and Ferguson, Missouri helped catalyze that seismic shift.

Reflections on Flint, Michigan: The Role of the Legal Profession in Healing the Flint Community

In 2016, lead seepage into the drinking water in Flint, Michigan, caused a massive public health crisis, leading then President Obama to declare a federal state of emergency. The problem was traced to 2014, when the city switched its water supply, which resulted in significant complaints about water quality from majority-Black Flint residents, 40% of whom live in poverty (U.S. Census Bureau, 2018) Ultimately, the City switched back to its original water supply in late 2015, but the damage to the pipes had been done, resulting in major corrosion and the leaching of lead into the water. High blood lead levels pose a significant health risk, especially to children and pregnant women, and can cause learning disabilities, neurological problems and other health problems. (U.S. Environmental Protection Agency, 2019).

The crisis in Flint unleashed a familiar clash of political and economic realities across a complex set of stakeholders, communities, and power centers. Across the United States and globally, it is a sad truth that where a particular trade-off has to be made about who should pay for the cost of a decision that will save money or meet other state ends, racially and economically vulnerable populations often will get the bad end of that deal (Washington & Foster, 2016). The stark racial dynamic on display in Flint served to catalyze the community, state, and federal actors as much as the legal implications of government sanctioned poisoning of a community's public water supply. Flint thus triggered both a community response to demand political change, as well as a legal response to hold state or other actors accountable for the failure of environmental and equal protection. Flint reverberated especially in the broader environmental justice movement and led subsequently to some of the country's most dramatic legal protections of public resources like water.

Holding systemic bad actors accountable through the justice system is the legal profession's greatest calling card, but it is a time consuming, long, and sometimes risky strategy. Think of the "standards of evidence" required in different justice settings. For example, some would say what happened in Flint constitutes "reckless indifference" that is worthy of criminal culpability. It was more than negligence (a lower standard of evidence, thus easier to prove). But states, and state officials, are typically immune from prosecution unless the facts and the causality are direct and explicit. Nevertheless, the past 15 years has seen the legal profession increase its advocacy and effectiveness as a tool to tackle gross corruption, as well as state efforts to disenfranchise specific populations and communities. There is a tension between the sufficiency of laws and the enforcement of the laws—whether substantive (e.g., the levels of lead in water)—or "procedural" (e.g., how do we hold decision makers and institutions accountable). But either focus must encompass improved protection and awareness of particularly vulnerable populations. We can make sure that communities do not have to be exposed like this, and elevate the cases where some populations are overexposed and environmental injustice persists.

In public health crises like Flint, the legal profession historically targeted the use of both civil and criminal lawsuits to right systemic wrongs. Well-known court cases featured in movies like *The Verdict*, *Erin Brockavich*, *A Civil Action*, and *Silkwood* recount vividly the "David and Goliath" struggles of individuals and communities to hold private and public systems and actors accountable. But the feasibility and reality of major litigation is less rapid and thrilling than a Hollywood movie. And what about the case of a government entity that presides over the veritable poisoning of an entire population, as happened in Flint? The public sector traditionally protected itself from tort suits through the doctrine of sovereign immunity—a legal doctrine that means "the king can do no wrong," shielding states and the federal government from liability when they're performing a core government function (Engstrom, 2016). In Flint, even if a plaintiff can convince a jury that she is suffering from lead poisoning, the defendant might be able to sow doubt concerning whether the lead that caused her impairment came from the Flint water supply and not another source. How could the legal system ensure that the people of Flint were fairly compensated for this catastrophe?

Flint helped advance a question/reflection: that our society has outgrown doctrines like sovereign immunity, which serve to reinforce disparities and a racist system. Where there are no longer kings, is it appropriate and just to shield the public sector from accountability? It was clear that the civil justice system was not equipped to meet the challenge of Flint, and that there was a generation of children in Flint, Michigan whose lives were irreparably changed by preventable lead exposure—and who would never, actually, recover a penny or be made whole. This reality called on the legal community to show up and pursue novel strategies and radical approaches to righting the balance of power. For example—if corporations could be treated as "people" under the law, could the city of Flint be treated as a "person," with the risks and protections that flow from that kind of legal framework? Could the water system be treated as a "person"? Statutes and case law have now firmly established at the federal and state levels that governments do not have the breadth of sovereign immunity previously shielding them from their negligent and tortious actions, and governments may be held accountable, with individuals who perpetrated gross negligence, even as a government actor, facing individual criminal penalties of both jail time and fines.

Flint—and Ferguson, described below, surfaced the notion that, if a central responsibility of the legal profession is to ensure the proper, fair, and equitable application of laws in our systems and governments, the legal profession cannot accomplish this task with 2016 tools. Where something as basic as access to clean water is not protected—indeed, was actively and secretively denied—Flint became the visible proclamation for communities of color that neither the law nor the legal profession can protect them from entrenched bad actors and systems.

In the years since Flint, legal advocates have more systemically partnered with the environmental community to both study and link sustainability, equity, and justice. For example, the Earth Law Center reviewed 200 case studies regarding societal impact on nature and indigenous populations concluding that human rights and nature's rights are inextricably bound (Wilson, Bender, & Sheehan, 2016). Environmental justice is now broadly defined to include more than mere legal case law, statutes, and causes of action, but also includes a professional valuing of a safe environment for all people regardless of their ability to pursue, afford or even know about a legal course of action. Environmental justice has become a fundamental societal value.

Further, it has also become a global value as international law has recognized that one national state's impact on the environment directly and indirectly impacts other nation states. The International Court of Justice now routinely addresses trans-boundary environmental issues, with its Chamber for Environmental Matters growing from seven members during its founding in 1993 to over 75 members in 2030.

Reflections on Ferguson, Missouri: The Role of the Legal Profession in Healing the Ferguson Community (Benavides, Benson, & DiAquoi, 2015)

In 2014, Michael Brown, an unarmed Black teenager, was shot and killed by Darren Wilson, a White police officer, in Ferguson, MO, a suburb of St. Louis. According to a report of the U.S. Department of Justice following the incident, Brown had stolen from a nearby convenience store and assaulted the store clerk who tried to stop him. Wilson subsequently encountered Brown and Johnson as they were walking down the middle of the street, realized the two men matched the robbery suspects' descriptions and blocked them using his cruiser. Following an altercation between Brown and Wilson, Wilson fired at Brown a total of twelve times; Brown was unarmed and moving towards Wilson when the final shots were fired. Witnesses claimed that Brown had his hands up in surrender when he was shot.

The shooting prompted protests that roiled the community and region for weeks, connecting with an emerging national movement protesting police killings and brutality known as Black Lives Matter (Day, 2015). In November, 2014, the St. Louis County prosecutor announced that a grand jury decided not to indict Mr. Wilson. The announcement set off another wave of protests. In March 2015, after an investigation of the Ferguson Police Department, the U.S. Department of Justice called on Ferguson to overhaul its criminal justice system, declaring that the city had engaged in constitutional violations (Jweied & Yang-Green, 2016), and noting: "Ferguson's police and municipal court practices both reflect and exacerbate existing racial bias, including racial stereotypes. Ferguson's own data establish clear racial disparities that adversely impact African Americans."

The legal story underpinning the tragedy of Ferguson was a complex web of intersecting laws, policies, and practices that misaligned tax, financing, and government roles, and doomed a fragile community to intractable racial and power dynamics. As the U. S. Department of Justice investigated and subsequently released a report detailing the surrounding landscape of Michael Brown's short life, it emerged that the legal community in particular was a key activator within the community to suppress change (Podziba, 2015). For example, from racist zoning and housing policy to court mandated fines and rules that set up low income, disproportionately minority communities to fail—Ferguson and the surrounding metropolis had built a municipal system that had oppression as its central economic driver (Balko, 2014). As highlighted in the Department of Justice's report, there was economic incentive to charging the petty crimes; with 90 municipalities in St. Louis County, each of which have their own police force and courts, they depended on fines and fees for court and police revenue.

The events in Ferguson—connected as they were to tangible issues of policing and municipal finance—demanded simultaneous reflection on the underlying—or blatantly obvious—issues of racial bias, discrimination, and fear. Much of the public debate initially focused on the criminal liability of the police officers involved and the role of local grand juries in seemingly shielding these officers from criminal prosecution, but local criminal prosecutions were not the only legal mechanism for holding police officers and other government officials accountable (Dodd, 2015; Washam, Merkle, Murtaugh, & LaFontain, 2014). As solutions to Ferguson's issue were considered, other mechanisms, such as political advocacy, alongside the implementation of race-conscious legislative and community approaches arose.

It is true that the cost, and the journey, was steep, posing the question, "Could Ferguson only be transformed once a century of flawed, segregationist policies was rectified?" (Rothstein, 2014). After all, federal, state, and local policy served to segregate Ferguson and St. Louis. Some of the historic policies designed to reinforce segregation in St. Louis included racially explicit zoning, segregated public housing projects, racially exclusive government subsidies for suburban development, and inadequate municipal services in black neighborhoods. It is in this landscape that one can see in highlights the pervasive, negative role of law and policy to reinforce segregation, as well as the need for communities to be armed with legal strategies and experts to undo the legacy of segregation (Rothstein, 2014). The overt dynamics of racial and economic tension were baked into Ferguson's civic life, and could only be removed through intentional, race conscious policy and advocacy. The legal principle of "disparate impact," which looks beyond the intent to discriminate to "disparate treatment," again became widely used to demonstrate that it is not enough to stop at what was intended (and provable) but to awake to the reality of the unequal impact of laws, policies, and behavior.

Like other sectors, the legal profession has been forced to confront whether progress toward freedom and equality, values embedded in our nation's constitution, can be simply linear and cumulative, or is more elastic, catapulting forward and bouncing backward, but always in motion and advancing. The legal profession's role in securing and promoting that progress is both undeniable, and burdened with limitations. In the face of the legal profession's very real ineffectiveness in redressing wrongs in Flint—and in reinforcing deeply segregationist systems in Ferguson, it was difficult to envision the seismic positive change that would advance a necessary revival of the legal profession in 2030. Indeed—that revival became even more important where crises like Flint and Ferguson risked destabilizing an entire population or region. But for the transformational election of Donald Trump in 2016, these frameworks might have remained academic hypotheses, with minimal relevance outside the legal profession. But the devastating impact of Trump's election and the subsequent administration, bolstering nationalistic and discriminatory practices and policies, rocketed the legal profession to the forefront, demanding its unique skills to protect vulnerable populations including racial and ethnic minorities, immigrants and others, and democratic values like voting. This new reality cemented the link of the legal profession with community organizing and political power, leading to a comprehensive retooling of the legal profession's values, activities, and vision of systemic change from 2020–2030.

Radical new legal theories helped test these principles, and discard repressive doctrines like sovereign immunity, leading to the eradication of police brutality by the "bad apples" in an otherwise law-abiding force. This required significant political will and leadership during and following the Trump era. For example, equipping law enforcement with exponentially better training, benefits and support, and vastly higher salaries, while holding them to a much higher standard of behavior with consequences for going outside the laws or scope of training, served to subvert the dominant paradigm of poorly trained and supported law enforcement agencies ill equipped to counter the flawed segregationist policies endemic to communities like Flint and Ferguson. Engaging public insurers to tackle the risk and expense of racist police brutality began to realign community perspectives regarding the financial, social, and community cost of police brutality.

Bold legal theories used the equal protection and due process clauses to assert that citizens, particularly African Americans, were not only legitimately fearful and at risk of being targeted by state actors, but in fact would not be protected. This led political and sector leaders to press on legal action under new radical theories that posited, for example, that African American citizens essentially were forced to subsidize their own potential gun injury or death by police actors who were unaccountable to the government. Under this analysis, police brutality came to be seen as a violation of tax laws, which mandate that minority citizens have an expectation to receive the same protection as White citizens, or should not be required to fund public entities at the same level.

The essence of the 2020 change point? That lawyers are a crucial bulwark in support of a civil society, and the political landscape will always pose the opportunity for the most radical change, but requires a concomitant synchronicity of coordination, resources, and leadership. While lawyers are the natural advocates for the poor and silenced, they too exist in a political context—as is reflected in the percentage of lawyers serving in political positions. And so, naturally, the transformation towards increased equity and access for vulnerable populations will depend on a positive, supportive political environment, which can only be ushered in by truly engaging in the democratic process. Is this even possible in a system where only half of the citizenry voted in the presidential election? Can "justice" arrive through a political election rather than via litigation? And if so, what is the legal profession's role in guiding that process?

HOW DID WE GET HERE IN 2030?

While the Flint and Ferguson experiences helped the legal profession grapple with philosophical concepts of equity, justice, and alignment with other sectors, a critical facet of the legal profession's transformation over the past decade was grounded in the adoption of rigorous practices of research, evaluation and data collection—a historically challenging endeavor for the legal community (Jweied & Yang-Green, 2016). Led by the American Bar Foundation whose mission is to serve the legal profession, the public, and the academy through empirical research, publications, and programs that advance justice and the understanding of law and its impact on society, a small set of researchers and social scientists sought to conduct and disseminate research findings to the organized bar, scholars, and the general public. The results were published and adopted in a wide range of forums, including leading academic journals, law reviews, and academic and commercial presses (American Bar Association, n.d.; Research).

The legal community—historically insular—also benefited from the increased transparency and accountability that partnership models like medical-legal partnership demanded, thereby hastening the move toward more efficient, less siloed access to legal aid services and expertise.

The legal community—including the for- and nonprofit sectors as well as pro bono resources in corporate and private law firms—had to more closely align its activities and priorities with multiple public and private stakeholders, and invest in leaders who could innovate across both sectors, and leverage scarce legal resources most effectively. With access to better data about how legal interventions can be measured, and improved quality and efficiency for the legal profession, the legal sector began to tackle the pervasive fragmentation and inequity in access. While the legal profession has been historically ill-equipped to partner with other professionals, especially in the public-interest sector, this negative attribute was also ameliorated over the past decade, as incentives to promote inter-professional teamwork and means to foster, and scale, innovations in access to justice became more readily available. Community courts elicited evidence from a wide swath of community stakeholders rather than merely the parties involved in a civil and criminal case. Reconciliation approaches became an integral part of plea agreements where victims agreed to their use. The criminal justice system looked at the disproportionate impact it had on certain communities, such as those with mental illness, and instituted preventative measures working closely with healthcare professionals and social workers. Tribal law was routinely used as a source of community solution and example and expanded in its own value across indigenous populations and areas.

Prescription for Legal Profession/Sector to Meet the Challenges of 2030

Our worlds—and sectors—are converging, driving professions and others to adopt each other's language, strategies, and business models. We saw it in the now-universal TED talks, which taught us that "technology, entertainment, and design" go together and can help us understand other domains, like justice, health, or art. Hyper-specialization is on the way out, and cross-sector practice is our future.

How did the legal sector shift to respond to these opportunities? In one example, it did so by building the capacity to correlate health outcomes with specific legal needs and interventions. Other examples include the standardization of cross-sector practices across law, health, business, and other professional schools, inculcating trainees with the ethic and practice of multi-disciplinary work; and finally, the recognition of the integral, unique nature of legal skills and analysis for the transformation and accountability of society and government. To improve access to justice in the years leading to 2030, the legal sector looked both within itself, and to other sectors for guidance on vision, values, quality and evaluation metrics, capacity-building, and sustainability.

NOTES

1. Each "Sector Visioning" chapter begins with an abstract prepared by the book editors and attributed to Zindzi in keeping with the storyline of the book. Zindzi is introduced in Chapter 2.
2. See https://www.pewforum.org/2013/07/11/public-esteem-for-military-still-high/
3. Matthew, B. *The law as healer: How paying for medical-legal partnerships saves lives and money.* See the Brookings Report (2017) at https://www.brookings.edu/wp-content/uploads/2017/01/es_20170130_medicallegal.pdf

REFERENCES

American Bar Association. (2016). *Historical trend in total national lawyer population* [Data file]. PDF retrieved at https://www.americanbar.org/content/dam/aba/administrative/market_research/total-national-lawyer-population-1878-2019.pdf

American Bar Association. (2017). *Resources for lawyers: Legal profession statistics.* Retrieved from http://www.americanbar.org/resources_for_lawyers/profession_statistics.html

American Bar Association (n.d.). Retrieved at http://www.americanbarfoundation.org/research/index.html

Balko, R. (2014). *How municipalities in St. Louis County, MO profit from poverty.* Retrieved from https://www.washingtonpost.com/news/the-watch/wp/2014/09/03/how-st-louis-county-missouri-profits-from-poverty/

Benavides, V., Benson, T., & DiAquoi, R. (2015). *Lessons from Ferguson: Leadership in times of civil unrest.* Cambridge, MA: Harvard Education Press. Retrieved from http://hepg.org/hep-home/case/lessons-from-ferguson

Cohen, M. A. (2016, December 24). The American Bar Association's greatest hits (lost tracks). *Forbes.* Retrieved from https://www.forbes.com/sites/markcohen1/2016/12/24/the-american-bar-associations-greatest-hits-lost-tracks/#6ab30c2b3f51

Cohen, M. A. (2017, February 20). The all-out assault on the rule of law. *Forbes.* Retrieved from https://www.forbes.com/sites/markcohen1/2017/02/20/the-all-out-assault-on-the-rule-of-law/#5948bde977af

Cohen, M. (2018). Legal innovation is the rage but there's plenty of resistance. *Forbes.* Retrieved from https://www.forbes.com/sites/markcohen1/2018/08/30/legal-innovation-is-the-rage-but-theres-plenty-of-resistance/#775c0c0b7cdd

Cuban, B. (2017). *The addicted lawyer: Tales of the bar, booze, blow, and redemption.* Brentwood, TN: Post Hill Press.

Day, E. (2015, July 19). #BlackLivesMatter: The birth of a new civil rights movement. *The Guardian.* Retrieved from https://www.theguardian.com/world/2015/jul/19/blacklivesmatter-birth-civil-rights-movement

Dodd, L. G. (2015). The rights revolution in the age of Obama and Ferguson: Policing, the rule of law, and the elusive quest for accountability. *Perspectives on Politics, 13*(3), 657–679. https://doi.org/10.1017/S1537592715001231

Engstrom, F. N. (2016, February 16). The Flint water crisis: Professor Nora Freeman Engstrom answers critical legal questions. *Stanford Lawyer Magazine: Stanford Legal Aggregate.* Retrieved from https://law.stanford.edu/2016/02/16/the-flint-water-crisis-professor-nora-freeman-engstrom-answers-critical-legal-questions/

Farrington, R. (2014, December 18). Law school and student loan debt: Be careful. *Forbes.* Retrieved from http://www.forbes.com/sites/robertfarrington/2014/12/18/law-school-and-student-loan-debt-be-careful/#2d2da13d4f06

Harper, S. J. (2015, August 25). Too many law students, too few legal jobs. *The New York Times.* Retrieved at http://www.nytimes.com/2015/08/25/opinion/too-many-law-students-too-few-legal-jobs.html?_r=0)

Jweied, M., & Yang-Green, A. (2016, February). White House legal aid interagency roundtable: Civil legal aid research workshop report for U.S. Department of Justice's National Institute of Justice and Office for Access to Justice with the National Science Foundation (NCJ 249776). Retrieved from https://www.ncjrs.gov/pdffiles1/nij/249776.pdf

Lerner, G. (2006). How teaching political and ethical theory could help solve two of the legal profession's biggest problems. *The Georgetown Journal of Legal Ethics, 19*(3), 781–793.

Olson, E. (2016, February 4). High rate of problem drinking reported among lawyers. *The New York Times*. Retrieved from http://www.nytimes.com/2016/02/05/business/dealbook/high-rate-of-problem-drinking-reported-among-lawyers.html?_r=0

Rhode, D. L. (2015, May 27). Law is the least diverse profession in the nation. And lawyers aren't doing enough to change that. *The Washington Post*. Retrieved from https://www.washingtonpost.com/posteverything/wp/2015/05/27/law-is-the-least-diverse-profession-in-the-nation-and-lawyers-arent-doing-enough-to-change-that/?utm_term=.67ec99c33271

Podziba, S. L. (2015). Negotiating social conflict: Imagining civic fusion approach in Ferguson, Missouri. *Negotiation Journal, 31*(4), 441–445. Retrieved from https://onlinelibrary.wiley.com/doi/abs/10.1111/nejo.12124

Regenstein, M., Trott, J., Williamson A., & Theiss, J. (2018). Addressing social determinants of health through medical-legal partnerships. *Health Aff (Millwood), 37*(3), 378–385.

Rothstein, R. (2014, October 15). The making of Ferguson. *Economic Policy Institute*. Retrieved from http://www.epi.org/publication/making-ferguson/

Scheiber, N. (2016, June 17). An expensive law degree, and no place to use it. *The New York Times*. Retrieved from http://www.nytimes.com/2016/06/19/business/dealbook/an-expensive-law-degree-and-no-place-to-use-it.html?_r=0

Spahn, H. (n.d.). A dual degree: Is it right for you? *Admissions Consultants*. Retrieved at https://admissionsconsultants.com/lawschool/dual-degree/

Sullivan, W. M., Colby, A., Wegner, J. W., Bond, L., & Shulman, L. S. (2007). *Educating lawyers: Preparation for the profession of law*. Stanford, CA: The Carnegie Foundation for the Advancement of Teaching. Retrieved from http://archive.carnegiefoundation.org/pdfs/elibrary/elibrary_pdf_632.pdf

U.S. Census Bureau. (2018). *Quick facts: Flint, MI*. Retrieved from http://www.census.gov/quickfacts/table/PST045215/2629000

U.S. Environmental Protection Agency. (n.d.). *Basic information about lead in drinking water*. Retrieved from https://www.epa.gov/ground-water-and-drinking-water/basic-information-about-lead-drinking-water#health

Washam, L., Merkle, Z., Murtaugh, M., & LaFontain, J. (2014, August 19). A collection of legal commentary on the events in Ferguson. *Saint Louis University Law Journal*. Retrieved from http://www.slu.edu/colleges/law/journal/a-collection-of-legal-commentary-on-the-events-in-ferguson/

Washington, S. H., & Foster, S. R. (2016). The legal discourse surrounding the water crisis in Flint, Michigan: Interview with Sheila R. Foster. *Environmental Justice, 9*(2), 59–64. Retrieved from https://www.liebertpub.com/doi/full/10.1089/env.2016.29004.shw?src=recsys&

Williams, J. C., Platt, A., & Lee, J. (2015). Disruptive innovation: New models of legal practice. *WorkLifeLaw*. University of California Hastings College of the Law. Retrieved from https://repository.uchastings.edu/faculty_scholarship/1279/

Wilson, G., Bender, M., & Sheehan, L. (2016). *2016 update: Fighting for our shared future: Protecting both human rights and nature's rights*. Retrieved from https://static1

.squarespace.com/static/55914fd1e4b01fb0b851a814/t/586d58835016e13b
1e98820a/1483561101515/ELC+Co-Violations+Report+-+2016+Update.pdf

Zeidel, M., Yu, S., & Zerehi, S. (2015, October). Learning to be a peacemaking
lawyer: Law student perspective on building peacemaking into law school
curricula, building paths to practice for new lawyers, and interdisciplinary training. *Family Court Review, 53*(4), 526–544. Retrieved from https://
onlinelibrary.wiley.com/doi/abs/10.1111/fcre.12182

CHAPTER 7

BUSINESS

Doing Well and Doing Good

Eric Barels and Bob Willard

ZINDZI'S ABSTRACT[1]

The business community is evolving to meet the challenge of the Anthropocene. While much of the 20th century was dedicated to increasing wealth for companies and their stockholders, in the 21st century businesses value equity and sustainability almost as much as their customers and employees. They have moved beyond sharing these values because of legal requirements or public relations campaigns to a place where businesses understand that their own survival is dependent on how organizations in addition to individuals take action to ensure a sustainable, equitable future. Our first contributor traces this evolution and shares examples of the shift toward greater corporate responsibility for big and small businesses. Our second contributor provides a model for businesses at different stages of their sustainability maturity, providing a pathway for even greater corporate impact.

Visionary Evaluation for a Sustainable, Equitable Future, pages 127–141
Copyright © 2020 by Information Age Publishing
127

INCORPORATING SOCIAL IMPACT INTO BUSINESS
by Eric Barela

In America, traditionally, capitalism and social values have largely existed side by side. Now, in the first few decades of the 21st century, we are witnessing an unprecedented integration of business and social values. Whereas businesses previously were involved primarily in charitable giving, they are now routinely contributing, both directly and indirectly, to the communities in which they operate. Here, communities encompass a geographic unit as small as a specific neighborhood to the entire planet. Businesses are also now going beyond charitable giving alone and actively investing in communities and partnering with governments and nonprofits. More significantly and perhaps with the greatest impact, businesses are now altering the quality standards for their business practices and processes from their carbon footprint to their internal equity standards to their supply chains. Businesses of all sizes and in all sectors have been on a steady march toward increasing participation in and responsibility for social progress. Now in 2030, business practices and business values are vital to the sustainability and equity of people and planet.

Social Impact in Business: Definition and History

Social impact in business (also known as corporate social responsibility, or CSR) is viewed as those actions of a company that encourage public good and, in doing so, go beyond the interests of the enterprise and what is required by law (McWilliams, Siegel, & Wright, 2006). Essentially, CSR is what a business does with its available resources to achieve impact beyond profit. Such activities focus on offering up a business's resources to improve social equity and/or environmental sustainability. Traditionally, CSR has taken the form of employee engagement in community volunteering, grant programs aimed at social impact, and/or sustainability initiatives focusing on environmental health.

The roots of business involvement in social impact traces to the Industrial Revolution (Wren & Bedeian, 2009). As factories began to emerge in urban areas around the world, a concern arose around working conditions, especially through infamous events such as the Triangle Shirtwaist Factory fire of 1911, which highlighted egregious corporate work practices. Factory workers were often subjected to working long hours in substandard working conditions. By the late 1800s, organizations began to arise to help workers cope with the harshness of factory life, including poverty, child labor, and unionization. One such organization was the Young Men's Christian Association, or YMCA. The YMCA was established in London in 1844 and quickly established itself as a provider of community-related welfare and social programs in the UK and around the world (Heald, 2005).

There was continued business focus on the social conditions of workers in the 1950s and 1960s, as employees began to work at companies for longer periods of time. The business sector then took on the responsibility to either directly support employees with needed services or to make it easier for employees to access external services. Businesses began to engage in company-wide philanthropy, mostly in the form of donations to external organizations, such as the United Way or the American Red Cross. It was during this time that the imperative to support employees began to shift from outside organizations to internal management. Employees who were provided with social service supports by their employers were more productive and often remained loyal to the company. An example of this is the Kaiser Permanente Health Plan, a not-for-profit health plan created in 1945 by industrialist Henry J. Kaiser in his attempt to provide his construction worker employees with affordable health insurance and medical care.

The 1970s and 1980s saw an even greater expansion of social impact beyond the corporate walls. Businesses began to be more mindful of improving society at large, as businesses began to see social impact as "an effective lens through which to examine the actions businesses can take toward ensuring mutual long-term well-being and sustainability" (Schwab, 2015). It was also during this time that social impact practices began to encompass the areas we associate it with today: direct employee support, social betterment, and environmental sustainability (Carroll, 2008). Many established businesses began to set up corporate foundations, which maintained close ties with the parent company and were often initially established with profits from the business. These foundations typically engaged employees in supporting causes that were important to them personally and that were important to the business. For example, the Walmart Foundation was founded in 1979 and, responding to employee interest in improving the communities where they worked, focused on economic opportunity, environmental sustainability, and community resilience.

In the 1990s, social impact practices became the norm for many large companies. With increasing globalization, businesses such as IBM and Nike began to see the potential of social impact efforts contributing to their bottom lines. Businesses began to recognize general public trends toward sustainability and equity. It was during this time that the purpose of adopting social impact practices shifted from ethics (i.e., business responsibility) to performance (i.e., increased profit). It was starting to make good business sense to operate with societal benefit in mind. Companies were able to see how achieving social impact could improve business, especially using their brand to attract loyal customers, while also making the world a better place to live. In addition, companies found they had an easier time of scaling up operations if they were perceived to be committed to helping the communities where they were setting up shop, in part due to perceived reputation and legitimacy (Kurucz, Colbert, & Wheeler, 2008). For example, after the 1988 Exxon Valdez oil spill, the Exxon brand lost credibility because it was seen as not being responsive to the needs of the surrounding community. As a reaction to this and other disasters, such as the 1984 Union Carbide Bhopal gas tragedy, large corporations began to be more cognizant of and transparent about their efforts to achieve social impact to build trust with their surrounding communities and to have that trust associated with their brand.

The "profit-driven" orientation behind the implementation of social impact practices continued into the early 2000s and informed several trends. The first was the dawning of companies focused on social impact and profit in equal measure, such as social enterprises and B Corporations. These types of companies have been able to capitalize on the notion that creating a better world is also good for business. An example of a social enterprise is Tom's Shoes, which was established in 2004 after founder Blake Mycoskie, who was learning to play polo in Argentina, met a woman who worked with a nonprofit that delivered shoes to low income children. Seeing the desperate need and the transformative power of action and product, Mycoskie started the company, then called Shoes for Tomorrow, based on the buy-one, give-one concept. The timing was right as the public and shareholders were increasingly interested in a business's social impact in addition to its bottom line.

This increased focus on social impact practices increasing a company's performance has led to a second trend, a heightened focus on measuring such efforts. A company's stakeholders (shareholders, employees, communities, customers) have wanted to know how social impact practices are making the world a better place. A report from Corporate Citizenship (2016) characterized this evolution as companies initially wanting to know how much they gave away, then how many people benefitted, followed by what was the actual social impact. Companies are recognizing that it's no longer enough to report on what is being produced or offered. Social impact occurs when there are concrete, positive social outcomes that result, in an attributory or contributory manner, from the social impact activities that companies produce, offer or engage (Barela, 2016).

The Triple Bottom Line as Part of a Company's DNA

In 2030, all types of businesses are now focused on the triple bottom line (3BL) of profit, planet, and people. The 3BL as a concept is not new (Elkington, 1999). It helped to shape some of the trends outlined above. However, businesses have now shifted their approaches to achieving results in economic prosperity (profit), environmental sustainability (planet), and social equity (people). Many businesses have become intentional about organizing themselves to achieve social equity and environmental sustainability goals while also remaining economically viable.

Profit is perhaps the component of the 3BL that is most easily and deeply understood by businesses. Maintaining economic prosperity is a defining characteristic of a business. Now in 2030, it has become clearer to businesses of all sizes that working toward social impact can also positively affect profit margins in terms of attracting and retaining top talent, shareholders, and a strong customer base.

One way that businesses have realigned themselves is by expanding their notion of who is holding them accountable. In the past, businesses answered to their boards of directors and/or their shareholders with an often singular focus on profit. While such governing bodies still are integral to the business model, the notion of accountability expanding from shareholder to stakeholder has become a common business focus. A shareholder is one who owns a portion of the company and directly benefits from its profits. A stakeholder is one who is affected either directly or indirectly by a company's actions. Stakeholders include shareholders, employees, customers, and people who live in the communities where the business operates.

This expansion of accountability to include those who are affected by a company's social impact practices has fundamentally reshaped how companies organize themselves and how they communicate their impact. Companies have both hired more internal staff to implement social impact efforts and hired more people to measure and study the effects of social impact business practices (e.g., evaluators). The importance of accurate and appropriate measurement of social impact business practices has become even more important as employees, current and potential, have begun looking closely at a company's impact and as the impact investing field (i.e., investing in companies based on the social impact of their business) has matured.

Employees and Corporate Social Impact

In 2030, employees are not only interested in a company's social impact but also in their ability to contribute to that impact, creating a growing trend of companies individualizing social programs targeted to their employees. Employee participation began in the latter half of the 20th century when many businesses collected money from employees that would be consolidated and given to a handful of management-determined charities, such as the United Way or Easter Seals. Businesses subsequently offered volunteering and donation-matching programs that allowed employees to support the organizations they individually wanted to support. These programs were highly successful both in increasing employee participation and pride. For example, supermarket chains of all sizes allowed for both employees and customers to determine where donations were sent. At Faletti Foods in San Francisco, customers who provided their own grocery bags were able to donate the bag charge to a variety of local nonprofits selected by employees. VMWare allowed employees to give their time and money to organizations and causes they were passionate about. In 2016, VMWare reported that 85% of its employees participated in these programs. According to the Committee Encouraging Corporate Philanthropy (CECP), the average rate of employee participation in corporate philanthropy in 2016 was 31% (CECP, 2016).

Social impact practices were also used by businesses to attract and retain top talent. A 2015 study commissioned by the IBM Institute for Business Value found that 22% of millennials surveyed viewed solving social or environmental challenges as one of their top two long-term career goals. While much has been written about millennials and their need to be a part of something bigger than themselves in their professional lives, the IBM study showed some surprising results for Gen Xers and Baby Boomers. When asked the same question, 20% of Gen Xers and 24% of Baby Boomers surveyed had the same long-term career goal (IBM Institute for Business Value, 2015). It is not only millennials who felt the need to be a part of something bigger than themselves at work. As competition gets more intense for positions in sought-after sectors such as technology, offering programs designed to achieve social impact worked to attract top talent from all age groups who had their pick of offers. According to the 2016 Deloitte Impact Survey, 47% of respondents noted that their companies did not offer volunteering programs (Deloitte, 2016). Now, in 2030, this percentage has dropped significantly as companies routinely offer individualized ways for their employees to participate in social impact.

In addition to using social impact programs to recruit top talent, businesses have also used them to retain that talent as they progressed in their careers. According to the 2016 Deloitte Impact Survey, volunteering could be used to develop employees. Among surveyed hiring managers, 92% agreed that volunteering improved employees' broader professional skill sets. The same percentage (92%) agreed that volunteering was an effective way to improve leadership skills. In these ways, such efforts contributed positively to a company's profit bottom line.

Another way that businesses worked to achieve social impact was in the area of diversity and inclusion in the workplace. This was not new. A survey of businesses in the early 1970s showed that nearly all companies were working to address the hiring and training of employees from historically-underrepresented groups (Eilbert & Parket, 1973). However, ensuring that all employees have an equitable chance to be hired, paid appropriately, and promoted has become even more important. In 2016, while private sector employment ethnicity and gender percentages resembled those of the general U.S. population, managers were overwhelmingly White (87% vs 63% in the general U.S. population) and male (71% vs 49% in the general U.S. population).[2] According to the Pew Research Center, at this same time, women were being paid 83 cents of every dollar paid to a man. However, when gender and ethnicity were combined, Hispanic and African American women earned 56 and 58 cents for every dollar earned by a White man, respectively (Patten, 2016). Companies have been working to eliminate the gender pay gap. By 2016, over 100 companies, from Adobe to Zillow, had signed the Equal Pay Pledge established by the Obama White House. Cities and states even began to enact equal pay laws that prohibit employers from asking about salary histories. This has become even more important as America has moved toward a majority–minority country and as the workforce needs of companies have increased, requiring bringing in global talent. In 2030, employees are actively looking to workplaces that align with their personal values, reflect their own and their communities' realities, and that actively engage in social impact.

Mixing For-Profit and For-Good: Social Enterprises and B Corps

In 2030, many businesses are structured around the concept of social impact. This restructuring has essentially expanded social impact efforts into an actual business. The establishment of social enterprises and Benefit Corporations (B Corps) represent this fundamental reorganization designed to deliver on the 3BL. Social enterprises are companies that combine the social impact of a mission-driven organization with the market-driven approach of a business. They can be nonprofit or for-profit organizations. Goodwill is one of the earliest social enterprises, established in 1902 with the purpose of providing economic self-sufficiency through its sale of used goods. There have been many other social enterprise models such as Warby Parker, which sells eyewear in developed markets and then contributes proceeds on each pair sold to programs providing people in the developing world with better eyesight.

B Corps took the concept of the social enterprise one step further. Businesses receive B Corp certification if they meet rigorous standards of social and environmental performance, accountability, and transparency. The fundamental purpose of B Corps has been to operate in such a way that they are intentional about achieving social impact in a transparent manner. B Corps must be certified by B Labs, which is responsible for maintaining and enforcing strict standards meant to drive impact. In 2016, there were over 1,700 B Corps operating in over 30 countries across 60 industries (Kassoy, Houlihan, & Gilbert, 2016). Examples of B Corps include Recycle-Bank, LEAP Organics, Hives for Lives, and Moving Forward Education.

These numbers have increased substantially in the years leading up to 2030 and further bolstered the public belief that businesses are a key partner in social impact.

In 2030, social impact practices in business are improving both a company's bottom line and the state of the world. Businesses are working towards the 3BL, three main ways:

1. Businesses focus more on people, whether it be employees who are looking to the company to provide equitable services, shareholders who care about where they invest their dollars, or customers who want products and services that reflect their values.
2. Certifications and collective standards for measurement have grown in importance, accessibility, and meaning so that stakeholders inside and outside the company could better understand social impact efforts.
3. Companies redesign themselves to focus more on social impact, from improving supply chains to becoming B Corps or social enterprises.

These trends helped businesses of all sizes innovate so they could deliver on all three components of the 3BL: profit, people, and planet. These trends and innovations have created a culture across the business world that recognizes the large footprint of the business community and the need for the business community to walk side by side with others toward societal equity and sustainability.

IN THE BUSINESS OF SUSTAINABILITY[3]
by Bob Willard

Let's suppose you've crafted a compelling business case to support a company undertaking a significant environmental or social initiative. Your proposal includes three justifications for the project: it helps the company *do the right thing* by causing less harm and doing more good for the environment, society, and employees; it enables the company to *capture opportunities* such as new revenue streams and expense savings; and it helps the company *mitigate risks* that could arise if it did *not* do the project. Where the company is on its sustainability journey determines which of those three components in the business case will best grab the attention of the decision-makers and win their support. Mapping the three justifications to the five-stage sustainability journey helps us choose which justification to highlight.

The big three justifications were routinely used to support business decisions across industries and sectors and through the early 1990s but their relative importance has shifted from that time. Decision-makers now weight them differently as companies progress on their journeys to becoming sustainable enterprises. When proposing sustainability projects, emphasizing the justification that best matches the company's maturity level on the sustainability spectrum helps decision-makers more quickly see the project's relevance to business success.

The Big Three Justifications

There are three reasons that companies typically undertake anything new: do the right thing, capture opportunities, and mitigate risks. Some combination of them is always in play when making big business decisions. They frame the rationale behind any big business decision.

The dominant mental model in the business community in the last two centuries has been to do the right thing. Unfortunately, it is also the mindset still promoted by many business schools. It positions being a steward of the environment and society as an *either–or* choice: *either* do the ethically right thing for society and the environment, *or* aggressively capture financial opportunities and mitigate risks.

In the 21st century, doing the ethically right thing has moved from the margins into the mainstream. Improving company impacts on the environment and the community can lead to capturing new financial opportunities and mitigating new risks. It is now an *if–then, both–and* relationship, not an *either–or* trade-off. Doing the right thing has morphed from being an anchor in the old business paradigm to being a driver of success in the new economy.

Three Justifications Mapped to the Five-Stage Sustainability Journey

The five-stage sustainability continuum applies to any business. Companies mature from unsustainable business models in Stages 1 and 2, to a more sustainable business model in Stage 3, to a strongly sustainable business model in Stages 4 and 5. During the journey, executive mindsets evolve from thinking of "green," "environmental," and "sustainable" initiatives as expensive and bureaucratic hassles, to recognizing them as catalysts for strategic success. Now, let's examine how the three justification factors are weighted differently by decision-makers as a business moves from stage to stage on its sustainability journey.

Stage 1: Pre-Compliance
It's risky to linger here. In this phase, a company flouts environmental, health, and safety regulations. It cuts corners and tries not to get caught if it breaks the law or uses exploitative practices that cheat the system. It

employs unqualified staff and forces them to work in a dysfunctional, abusive workplace. It is careless with its waste. These businesses happily externalize their negative ecological and social impacts. This stage is often associated with corrupt jurisdictions.

Society is starting to demand that all businesses be more accountable for their collateral social and environmental damage. Whistle-blowers are more courageous. Social media leaves no place to hide. If Stage 1 companies don't clean up their acts, they will be exposed and put out of business by regulators, activist nongovernmental organizations, or customers who vote with their wallets and move to more responsible companies. Stage 1 companies are driven to Stage 2 by sticks, more than by carrots.

That is, 80% of the justification to move from Stage 1 to Stage 2 is to *mitigate risks* of getting caught. That's the justification to underscore in the business case when proposing sustainability initiatives to Stage 1 companies. The weight of the *capture opportunities* justification for the move to Stage 2 is about 20% the opportunity is to stay in business. The *do-the-right-thing* justification is not on the radar screen.

Stage 2: Compliance

In this stage, the company manages its liabilities by obeying all labor, environmental, health, and safety regulations. It respects industry organization standards, regulations, and bylaws. It does what it is legally or professionally bound to do. It complies with local regulations for the handling of its waste. Its staff is professionally qualified, respected, and well-treated. But extra environmental efforts and provision of products and services to the underserved is given lip service, at best.

A Stage 1 business's actions are illegal, unprofessional, and unsustainable. A Stage 2 practices are legal and professional, but they're still unsustainable. They may still cause environmental harm with their waste practices, water use, energy sources, and supply chains, but they are not legally required to stop or to be restorative. They don't feel much stewardship for the health and well-being of their communities or the environment, beyond token philanthropy. They are compliant.

Their missions are to grow the business and to improve their bottom lines. Ironically, that desire makes up 80% of their motivation for moving *beyond* compliance to Stage 3. They want to *capture new opportunities* to save money and generate more income. Who wouldn't? *Risk mitigation* may be a background justification (10%) for doing more, if the company starts to sense that its social license to operate may be in jeopardy if its behaviors do not reflect the growing unease of its stakeholders about environmental and social issues. And the *do-the-right-thing* justification may be starting to stir (10%).

Stage 3: Beyond Compliance

A business voluntarily moves to Stage 3 when it realizes that it can save money with operational "eco-efficiencies." It's in this stage that the company earns the label "eco-friendly" or "green." There are typically four types of low-hanging fruit in the fruit salad of "eco-savings": reducing the firm's energy, water, materials, and waste bills. Best practices in these areas are well documented. They are amazingly straightforward once company leadership decides they want to move into Stage 3 and reap the savings.

First, it finds eco-efficiencies in its current operations and processes; then it re-engineers some of its processes to capture more savings; then it acknowledges that it is mutually accountable for impacts throughout its value chain and starts to work with suppliers to improve their environmental performance; and then it starts to create more green, healthy, and sustainable products and services for its customers.

As a company approaches the end of Stage 3, it may also see the benefits of increasing its contributions to the well-being of the local community and society at large. However, the hard-nosed business case to support undertaking socially beneficial initiatives may be more challenging than the business case for environmentally beneficial initiatives. Fortunately, there are good tools available to help with that. For example, the Sustainability ROI Workbook[4] is a free, open-source Excel workbook that allows all potential expenses, benefits, and co-benefits of environmental and social initiatives to be framed on a CFO-friendly format.

As businesses explore possibilities in Stage 3, they discover the value of moving to Stage 4. They come to realize that they may make 31–81% more profit if they simply implemented proven best sustainability-related practices, while avoiding a 16–36% erosion of profit if they did nothing.[5] So, the justification to highlight with decision-makers in Stage 3 companies to help them see the benefit of doing more is the same as it was for moving to Stage 3 in the first place: *capture (more) opportunities* (80%). The weights given by decision-makers to the *mitigate risks* and *do-the-right-thing* justifications are usually low: 10% and 10%, respectively.

Stage 4: Integrated Strategy

By Stage 4, the company is well on its way to transforming into a sustainable business. It re-brands itself as a company committed to sustainability and institutionalizes sustainability factors into its governance systems and policies. It injects sustainability principles into its values and the company DNA. It integrates sustainability approaches into its business strategies, measurement and management systems, and recognition and reward systems.

Stage 4 companies also set long-term aspirational goals and short-term targets for their environmental and social efforts. The goals and indicators may be expressed using the consensus-based Sustainable Development Goals framework, the science-based Future-Fit Business Benchmark[6] framework, the framework used in the B Corp Business Impact Assessment Questionnaire,[7] or others. Stage 4 businesses publish periodic reports on their progress toward their goals, perhaps using an integrated report[8] format to connect the dots between progress on their environmental and social goals and improvements in their financial results. That is, they not only integrate sustainability into their business strategies, they integrate it into their culture.

So, what's left? Hasn't the business gone as far as there is to go on its sustainability journey? Yes and no. What drives any organization to Stage 5 is the emergence of the *do-the-right-thing* justification. It becomes the dominant (80%) rationale, with *capture opportunities* (15%) and *mitigate risks* of inaction (5%) in the background. In Stage 5, doing the right thing really matters to decision-makers, so that part of the business case should be emphasized.

Stage 5: Purpose and Values

About 80% of the behaviors of companies in Stage 4 and Stage 5 look similar. They both deploy business strategies that respect the health of the environment and community, and the ongoing business health of the firm. It's the motivation that differs. Stage 4 companies "do the right thing" *so that* they are successful businesses; the co-benefit is that they also do the right things. Stage 5 companies "do the right thing" *so that* they fulfill their purpose and values by contributing to a better world; the co-benefit is that they are also successful businesses. The benefits and co-benefits are flipped. The dotted line between Stage 4 and Stage 5 in Figure 7.1 denotes this motivational difference.

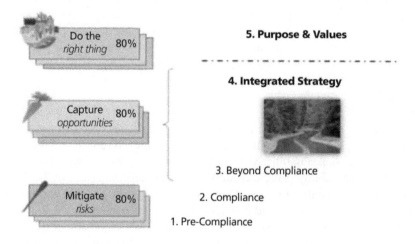

Figure 7.1   Dominant justification for moving to the next stage.

The values of Stage 5 companies usually mirror founder/CEO values. Some founder-owned and founder-led companies start and end in Stage 5 without ever entering the other four stages. Examples are Seventh Generation founded by Jeffrey Hollander; Patagonia led by Yvon Chouinard; and my publisher, New Society Publishers, founded by Chris and Judith Plant. Purpose-driven B Corps are in a similar situation. They not only cause little or no harm to the environment and society, they intentionally have positive impacts on them.

Stage 5 companies are leaders. They help others discover the benefits of being Stage 5 companies. They collaborate to lead the change to resilient human society nested in a healthy environment. They use their influence for good.

If you were to ask most executives in the 1980s and 1990s why they weren't more environmentally and socially responsible, they would have thought it was a trick question. The answer was too obvious. They would be at a competitive disadvantage if they tried to become too "green" or became too distracted by helping the underserved in their communities. It would be too costly. Just keeping up with all the workplace and pollution regulations was a burdensome expense. There was no business case for doing more. These companies were stuck at early stages in their sustainability journeys. Many still are.

In the 21st century, there is a strong three-justification business case for companies to become more environmentally and socially responsible. The appeal of the three justifications will differ at each stage, so we need to meet executives where they are and emphasize the most germane justification for where the company is on its sustainability journey. The other justifications are nice-to-have companion passengers, but the most dominant justification is the driver.

As time has progressed, we have helped monetize and personalize the company-level and project-level business cases for sustainability in order to have those who are asking about sustainability options for the companies obtain answers to the questions that they are *really* asking: "Is there a business case for *my company* being more proactive on sustainability?" and "Is there a necessary and sufficient business case for *my sustainability project* that will win CFO approval?" Their answers will be more credible than ours because they created them.

Maybe it's time we stopped being on the defensive and *we* started to ask our own tough questions. When I bought my first hybrid car, people would ask whether I could really save enough gas to offset the extra expense of the car. At first, I scrambled to do a retroactive cost-benefit analysis to justify my purchase. Looking back, I realize that I got sucked into a defensive business case exercise that was irrelevant. Maybe I should have answered, "I'll show you my business case for buying a hybrid if you show me your business case for buying an SUV." I bought the hybrid because I wanted it, the same reason most people use to justify purchasing their vehicle of choice. I used a values-based rationale. I expect they did, too.

So, maybe the next time we're asked whether there is a business case for sustainability we should try a similar retort: "I'll show you the business case for your company helping to create a more sustainable world if you'll show me the business case for your company helping to destroy it."

NOTES

1. Each "Sector Visioning" chapter begins with an abstract prepared by the book editors and attributed to Zindzi in keeping with the storyline of the book. Zindzi is introduced in Chapter 2.
2. The author calculated these numbers directly from the U.S. Equal Economic Opportunity Commission website. The 2016 numbers are the latest published and were found in the document *2016 Job Patterns for Minorities and Women in Private Industry*. Retrieved at https://www1.eeoc.gov/eeoc/statistics/employment/jobpat-eeo1/2016/index.cfm#select_label
3. Reprinted by permission from https://sustainabilityadvantage.com blogs dated July 1, 2018 and December 2, 2018.
4. See https://sustainabilityadvantage.com/books-dvds/roi-workbook/
5. See https://sustainabilityadvantage.com/books-dvds/new-sustainability-advantage/
6. See http://futurefitbusiness.org/
7. See https://bimpactassessment.net/
8. See http://integratedreporting.org/resource/international-ir-framework/

REFERENCES

Barela, E. (2016, October). *Corporate social responsibility*. Presented at Impact Convergence, Atlanta.

Carroll, A. B. (2008). A history of corporate social responsibility: Concepts and practices. In A. Crane, A. McWilliams, D. Matten, J. Moon, & D. Siegel (Eds.), *The Oxford handbook of corporate social responsibility* (pp. 19–46). Oxford, England: Oxford University Press.

Committee Encouraging Corporate Philanthropy. (2016). *Giving in numbers, 2016 edition*. Retrieved from http://cecp.co/wp-content/uploads/2016/11/GIN2016_Finalweb-1.pdf?redirect=no

Corporate Citizenship. (2016). *Hard outcomes or hollow promises? Realising the true impact of corporate community investment*. Retrieved from http://corporate-citizenship.com/our-insights/hard-outcomes-hollow-promises-realising-true-impact-cci/

Deloitte. (2016). 2016 Deloitte impact survey: Building leadership skills through volunteerism. Retrieved from https://www2.deloitte.com/content/dam/Deloitte/us/Documents/us-deloitte-impact-survey.pdf

Eilbert, H., & Parket, I. R. (1973). The current status of corporate social responsibility. *Business Horizons, 16*(4), 5–14.

Elkington, J. (1999). *Cannibals with forks: The triple bottom line of 21st century business.* Hoboken, NJ: Wiley.

Heald, M. (2005). *The social responsibilities of business: Company and community, 1900–1960.* Cleveland, OH: The Press of Case Western Reserve University.

IBM Institute for Business Value. (2015). *Myths, exaggerations, and uncomfortable truths: The real story behind millennials in the workplace.* Retrieved from http://www-01.ibm.com/common/ssi/cgi-bin/ssialias?subtype=XB&infotype=PM&appname =GBSE_GB_TI_USEN&htmlfid=GBE03637USEN&attachment=GB E03637USEN.PDF

Kassoy, A., Houlahan, B., & Gilbert, J. C. (2016). *Impact governance and management: Fulfilling the promise of capitalism to achieve a shared and durable prosperity.* Washington, DC: Center for Effective Public Management at Brookings. Retrieved from https://www.brookings.edu/wp-content/uploads/2016/07/b_corps.pdf

Kurucz, E., Colbert, B., & Wheeler, D. (2008). The business case for corporate social responsibility. In A. Crane, A. McWilliams, D. Matten, J. Moon, & D. Siegel (Eds.), *The Oxford handbook of corporate social responsibility* (pp, 83–112). Oxford, England: Oxford University Press.

McWilliams, A., Siegel, D. S., & Wright, P. M. (2006). Corporate social responsibility: Strategic implications. *Journal of Management Studies, 43*, 1–18.

Patten, E. (2016, July 1). *Racial, gender wage gaps in U.S. persist despite some progress.* Pew Research Center. Retrieved from http://www.pewresearch.org/fact-tank/2016/07/01/racial-gender-wage-gaps-persist-in-u-s-despite-some-progress/

Schwab, K. (2015, January 6). *Business in a changing world: Stewarding the future.* Retrieved from https://www.foreignaffairs.com/articles/global-commons/2015-01-06/business-changing-world

Wren, D. A., & Bedeian, A. G. (2009). *The evolution of management thought (6th ed.).* Hoboken, NJ: Wiley.

CHAPTER 8

HEALTH

Building Our Power to Create Health Equity

Jeanne Ayers

ZINDZI'S ABSTRACT[1]

In recent decades, the health field has been actively committed to equity. Now in 2030, there is a widespread understanding that creating and supporting healthy populations requires approaches that go far beyond access to affordable, quality medical care. Health results from decisions about all aspects of community life. The materials offered regarding health, often very personal, draw special attention to how one engages in praxis while using all of the other Visionary Evaluative Principles. You'll see how the contributor's deep commitment to equity anchors her way of living in the world , how systems thinking and intersectionalities are a constant area of her attention, how she facilitates transparency and understanding of values, and how she keeps iterating learning, action, and inquiry. You will see a variety of uses of evaluative inquiry to support action.

Visionary Evaluation for a Sustainable, Equitable Future, pages 143–160
Copyright © 2020 by Information Age Publishing
All rights of reproduction in any form reserved.

143

WHAT HEALTH EQUITY LOOKS LIKE IN 2030

Today, in 2030, there is a widespread understanding that creating and supporting healthy populations requires approaches that go far beyond technical solutions and access to affordable, quality medical care. As a result, sustainable investments in prevention have increased through a focus on policy, system, and environmental change. The long-standing, disproportionate focus on illness care and individual behaviors has begun to diminish. Although the United States health system continues to be complex and continually changing, the gaps between the United States and other developed countries is narrowing. The rate of growth of health care expenditures has begun to level off, as have the persistent internal health disparities that marked the U.S. experience for generations. In the United States, decreasing the disparities in health outcomes by race, ethnicity, and income has resulted in measurable improvements in health for the entire population. These gains can be traced back to a growing commitment to health equity that emerged early in the 21st century. This commitment challenged the prevailing dominant assumptions of the effectiveness of technical, programmatic, individualistic solutions. It became apparent that advancing health equity would require a "both–and" approach that recognized the interactions between medical services and a complex set of community conditions created in the broader system and policy environment. The commitment to advancing health equity compelled the health sector to explore systems approaches to navigate this complexity.

BOX 8.1

Health equity is when every person has the opportunity to realize their health potential—the highest level of health possible for that person—without limits imposed by structural inequities. Health equity means achieving the conditions in which all people have the opportunity to attain their highest possible level of health. (Minnesota Dept. of Health, 2014, p. 11)

Now in 2030, many states and organizations have adopted a set of strategic practices rooted in an understanding of complex adaptive systems to achieve the aim of health equity. Three core practices designed to build the collective power of communities' to transform the systems that create health are in widespread use. These include:

1. Organize narrative, data, and knowledge to expand the understanding of what creates health.
2. Organize resources, policy, and systems with equity as the aim.

3. Organize people and strengthen communities' capacity to create their own healthy futures.

Encouraging intentional adoption of these practices and being transparent about their purpose served as a major breakthrough. They assisted those in the health field to stretch beyond more limited reductionist service-provider approaches to include building a growing network of people working to address the root causes of health inequities.

In 2030, there is a widespread recognition of the profound impact on health that results from decisions about all aspects of community life. Community groups and policymakers have embraced a systems approach that considers the health impact of decisions across a wide spectrum of sectors. Increased transparency of values and assumptions guides decision-making. Increasingly, the public is beginning to understand that health is not a commodity or a static state but is created through a system of fragile and dynamic interactions among all aspects of community life and the natural environment. There is recognition that belonging and inclusion are important for health. Understanding these dimensions of health has effectively built public commitment and political will to find equity-driven solutions and energized a new era of community participation, collaboration, and collective action.

Changes in professional training and practice are amplifying these patterns. Professional development efforts incorporate the data analytic and evaluation skills as well as the participatory processes and systems thinking necessary to strengthen and reinforce these practices. These approaches are effectively strengthening the capacity of communities to recognize inequities, see them as the source of an unsustainable pattern, and hold themselves collectively responsible for outcomes.

In the last 10 years, many evaluators have come to see themselves as part of the health equity movement. Professionals, governmental personnel, and community organizers are partnering with evaluators to accelerate transformational change. For example, evaluators have become valued members of planning and implementation teams where they focus on strengthening adoption of a systems approach. They help to identify patterns and build evaluative thinking by making merit, worth, and significance part of everyone's conversations. When evaluators lead the continuous reflection on learning as it is occurring, they reinforce the transparency of values, strengthen the group's focus on purpose, and support a practice of interrupting the work and adjusting course when necessary.

Early in the 21st century, innovators working separately in the public health, evaluation, and community organizing sectors became increasingly conscious of the patterns within the system and the assumptions, practices, and decisions that were forming these patterns. New practices were adopted and introduced through a growing and informal network of relationships. Consequently a dispersed and expanding network of leaders and organizations have contributed to the changes we are seeing today. In this writing I share the story of my developing leadership and experience during this time of transition.

BUILDING A HEALTH EQUITY MOVEMENT (KEY EVENTS)

The landmarks of political, economic and social history are the moments when some condition passed from the category of the given into the category of the intolerable ... I believe that the history of public health might well be written as a record of successive re-definings of the unacceptable.

—Sir Geoffrey Vickers, "What Sets the Goals of Public Health?" (1958)

Recognizing a Deep Discontent With Patterns of Health Inequities and Disparities

The first step to effective action requires understanding ourselves, our values, and the challenges we are facing. For many of us involved in the emerging movement for health equity in the early 2000s, the change began as we recognized racial and economic inequities as a violation of our values and a threat to everyone's health. This was certainly true for me. As a public health professional, nurse, parent, and active member of my community and faith congregation, I had dedicated over 20 years of my life to working to create healthy communities. But as disparities in health outcomes by race, ethnicity, income, and sexual orientation were documented over and over across a wide array of health indicators, I began to question myself, and my professional practice. The root causes of these disparities were clear: To be healthy, people needed equitable access to education, transportation, housing, income, safety, health care, and environmental justice. Inequities in these "social determinants of health" led to negative differences in physical and mental health outcomes for populations of color, American Indians, and low-income people.

Persistent health inequities were being socially created through our decision-making processes and people with less power had less influence over these critical decisions. The disparities in health we were seeing were the physical manifestation of inequities in power and served as a clear indictment of our approaches. I experienced a sense of urgency and responsibility as it became apparent that we needed to build our collective capacity to influence power, social policies, and politics to impact historical patterns of structural discrimination.

BOX 8.2

Health disparity is a population-based difference in health outcomes (e.g., women have more breast cancer than men).

Health inequity is a health disparity based in inequitable, socially-determined circumstances (e.g., American Indians have higher rates of diabetes due to the disruption of their way of life and replacement of traditional foods with unhealthy commodity foods). Because health inequities are socially determined, change is possible.

Structural inequities are structures or systems of society—such as finance, housing, transportation, education, social opportunities, and so on—that are structured in such a way that they benefit one population unfairly whether intended or not (Minnesota Dept. of Health, 2014, p. 11).

There was a growing understanding across many sectors that we needed to shift from expert-driven, professionally focused solutions and services where we were working "for" people to approaches that recognized and embraced the complexity of problems and strengthened a community's capacity or power to assure the conditions for health for themselves. We needed to learn to create widespread transformative change in power relationships.

Significant transformation came only after many people and organizations intentionally began to change practices, align their efforts, and work seriously to build the power for change. While I did not have the language for a formal understanding of complex adaptive systems at the time, I will use this lens to share how the health equity movement formed in my state.

Moving From Reductionist Thinking to Systems Thinking

Public Health Strategies

I started by having uncommon conversations with a small set of public health colleagues (having first met on March 4th, we called ourselves the March Forth group). We recognized the challenges we faced in fulfilling the mission of public health. "Public health is what we, as a society, do collectively to assure the conditions in which (all) people can be healthy" (Institute of Medicine, 1988). We began developing a shared analysis of the root causes of health disparities and their relationship to historical patterns of discrimination and ultimately to inequities in power. We learned to be more transparent by identifying and communicating our values and aims. We realized we needed to build public understanding, public commitment, and the political will to enact changes to redress social and racial inequities in the opportunity to be healthy. The complexity of the system and scale of necessary transformation were daunting. To change these forces and achieve our public health purpose we would need to build collective power. As Martin Luther King, Jr said in 1967, "... power, properly understood, is nothing but the ability to achieve purpose."

The field of public health did not have a robust set of practices focused on system change at the time. While my March Forth colleagues bonded through shared values and a sense of urgency, we were constrained by professional and organizational strategies that were reductionist, service-oriented, and transactional in nature. Even our advocacy experience focused mostly on mobilizing around seeking funding for specific prevention strategies and rarely if ever addressed building collective power for system change. Common public health approaches included providing data, holding conferences, and offering expert testimony on policy or program proposals. There was even an initiative to "re-brand public health" to build public support for prevention. But the one thing we did not discuss was "power."

Community Organizing Strategies

When I first encountered ISAIAH[2] in 2004, its members were organizing over 90 congregations across Central Minnesota and the Minneapolis-Saint Paul Greater Metro area around issues of education, immigration, transportation, and housing. ISAIAH did not consider this a "health" or "health-care" focus because they did not see issues of social, racial, and economic justice as health issues. Their view was influenced by the dominant belief that health was created primarily by access to medical care and an individual commitment to good personal habits.

From my perspective as a public health professional, however, ISAIAH's work was completely aligned with the mission of public health. They were working to change the very conditions that determine a community's health. As a public health person I thought it would be helpful if I could "educate" community leaders on health and the determinants of health, but they were not responsive. It was only when I demonstrated an ability to lead, build a team, and bring people to meetings that I was able to engage others in the challenge and opportunity I envisioned. As I became an active leader, I helped ISAIAH see that the work of the organization could gain coherence and be strengthened by being framed within a health and health equity lens.

ISAIAH's practices had its roots in community organizing theory and political and civic science. They built upon a rich history of rigorous organizing practice and deep commitment to leadership development. The tools, methods, and tactics were focused almost exclusively on two key approaches: "organizing people" and "organizing money and resources." In a process parallel to public health, they were discovering that the complexity of the system required them to stretch and adapt to achieve their aims of racial and health equity. I joined the organization just as they began interrogating the limits and constraints of their traditional practice and expanding their approach to include "organizing worldview and narrative." ISAIAH began by transparently connecting their leaders to a shared vision of "hope, community, and shared abundance."

Intentionally organizing worldview and narrative energized a break-through in ISAIAH's organizing practice. This approach served to break down silos across issues and advocacy campaigns and connect the work and relationships to the bold long-term vision of healthy, thriving communities with social and racial justice for all. ISAIAH's courageous public commitment to racial and health equity served as an inspiration and invitation to public health to tackle inequities.

By this time, I was an active leader in ISAIAH and was developing skills and experience in community organizing. I believed the three practices—"organizing people," "organizing resources," and "organizing narrative"—could equip the field of public health to fully embrace its mission "to assure the conditions in which (all) people can be healthy."

Developing an Expanded Network of Leaders

Leading within ISAIAH required a deep mutual learning process. At one point after we started to gain traction in our health equity work, the executive director turned to me and said, "We would have gotten here two years earlier if you had been willing to own your role as the leader." (Community organizers are frequently blunt with their feedback.) I was startled because I thought I was leading by "sharing" the leadership. I had been concerned about being too directive and had taken what I considered to be a facilitative and less direct approach in the belief that this was the way to bring other people along. Her point to me was that sometimes the movement needs the clarity and courage of someone stepping forward and owning the leadership role that they have the experience, knowledge, and skills to take or may already be exercising. Clearly and transparently owning our own leadership strengthens our sense of commitment, responsibility, and accountability.

The public health culture tended to view leadership and power as a scarce commodity equated with positional roles and titles. In the public health profession and other credentialed fields, claiming leadership might arouse pushback or professional jealousy. In this arena, there are group norms that tend to work to contain the power of any one leader or group and create a pattern of "leveling" at an individual and organizational level. The process of "leveling" is predicated on a belief that leadership had to be "fair," "equal," "formal," and "earned through position" or agreed to through consensus. This process of leveling played out repeatedly in my own work within organizations and between organizations and funders. The pattern served to decrease the capacity of those in public health by guarding against those who would seek to build collective power and create change.

Community organizers, however, generally saw power in developing an expanded network of leaders. They recognized that the work of building the community's capacity for power required an abundance of leaders. Leaders were seen as people who had others willing to follow them. The more people who came forward to take leadership roles, the stronger the community's capacity for making change happen. So, everyone was called to lead.

Leadership development in ISAIAH occurred through conversations, appreciative inquiry,[3] interactive training, public roles, evaluative reflection, and community action. As community organizers, ISAIAH posed questions about whose values and futures were at stake and who was making the decisions. Leaders were equipped with tools and skills to become more effective at creating transformative change in their community—teaching ordinary people to unleash their capacity to impact the social, political, environmental, and economic decisions affecting their lives. There was a robust practice of asking questions to help recognize and disrupt the dominant processes creating inequities. Leadership was not based on charisma but was focused on helping people build their personal capacity to influence. People became influential by (a) understanding self-interest and purpose, (b) investing in relationships, and (c) taking action.

Organizers used several evaluative strategies. One approach was to immediately evaluate every meeting and the roles of every leader within the meeting. There was a particular focus on understanding the tension that was produced. To the organizers, tension created the basis for learning and action. The sources of tension were deliberately evaluated for evidence of people sharing their values, and building their collective capacity to act. Tension could serve to deepen relationships and accountability and develop a shared understanding of a challenge and the action necessary. It also could serve to create urgency. If there was no tension, the organizers would question if the meeting was successful. This experience led me to believe public health would benefit from building the practice of welcoming and learning from tension.

I learned to recognize patterns that were not "fit to purpose." ISAIAH challenged me to engage in a mutual learning and co-creating process and I developed the skills and perspective of a community organizer. If it hadn't been for the investment ISAIAH made in my leadership, I don't know if I would have had the breakthroughs on understanding power that guided my later work in the Minnesota Department of Health. The strategic practices and evaluative strategies of the organizers were clearly connected to being serious and intentional about building their power to influence change. Public health professionals did not have that kind of practical experience or training. In public health, we had a limited set of approaches that included services, education, research, dissemination, "collaborative convening," and conferences.

BOX 8.3

Appreciative Inquiry (AI) is a theory and practice for approaching change holistically. It is based on the belief that social systems are envisioned and made by those who live and work within them. It leads people to imagine and create their social systems from their most positive core values, visions, achievements, and practices (Watkins & Mohr, 2001).

Engaging in Purposeful Collaboration for Collective Action

Typically in public health, professionals spoke of community engagement but meant that community members would be brought in to inform the professionals' work. Community organizers, however, thought in terms of building the community's capacity for power. So, when ISAIAH brought people into the decision-making process, these people represented—and were accountable to—diverse community groups. In speaking from the perspectives of the groups they represented, these community members often changed the conversation because their experiences challenged prevailing assumptions. Perhaps most importantly, when the people convened in decision-making spaces, they had the responsibility to co-create and enact any actions or plans that were formed. This was a very different way of engaging community than the methods typically used in public health or professional organizations.

Central Corridor Campaign

A coalition of community organizers, including ISAIAH, came together to change a proposal that would eliminate three stops from a planned light rail project in St. Paul, Minnesota. The stops were situated in the Central Corridor, the area of the city with the highest concentration of racial and ethnic minority people. Those advocating for the removal of the stops said that they were simply trying to meet the federal criteria for matching funds: "Move the most people the farthest distance in the shortest amount of time."

The coalition understood that the elimination of stops on the light rail would disconnect the transportation network from the communities that were in most need of access to it. They organized all the way to the federal level to change the criteria. It was my first public experience with recognizing and naming structural racism.

BOX 8.4

Structural Racism is the normalization of an array of dynamics—historical, cultural, institutional and interpersonal—that routinely advantages White people while producing cumulative and chronic adverse outcomes for people of color and American Indians (Minnesota Dept. of Health, 2014, p. 11).

The battle over the Central Corridor took years. In the process, the coalition made the communities' values transparent, changed the decision-makers and decision-making space, altered the relationship with experts, identified the metrics that mattered, avoided a too-narrow approach, and kept the focus on strengthening the communities' ability to influence decisions.

As a result of these concerted efforts, the federal criteria were changed. The light rail stops in the most racially and ethnically diverse communities were restored and ridership subsequently exceeded expectations. More importantly from the community organizers' perspective, the work reinforced community relationships and substantially expanded people's belief in their capacity to create change. From my perspective, we were making major progress on improving a critical social determinant of health—access to opportunity via transportation—while we were building our collective capacity to assure future decisions would prioritize health and racial equity.

Healthy Heartland

In my role as chair of ISAIAH's Health Equity and Healthy Communities work, I had built relationships across Minnesota. But we needed to attend to the broader system to create transformative and sustainable change. So, we launched Healthy Heartland, a five-state collaborative to explore the intersections of health equity and community organizing. In 2010, I initiated an evaluation of Healthy Heartland. In this multi-state effort we engaged evaluators, public health professionals, and community organizers in conversations and reflections about their roles and shared issues. The evaluation aimed to identify ways we could measure the process of building power and creating policy change.

We were also striving to "build a body of work" across fields, issue silos, and geographic locations that would be recognizable as collective shared work. Seeing our efforts as collective work across a broader system would help build a movement. The aims of the evaluation included building a shared body of work, strengthening relationships across a broad region and across sectors, and developing the skills and knowledge to recognize patterns and strengthen practices that build collective power.

Shining the Light—10,000 Voices Campaign

In 2010, ISAIAH prepared over 150 people to lead conversations within their communities and governmental agencies reflecting on health and racial equity and structural racism. The iterative nature of this process was consistent with a systems-oriented evaluation process and served to strengthen a pattern of understanding, action, and relationships.

Strengthening a shared vision of health and racial equity gave ISAIAH and its public health partners a foundation and a platform for action. As part of the process, ISAIAH leaders met with all the gubernatorial candidates and proposed they meet again if elected. In December of 2010, Governor-elect Dayton and his transition team attended a meeting with a diverse group of over 1600 people who had gone through a deep reflection on racial equity and its impact on health, transportation, and education. The Governor listened to the recommendations and was moved by the stories and vision ISAIAH proclaimed. He then appointed Dr. Ed Ehlinger, a member of the original March Forth group, as commissioner and me as assistant commissioner of the Minnesota Department of Health (MDH).

FINDING EQUITY-DRIVEN SOLUTIONS

I arrived at the health department in 2011 with a clear sense of purpose and a deepening understanding of power. I understood that to achieve the aim of health equity we needed to intentionally build collective power with people serious about creating the conditions where all people thrive. It was apparent that health is almost completely connected to our living conditions and that our living conditions are determined by our "capacity to act" or power to create these conditions for all. The health and racial disparities we were seeing were really a physical manifestation of inequities in power. I felt ready to act!

In my first month as assistant commissioner at MDH, I planned to attend a meeting with a community group on housing and zoning issues. I met a colleague in the corridor who counseled me that housing was not in our "swim lane," and that we had to be cautious about meeting with community groups because they have "an agenda." The colleague then went into a meeting with our recognized "stakeholders"—health insurers. The challenge was clear. The pattern of assumptions and norms about our practice at MDH was constraining our ability to work collectively to achieve our aim of health equity.

Changing the Statewide Health Assessment

I realized we needed to develop a shared narrative aligned with a more complete understanding of what creates health as well as find a way to "re-set the table" to make it possible for community groups to be a natural part of the discussion and decision-making process. To accomplish this, we began by "organizing people." We expanded the Healthy Minnesota Partnership (Partnership) to 25+ organizations representing various constituencies including community and advocacy groups; as well as public health; state departments of housing, transportation, corrections, and human services; hospitals and insurance companies; and academic institutions.

The Partnership was charged with "developing a statewide health improvement plan that ensures the opportunity for healthy living for all Minnesotans." The broadened network of stakeholders worked through a public iterative process to develop a set of aims and metrics that integrated their values and knowledge and served to guide their collective action. They also grounded themselves in the data regarding health, the determinants of health, and health inequities.

The Partnership made a groundbreaking departure from usual public health practice when it directed the agency to broaden the Statewide Health Assessment (Assessment) to include indicators such as income, education, transportation, incarceration, and housing and, where available, analysis by race, ethnicity, and income. In this way the Partnership was organizing narrative, data, and knowledge to expand the understanding of what creates health.

The innovative introduction of the practices of "organizing people," and "organizing narrative" paired with the practice of "organizing resources, policy, and systems with equity as the aim," through the partnership represented a breakthrough in our ability to build power to change the conditions creating health. These practices resulted in partners aligning and strengthening efforts to decrease barriers to employment, increase minimum wage, improve paid leave, address healthy food access, and transportation. The experience demonstrated an early application of systems and evaluative thinking to public health practice.

Intentionally Building Power for System Change

I joined the department in 2011 with the goal of building collective power to influence the policies and systems that were creating inequities. I began by focusing on the power building strategies of "organizing people," "organizing resources," and "organizing narrative." In 2015, I was introduced to "Adaptive Action" and systems theory by Glenda Eoyang and Royce Holladay of the Human Systems Dynamics Institute. I learned that intentional application of a set of three to seven simple practices can create transformative change in human systems. I realized leaders would need to recognize and commit to a set of practices to effectively create sustainable change.

The Triple Aim of Health Equity

Armed with the recognition that the approach we were using was grounded in theory and research on power and systems change strengthened our commitment to be even more explicit in promoting these practices. To share and disseminate the three organizing practices, Commissioner Ehlinger codified them into what we began to call the Triple Aim of Health Equity:

1. Expand the understanding of health (organize narrative).
2. Implement a health in all policies approach with equity as the aim (organize resources).
3. Strengthen community capacity to create their own healthy futures (organize people).

Use of the term, Triple Aim of Health Equity, was intended to balance the Triple Aim of Health Framework promoted by the Institute for Health-Care Improvement (IHI, http://www.ihi.org/). Commonly considered an authoritative source on population health and health care at the time, IHI focused primarily on cost, access, and quality of medical services delivery in the health care sector. In contrast, the Triple Aim of Health Equity expanded that framework to invite people to also embrace their role in creating health by building the power to address the structural and social determinants of health.

As we expanded the people and networks engaged in the growing health equity movement we emphasized the iterative, learning nature of the process. It became apparent that our approach would benefit from application of an evaluative framework or evaluation thinking. We began to encourage asking these questions:

What: What is the pattern?
So What: What is the meaning of the pattern?
Now What: What can we do?

By the end of 2015, the three practices of the Triple Aim of Health Equity served as the focus of the department's strategic plan and had begun to guide action within all sections and programs in the agency. Naming and committing to these practices allowed a growing number of people and partners to engage in creating change. As staff adopted the Triple Aim of Health Equity, a pattern of change emerged in grant making, policies, contracting, hiring, laboratory procedures, community engagement, and advisory committee processes. The Triple Aim of Health Equity was used extensively in reports and initiatives to guide and describe MDH's systems approach to organize people, narrative, and resources to advance health equity.

Crafting the Seminal Report: "Advancing Health Equity in Minnesota"

The seminal report *Advancing Health Equity in Minnesota: Report to the Minnesota Legislature* is an example of the transformative impact achieved through an iterative application of the three practices of the Triple Aim of Health Equity (Minnesota Department of Health, 2014).

The commitment to expand the understanding of health and the root causes of health disparities emboldened community partners to raise issues with policy-makers. Policy-makers were increasingly receptive to community concerns as their own understanding grew. As a result, in 2013, the Minnesota Legislature formally directed MDH to write a report assessing Minnesota's health inequities and recommend best practices, policies, processes, data strategies, and other steps to promote health equity for all Minnesotans. I designed the legislative language to build upon the three practices of the Triple Aim of Health Equity. With this aim in mind, I invited 100 MDH staff to help write the report. I intentionally asked people to contribute based upon their interests not their hierarchical role in the department. I also made sure that people with positional power were invited in the same way. By inviting staff to lead sections of the process, I was building a network of leaders across levels of the hierarchy and program areas (*organize people*). Drawing on community organizing practices, we invited health department staff to engage their respective networks, organizations, and communities to develop the report. We used the increased visibility and urgency of a legislative directive to engage hundreds of groups across the state in conversations on health equity and structural racism.

We then brought the 100 agency leaders together in a convening. There we grounded our efforts in expanding the understanding of what creates health and health inequities with an intentional focus on race and structural racism (*organize narrative*). We used a set of questions to reflect on our practices, policies, and systems and their impact on health outcomes (*organize resources*). We asked questions to help identify structural barriers or inequities to health and reflect on who was most likely to be impacted by these barriers.

At the end of the convening, I asked, "How many of you can lead conversations like this with people you are in partnership with?" And they committed to 180 additional convenings. In six weeks, 1,000 people contributed to writing the health equity report (*organize people*). It became their report.

The *Advancing Health Equity* report (Minnesota Department of Health, 2014) explicitly led with a discussion about the relationship of race to the structural inequities that contribute to health disparities (that is, "redefining the unacceptable"). The report emphasized "Structural racism is perpetuated when decisions are made without accounting for how they might benefit one population more than another, or when cultural knowledge, history, and locally-generated approaches are excluded. When this

> **BOX 8.5**
> **Example Use of Questions on Path for Change**
>
> An example of how we've used transparent values to improve decision-making occurred at a diabetes-prevention meeting. At a meeting of health care leaders, we were working on improving the reach of a diabetes-prevention program. There was a general consensus that all participants in the meeting cared about the quality and integrity of the data being collected. Having reached agreement on the importance of high-quality data collection, the participants jumped to a solution that would have eliminated community groups from delivering the prevention program. To assure the integrity of the data, participants decided that the diabetes prevention program could only be provided by entities that used electronic billing. Yet, most community providers—who also happened to be the groups most deeply engaged with the populations experiencing the highest levels of diabetes—lacked the capability to bill electronically.
>
> The participants were initially reluctant to consider a different solution. Group members in favor of limiting providers to only those organizations with electronic billing implied that opposition to this requirement demonstrated failure to hold data integrity as a high value. Then it was pointed out that none of the groups most impacted had representation at the meeting. This led to additional conversation about the value of inclusivity and changed the membership of the group. With a broader set of groups represented the recommended solution changed. We agreed to provide additional technical assistance and support to the community-led efforts on diabetes prevention so that they could assure the integrity of their data while they provided service to the communities most impacted by diabetes. Reflecting on values and assumptions and recognizing whose values are guiding a process led to changing the decision-makers and the decision-making space.

happens, programs and policies can reinforce or compound existing race-based inequities" (p. 6). This public declaration of the pattern—and the meaning of the pattern—for the health of our state contributed to the ability of many organizations and leaders at all levels to effectively work together to change the policies and systems creating inequities.

Improving Decision-Making by Being Transparent About Values

Even today in 2030, I am still handing out a set of questions about values and assumptions in nearly every meeting I attend. The questions have successfully helped us interrupt our own practice and reflect on the patterns created by the policies, practices, and processes in our organizations The questions are not about a list of what's been accomplished but about what is valued and what is wanted (see Box 8.6). We continue to focus on building power for system change by employing a set of simple practices.

Expanding the Reach of the Triple Aim of Health Equity

By 2015 we were introducing the Triple Aim of Health Equity across an ever-expanding network of leaders and organizations and now in 2030 health equity leaders routinely use these practices to strengthen the movement for health and racial equity. The Commissioner promoted the Triple Aim of Health Equity through his many state and national leadership roles including the Association of State and Territorial Health Officials (ASTHO).

BOX 8.6
Asking the Right Questions Is a Path to Action for Change[4]

The central questions when looking at *existing policies* are:
- What are the outcomes?
- Who benefits?
- Who is left out?

The central questions to help design *new policies* are:
- What outcomes do we want?
- Who should be targeted to benefit?

The central questions to examining *processes* are:
- Who is at the decision-making table, and who is not?
- Who has the power at the table?
- Who is being held accountable and to whom or what are they accountable?

The central questions to help develop *new processes* are:
- How should the decision-making table be set, and who should set it?
- Who should hold decision-makers accountable, and where should this accountability take place?

The central questions to identify *assumptions* are:
- What values underlie the decision-making process?
- What is assumed to be true about the world and the role of the institution in the world?
- What standards of success are being applied at different decision points, and by whom?

The central questions to define *new assumptions* that will create the opportunity for health and healthy communities for all are:
- What are our values?
- What would it look like if equity was the starting point for decision-making?

(ISAIAH & the Kirwan Institute, 2010, p. 13)

Staff and partners wrote articles, reports, and documents, and conducted media interviews and events. We trained thousands of people and shared stories of the changes we were making in policies and processes widely with funders, grantees, organizers, and policy-makers. We worked to reach many layers and systems by working at the local, state, and national level to share learning, develop tools, and share resources. Today in 2030, the practices of the Triple Aim of Health Equity and complex adaptive systems are routinely embedded in training and organizational structures. What were new ways of thinking and practicing now serve as the foundation for a robust movement for health equity. Leaders in philanthropy have incorporated the learning and practices into their grant-making and regularly focus on supporting efforts to build the public and political will for policy, system, and environmental changes. Public health professionals, evaluators, and communities now expect to work together as partners to create policy and system changes and address structural and racial inequities.

BOX 8.7

Public Narratives are the "stories," shared in the public domain (e.g., in policy discussion or other decision-making places) that shape people's conscious perceptions, understanding analysis, and senses of responsibility and possibility. (Dave Mann, Grassroots Policy Project)[5]

CONCLUSION

I have described some of the practices or shifts that helped create opportunity pathways for health. The success of our efforts to create transformative change came through the connected actions of March Forth, ISAIAH, Healthy Heartland, The Healthy Minnesota Partnership, state and local government, community, labor and faith-based groups, philanthropy, and academia. The practices of organizing people, resources, and narrative created changes in concrete work products such as community meetings; data collection; analysis and reports; and changes in policies and processes and have resulted in very real improvements in disparities. Paying attention to a simple set of practices and the iterative evaluation of changes in patterns guided our efforts and helped us navigate toward our aim of health equity.

Critical to the work of the health equity movement was systems thinking. As we took a systems approach, we paid attention to power and equity and focused on developing relationships and identifying values. We committed to the practice of consistently directing our efforts toward the Triple Aim of Health Equity.

In this systemic approach to health improvement, communities and public health—not hospitals or medical industries—were at the forefront. The practices became a fundamental part of the strategy to continue to learn from a broad network of sectors (including professional, academic, health, and non-health sectors in many states) closely connected to communities and their residents. Evaluative thinking increased our capacity to see the patterns, the meaning of the patterns, and resulted in fundamental paradigm shifts toward a world of sustainable, equitable health for all.

NOTES

1. Each "Sector Visioning" chapter (Chapters 4–12) begins with an abstract prepared by the book editors and attributed to Zindzi in keeping with the storyline of the book. Zindzi is introduced in Chapter 2.
2. For more information about ISAIAH and its community organizing work, see Minkler, M. (Ed.). (2012). *Community organizing and community building for health and welfare (3rd ed)*. New Brunswick, NJ: Rutgers University Press.
3. Watkins, J., & Mohr, B. (2001). *Appreciative inquiry: Change at the speed of imagination*. San Francisco, CA: Jossey-Bass.
4. ISAIAH and The Kirwan Institute for the Study of Race and Ethnicity. (2010). *Shining the light: A practical guide to co-creating healthy communities*. Retrieved from http://www.kirwaninstitute.osu.edu/reports/2010/05_2010_Shining theLightOrganizingGuide.pdf
5. See https://grassrootspolicy.org

REFERENCES

Institute of Medicine. (1988). *The future of public health*. Washington, DC: The National Academies Press.

ISAIAH and The Kirwan Institute for the Study of Race and Ethnicity. (2010). *Shining the light: A practical guide to co-creating healthy communities*. Retrieved from http://www.kirwaninstitute.osu.edu/reports/2010/05_2010_Shiningthe LightOrganizingGuide.pdf

King, Jr., M. L. (1967). Where do we go from here? Address delivered at the Eleventh Annual Southern Christian Leadership Conference on August 16, 1967 in Atlanta, Georgia. In C. Clayborne (Ed.) (2001). *A call to conscience: The landmark speeches of Martin Luther King, Jr.* New York: IPM/Warner Books.

Minnesota Department of Health. (2014). *Advancing health equity: Report to the Minnesota legislature*. St. Paul, MN: Minnesota Department of Health. Retrieved from https://www.health.state.mn.us/communities/equity/reports/ahe_leg_ report_020114.pdf

Watkins, J., & Mohr, B. (2001). *Appreciative inquiry: Change at the speed of imagination*. San Francisco, CA: Jossey-Bass.

CHAPTER 9

FINANCIAL INVESTING

Valuing Social Returns

Georgette Wong

ZINDZI'S ABSTRACT[1]

One of the areas most impacted by people dedicated to having their actions reflect their values is in the area of financial investing. Today a wide swath of individuals, philanthropies, and investment companies routinely consider the social impact of the companies and funds in which they invest. They critically discern whether the intent, actions, and outcomes of the companies and funds align with their own values, especially with regard to equity and sustainability. Our next contributor traces the key events that have led to this shift—from the apartheid divestment movement, to the rise of impact investing, to philanthropies using their core financial assets in addition to their grant dollars to further their mission. These actions, among others, has led to a mindset shift of investors such that their social return on investment is as valuable as their financial return. This change created a systems approach to investment. In addition, diversity increased not only in investor circles but also in boardrooms. While there has been a move toward meaningful metrics, especially alignment with the Sustainable Development Goals and toward outcomes rather than just outputs, there is still much that financial investors and decision-makers can learn from taking on a Visionary Evaluative approach.

Visionary Evaluation for a Sustainable, Equitable Future, pages 161–174
Copyright © 2020 by Information Age Publishing
161

In 2030, people looking to create social change have widely adopted a new tool: their investments. People and organizations use their cash, stocks, and bonds, alongside the traditional tools of philanthropy and policy, to realize their visions and values. Often called impact investing; environmental, social, and governance (ESG) investing; or socially responsible investing (SRI), these investments consider financial returns as well as social and/or environmental benefits. These investments address a wide array of social challenges including equity, education, climate change, water quality and access, food systems, healthcare, housing, and job creation.

Whether wealthy individuals, foundations, corporations, pension plans, or government agencies, leading investors in 2030 practice ESG/impact investing as the natural course of business. Those who have not chosen this path are questioned as to why they are not including social and environmental factors in their investments, especially as the investments have been proven to have the same risk-adjusted rates of return as traditional (nonsocial) investment, while also contributing to ensuring a more sustainable world.

This chapter explores the history and growth of impact investing (including the importance of women, millennials, and people of color), actionable frameworks for financial investment, and the importance of measuring the impacts of these investments.

HISTORY AND GROWTH

How did impact investing become mainstream? Indeed, how did investing—where the best risk-adjusted financial returns are the most highly valued—come to use social and environmental criteria in their investment analyses? How did investing—which economic giants such as Milton Friedman said was only to maximize shareholder return—also include metrics for social and environmental change? To trace the arc of impact investing, we need to look to its beginnings.

Investing for social change has its origins in the 18th century, when the United Methodist Church and the Religious Society of Friends (Quakers) avoided investments in the slave trade, smuggling, alcohol, tobacco, and gambling based on religious values. There have been several key historical events that led to its more widespread adoption. First was divestment from South Africa to end apartheid in the 1980s. When the De Klerk administration took steps to end apartheid in 1993, $625 billion was being screened to exclude investment in South Africa (Barry, 2013). Second, in 2005, and signaling a growing global trend, then United Nations Secretary General Kofi Annan invited a group of the world's largest and most respected investors to draw up the Principles for Responsible Investment, a list of six principles that investors voluntarily utilized to integrate ESG practices into their investment strategies. These principles were launched at the New York Stock Exchange in 2006 and ranged from integrating ESG considerations into decision and policy making to reporting on ESG activities and progress. Since that time, the number of institutions committed to responsible investing has grown from 100 to over 2300 in the first 2 decades of this century (Principles for Responsible Investment, 2019). Third, the term "impact investing" was created in 2007 to show that the end result of investing—the social impact—was equally as important as financial returns. Fourth, and perhaps most importantly, is that evidence showed that risk-adjusted financial returns were equal to or greater than those of "traditional investments." The MSCI KLD 400 is the considered the oldest mutual fund focused on SRI. From its inception in May 1990 to March 2018, the MSCI KLD 400 has beaten the standard benchmark Standard & Poor's 500 by 0.5 percentage points annually (Kaissar, 2018). This is critical, as most investors have a legal responsibility (called "fiduciary duty") to earn the highest risk-adjusted financial return as possible for their clients.

The 2010s and 2020s witnessed a significant increase in dollars dedicated to socially responsible/impact investing (see Figure 9.1).

By the end of 2016, almost $9 trillion was invested using as guidelines ESG factors (Gorte & Voorhees, 2017).

Financial institutions have at least a century of measuring financial return and the risk it takes to earn that return. Measuring the social and environmental impacts of the investments, however, is a much younger endeavor.

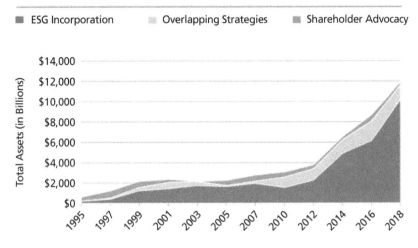

Since 1995, when the US SIF Foundation first measured US SRI assets at $639 billion, assets have increased 18-fold, a compound annual rate of 13.6 percent.

■ ESG Incorporation   Overlapping Strategies   ■ Shareholder Advocacy

Figure 9.1 U.S. sustainable and responsible investing growth 1995–2018.[3]
Source: US|SIF Foundation, 2018.

The link between investments and global challenges was bolstered when the United Nations adopted the Sustainable Development Goals (SDGs) in 2015. The SDGs aim to eliminate poverty, increase peace and prosperity, and protect the planet for all by today (2030). Targets included no poverty, zero hunger, gender equality, quality education, clean water, clean energy, reduced inequalities, decent jobs, economic growth, and climate action (United Nations, 2015).

In 2016, the Global Impact Investing Network ("the GIIN"), the largest global association of impact investors, urged all investors to measure their success against the SDGs. In 2018, the United Nations and GIIN estimated that between $5–7 trillion would be needed annually to reach the SDGs by 2030. Since 2016, large industry leaders such as United Bank of Switzerland (UBS) and Credit Suisse have aligned their investments with the SDGs, due to the leadership of executive management and the banks' most important clients.

SHIFTS IN MINDSET

Underlying this growth in sustainable investing are significant shifts in mindset for all players in the financial services industry. These mindset changes are: (a) investors now understand that the constraints of the natural world dictate the extent of investing; (b) wealthy families and foundations recognize that they, as individual actors and as a group, do not possess enough money to make significant social change and need to bring on other large pools of money; and (c) current CEOs and other business leaders recognize that the needs of all stakeholders are more important to profit than maximizing shareholder value.

Investing is comprised of two main groups: the clients (wealthy people, foundations and other organizations who have money) and the financial institutions (financial advisors, mutual funds, and other money managers) who aim to serve them. Both groups had traditionally been taught to separate their values from their investing, lest the investment performance suffer. Today, however, large global trends enable investors to earn a profit and invest with their values. For example, solar and other renewable energies are solutions to climate change and global warming. Water recycling and smarter techniques to grow food address the shortage of both water and food globally.

Clients are the key to profound change within financial services. Clients have the money, and financial services institutions will do what it takes to serve them. Thus, a change in client demand and preferences leads an entire industry to offer new products. In the early 2000s, foundations and wealthy individuals were the first to demand a new way of doing business for a practical reason: They realized that they simply did not have enough money to solve large global problems with only philanthropic dollars. Clients wanted to use their investment dollars as well. For example, up until the early 2000s, the vast majority of foundations relied solely on grants (approximately 5% of their dollars) to accomplish their missions. The other 95% of their money was invested to maximize financial return, even if those returns were derived from corporate activities that were directly opposed to a foundation's mission. For example, it was not altogether uncommon to find a health foundation investing in a high returning tobacco company or an environmentally focused foundation investing in oil companies. To put numbers to it, U.S. foundations in 2015 distributed $63 billion in grants. Yet, these foundations controlled $860 billion of assets (Foundation Center, n.d.).

The first mindset change is that investors now fully comprehend that business, humans, and all other life forms are dependent on nature and that companies cannot and should not live separately from the natural world. For many years, it has been orthodoxy that humans can and should control nature, and that growth of the financial markets was infinite. Investors now understand that growth only for the sake of growing profits is deleterious to our world. While profits are generally welcome, they are not if they come at the expense of people going hungry, or are subjected to discriminatory impact, or are poisoned by chemicals, or if swaths of rainforests which supply our world with oxygen are destroyed.

A second mindset change was that wealthy families and foundations understood that they needed to bring other large asset owners on board to use their investment capital to solve social and environmental issues. While foundations have a lot of money, total U.S. foundation assets (grants and endowments) represented only 0.18% of the $405 trillion in the global capital markets—cash, stocks, bonds, real estate, and derivatives (current figures as of May 31, 2016; Malvey, 2016). Thus, it was important that companies, pension plans and governments, and other investors that make up the remaining 99.82% of investable assets invest for impact.

With greater interest from potential clients, large financial firms such as Morgan Stanley, JP Morgan, and UBS entered the market with their products. The growth in SRI and ESG continues to increase, largely because of the preferences of women and younger generations. Whether from very wealthy families or from everyday families, these individuals now control trillions of dollars. Impact investing is no longer only for the super wealthy. In 2030, we are partly through the transfer of approximately $16 trillion in wealth from the Boomer generation to their spouses (predominantly women) and children (Harjani, 2015) who are Gen Y or millennials[2] (Bump, 2014). Many experts see this as the largest transfer of wealth in history. Women and millennials tend to look at the world from a more holistic lens. They have been conscious of what their money buys: Is the food organic?

Are the workers paid well? Is it a fair trade product? In the same vein, they are conscious investors and want their money to have a positive impact. Many individual investors and institutions want to ensure that their investments do not fund practices that are contrary to their personal or organizational values or missions. While both philanthropy and investment are used to create social good, millennials show greater confidence in the private sector to drive social change (Yeap, 2016) than older generations. The preferences of women and millennials will continue to drive change in financial markets for decades.

While the needs of clients and prospective clients influence financial firms, these firms are guided also by analyses that focus on returns, as well as the risk, whether related to politics or governance or other factors. Social and environmental analyses can reveal unhealthy amounts of risk or decreased risk in a given investment. They can also correlate to increased financial returns. Climate change provides an example of increased risk to investment portfolios. In fact, BlackRock, the largest asset manager in 2018 with $5.967 trillion under management, stated that climate change was a systemic risk (Williamson, 2019). The influential firm asserted that those energy companies most likely to be adversely affected by global warming must terminate their boards of directors if they didn't adequately manage the potential risk of damages to shareholders (Johnson, 2017).

One example of greater financial performance is female leadership and gender diversity. According to a 2017 analysis of 11,000 public companies globally by the Norwegian bank Nordea, companies with a woman in the top two roles have performed far better than a major global index over the preceding 8 years. On average, companies with a woman as the chief executive or chairperson at the end of the calendar year more than doubled the performance of the MSCI World Index in the following year. The annualized return for female-led firms was 25% since 2009, compared with just 11% for the broader market (McGregor, 2017). Proponents of gender-based investing use data from this study and other studies to argue for increased investment in women. They argue that by investing in companies that support women, they help women gain access to capital to start businesses, foster workplace pay equity, and support companies making products and offer services that advance the lives of women and girls.

Robust research has existed on women's leadership on company performance, yet in the second decade of this century, comparatively little had been done on the contributions of people of color to company performance. Research now indicates that people of color also outperform other managers, not because of their color or race per se, but because people of color often hold multiple perspectives and viewpoints at once. This ability to hold multiple perspectives—even those in opposition to each other—is extremely useful in investing. Investors and philanthropies started acknowledging this shift such as with the move by the Kresge Foundation in 2019 to place one quarter of its assets to firms owned by women and people of color (Welch, 2019).

The third and final shift in mindset comes from today's CEOs and other influential business leaders. While earlier generations of CEOs were taught in business schools that "maximizing shareholder value" was the only priority, this CEO generation in 2030 attended business schools that integrated sustainability and the concerns of all stakeholders (including employees, suppliers, and communities) into the curriculum. Without understanding the needs of all those who have an interest in the company and who may benefit or be harmed by company practices, companies are less likely to maximize profits (Jensen, 2000). Significantly, the Business Roundtable, which is an association of CEOs of top US corporations, issued a statement in August 2019 that redefined the purpose of a corporation. No longer focusing solely on profit maximization, 181 CEOs from companies such as JPMorgan Chase & Co. and Johnson & Johnson have committed to "lead[ing] their companies for the benefit of all stakeholders—customers, employees, suppliers, communities and shareholders" (Business Roundtable, 2019). While this statement alone holds import, more meaningful are the actions these businesses must take to prove this change is more than words alone.

FRAMEWORKS FOR SUCCESSFUL INVESTING: IMPACT FIRST, TOOL SECOND

In 2030, successful investors know that all their investments, whether labeled socially responsible or not, have an environmental and/or social impact. The most successful investors for social change possess a systemic view of the problems they are looking to solve and a long-term horizon to solve them. These investors are cognizant that their money may be having a detrimental impact on the planet and its people and that they could instead harness investments for a positive impact. As such, they look to solve problems and issues across sectors and at the root level. While most investors look for returns within a day, a year, or even a 10-year time frame, these successful investors have lengthened their timeframe to span multiple decades. They acknowledge that they individually do not have all the answers, and actively engage others from different sectors. These conversations lead to a 360-degree view of the problem and to possible solutions. They recognize that they may need to use all types of capital at their disposal to obtain the result they envision. These tools may include for-profit investments, philanthropic dollars, their reputations, as well as networks of employees, boards of directors, suppliers, and friends.

While most people focus first on the types of capital that they or their organization have, and secondarily on the change they want to create, the most successful social investors see the big picture first:

- What is the change my organization is trying to create? Is it systemic? If so, on what level(s)—local, regional, national, international?
- What is my organization's theory of change? How do we propose to get from A (present day) to B (the new reality)?
- As an individual or an individual organization, what impact can we have on a system?
- Looking beyond intent, how will we measure our impact and evaluate our progress?
- Will for-profit or nonprofit capital best support this change?
- Do we have the type of capital we need to make the change?
- If we don't have the right kind of capital for the impact, who does? How do we create collaborations with organizations with similar values and priorities so we can have the impact we seek?

In a vast departure from earlier decades, conventional wisdom in 2030 now holds that:

- Everything is connected. Investors want to better understand the problem and the system in which it is operating to affect long-term change.
- Rather than using one type of capital to affect change, people and organizations are 100% of their assets such as their investment dollars, philanthropic money, networks, influence, brand, and voice. All these tools are being used in concert together for the same aim.
- Investors are honest about their capabilities and their resources.
- Investors have greater ease with failure; they do not let risk stand in the way of trying something new. In the same way that investors are willing to try new products, they are willing to experiment in social change and "fail forward"—that is, feeding learnings from failures into new paths forward.
- Investors recognize that we must build or rebuild and reinforce entire ecosystems. While cash flow for one's own organization retains top priority for most mission-driven organizations to remain viable, leaders recognize that their partners must also be strong so that they can continue to reach their shared goals.
- Investors focus on results and outcomes, rather than outputs. The most important results could come from a nonprofit or a for-profit. The type of organization is secondary to their track record and results they obtain.

Accountability for Impact

While impact investing saw great interest and popularity from wealthy individuals and foundations, and even from the White House under President Obama and the Vatican under Pope Francis, the entry of the largest financial players (including JP Morgan, Morgan Stanley, Goldman Sachs, UBS, and BlackRock) in the early 2000s gave many pause. Was impact truly happening? Or were these large financial firms "impact washing," that is, just using the concept to bring in new clients? Furthermore, how could any organization—in the private, nonprofit or governmental sectors—be held accountable and/or rewarded for the impacts they create?

The keys to accountability proved to be: (a) investors who continued to push for meaningful accountability metrics, (b) alignment with the SDGs, and (c) experts who helped investors understand and simplify metrics and measurement. Fortunately, wealthy investors believe in the importance of outcomes, and experts have simplified the over 200 different sets of standards created to define impact in existence in 2015. The business community has looked to evaluators with expertise in social impact to lead the way beyond outputs, which are seen as insufficient. Instead, outcomes are routinely used; they are no longer seen as a means of proving success to donors or investors. Investors map the outcomes they desire at the beginning of their process, develop metrics tied to those outcomes, and then use the data gathered to make evidence-informed decisions throughout the process. Evaluators have been important in helping investors judge the impact of their resources and efforts. Evaluators have also enabled consistency, which makes comparison easy and ensures that the burden to meet a variety of standards is not being placed on the companies and social change organizations.

Because mainstream investors take impact as seriously as they do financial return, the most money flows to those investments that have the highest rates of risk-adjusted return and that show positive change through reliable and repeatable measures and metrics.

Progress in Equity Through Finance

Equity for people of color and women has made significant strides since the mid-2010s. Equity goes well beyond equality, which is the belief that all people are equal. Equity is a concrete phenomenon, created when behavior and systems enable all people to have equal access and opportunity to societal resources, opportunities, success, and rewards. A move toward equity also requires people to become more aware of their own roles and actions in both supporting equity and, at times, perpetuating inequity.

While the United States has become more ethnically diverse, the racial wealth gap remained stark in 2015: the typical African American household held just 6% of the wealth of a typical White household; the typical Latino household had just 8%. Three main factors contributed to these significant discrepancies: (a) differing levels of home ownership and appraisal for the homes; (b) disparate levels of college graduation and differing levels of debt incurred for that education; and (c) inequality in the labor market, as a result of employment discrimination and hidden bias (Shin, 2015). Lower levels of wealth mean greater difficulty in passing that wealth down to the next generation and/or spreading that wealth to a local community.

Finance was key to increasing equity in a number of ways. First, today (2030), there are more investors and decision-makers who are women and people of color. Not only do they have the ability and money to invest (as investors) and raise capital (as entrepreneurs), they are also valued for their ability to see opportunities that others in the "mainstream" do not have. Investors of any ethnicity or gender can choose to support women and people of color: with professional training and mentorship; by making the race/ethnicity/gender of an investment manager one of the criteria for manager selection; by including them in investment teams; and by investing in their enterprises. When women and people of color are empowered to create the options—not simply choose among the options that are presented to them—they create the future. A good example is the pressure that coalitions of families, mostly people of color and their allies, exerted the power of their investment dollars to prison reform issues in the late 2010s by choosing not to invest in private prison companies (Field, 2019).

Second, the public has become more aware of perpetuated inequality and the need for active, intentional rooting out of those inequities. Investors, money managers, and investment advisors are taking their responsibility seriously in creating more equitable systems as a routine part of their job. The most evolved organizations make advancement towards equity an integral part of job performance.

Third, investors are choosing to invest more locally and where they feel connected. They want to benefit the communities where they work and live. Investors know that their own well-being is inextricably bound with the progress of others.

Fourth, the move to more local investments has meant that communities are involved in the design, governance and ownership of selected investments and funds. One 2016 example was Emily Stone's Maya Mountain Cacao, based in Belize. This entrepreneur knocked on doors of 200 farmers to understand their needs. The farmers wanted 2 cents more per kilogram. The entrepreneur introduced a structural change: she required that 51% of revenue goes back into the community. In this way, she created more value for the community that she was taking out. She believed in equality and equity.

Continuing to Work Towards Equity

Despite progress towards equity, in 2030 we are still not at mass scale. To get there, more asset owners must invest and make clear they want more options from their financial providers, who will develop new investment products to meet this demand. This strategy was successful for climate change and can also be achieved for equity. Financial metrics must be improved, as they continue to be imperfect in their ability to capture the financial value of the things we value: a healthy environment, clean water, and social justice (Lake, 2017), to name a few. Economic inequality between the rich and everyone else may not be reflected in traditional investment analysis, but it will have a large impact on long-term investments (Thomas, 2017). While the big accounting firms continue to simplify metrics and evaluation, the systems are being refined, and independent third party verification is almost here. Financial leaders are increasingly looking to other sectors, such as evaluation, to help define, create, and implement measurement approaches.

Finally, an increase in equity will occur when social sector professionals and advocates expand their toolbox to harness the power of finance and investments to meet their missions and goals. To do so, they may need to overcome the tendency to believe that they are the "true believers" and the only ones who can hold the purity of social change. As metrics become clearer and partnerships and collaborations grow, the quintessential nonprofit social change organizations can have business as a partner in the solution. Examples include public–private partnerships (PPPs) from the 1970s and 1980s, when policy-makers recognized a need for additional funds to finance public infrastructure, and reached out for private capital. In the 2010s, PPPs had also begun to be used in innovative performance-based contracts to achieve social outcomes (Gover, 2017), such as for social impact bonds.

CONCLUSION

This chapter has demonstrated the way that investments can be an effective tool for social change. By 2030, several positive changes have occurred:

- Impact investing has reached a "tipping point" among investors and is now considered mainstream. In fact, it's just now called "investing."
- Investments have aligned with the SDGs in a meaningful way to measure outcomes.
- Instead of thinking about isolated incidents, people think about systems change—how everything is linked to everything else.
- While many still believe that businesses should maximize shareholder value, many also believe that businesses can and do have a

duty to their other stakeholders (their employees, the communities in which they work, the environment, their vendors, their clients). Businesses are, in fact, more profitable when they are more thoroughly integrated in the community.

- Investors tend to think more about the long-term versus the short-term. For example, as evaluators know, large intractable social issues such as wealth inequality must be measured over decades, even when financial measures are done on a daily or at best, 7–10 year basis.
- Investment in female entrepreneurs and/or entrepreneurs of color create the leadership of tomorrow, enable intergenerational wealth and equity, and build on the values of a nation founded on equality and opportunity.
- It is very common for investors to balance their own self-interest in their family's financial portfolio with their shared interest in a community, nation, or world.
- Money has tremendous power that we are harnessing for the benefit of society and the environment. Making change and doing well financially are no longer considered mutually exclusive, either to investors or to social justice advocates. In the 2010s, we learned to embrace our purchasing power as consumers, supporting businesses that aligned with our values. Now in 2030, people and organizations truly recognize their power as investors for social change. Investors work in effective partnerships with the social and government sectors to accurately develop solutions to global challenges. Investors can and do make the world a better place by lifting people out of poverty, stopping infrastructure projects that trample on the rights of Indigenous Americans, pushing towards a low-carbon economy, and strengthening our local communities. In doing so, the identity of an investor is fortified: he or she is no longer an individual but part of something greater than him- or herself. Money becomes a tool of self-identity and self-expression. While we individually can use our money to support our values and make profits, lasting impact comes from partnering with values-aligned people and organizations to "be the change we want to see in the world."

NOTES

1. Each "Sector Visioning" chapter begins with an abstract prepared by the book editors and attributed to Zindzi in keeping with the storyline of the book. Zindzi is introduced in Chapter 2.
2. Gen Y or Millennials are people born between 1982–2004. See Bump, 2014.
3. For more information about Figure 9.1, see the PDF of the US|SIF Foundation's 2018 trends report highlights in the foundation's *Report on US Sustain-*

able, Responsible, and Impact Investing Trends. Retrieved from https://www.ussif
.org/files/2018%20_Trends_OnePager_Overview(2).pdf

REFERENCES

Barry, M. D. (2013, August 9). History of socially responsible investing in the
U.S. *Thomson Reuters.* Retrieved from http://sustainability.thomsonreuters.
com/2013/08/09/history-of-socially-responsible-investing-in-the-u-s/.c

Bump, P. (2014, March 25). Here is when each generation begins and ends, according to facts. *The Atlantic.* Retrieved from https://www.theatlantic
.com/national/archive/2014/03/here-is-when-each-generation-begins
-and-ends-according-to-facts/359589/

Business Roundtable. (2019, August 19). Retrieved from https://www.businessround
table.org/business-roundtable-redefines-the-purpose-of-a-corporation-to
-promote-an-economy-that-serves-all-americans

Field, A. (2019, January 7). 30+ A-list celebs and athletes will divest from private
prison investments. *Forbes.* Retrieved from https://www.forbes.com/sites/
annefield/2019/01/07/30-a-list-celebs-and-athletes-will-divest-from-private
-prison-investments/#422c4ce64ebf

Foundation Center. (n.d.). Aggregate fiscal data of foundations in the U.S., 2015.
Retrieved from http://data.foundationcenter.org/

Gorte, J., & Voorhees, M. (2017, March 6). *Five investment trends behind growth in
sustainable and impact investing.* Retrieved from http://www.investmentnews.
com/article/20170306/BLOG09/170309981/5-investment-trends-behind
-growth-in-sustainable-and-impact-investing

Gover, J. A. (2017, July 19). *What is a public–private partnership?* Retrieved from https://
medium.com/@beeckcenter/what-is-a-public-private-partnership-c6c935
69a471

Harjani, A. (2015, January 13). Coming soon: The biggest wealth transfer in history. *CNBC.com.* Retrieved from http://www.cnbc.com/2015/01/13/coming
-soon-the-biggest-wealth-transfer-in-history.html

Jensen, M. C. (2000, July 24). Value maximization and stakeholder theory. Retrieved from
http://hbswk.hbs.edu/item/value-maximization-and-stakeholder-theory

Johnson, I. (2017, March 15). World's biggest fund manager issues "Darth Vad-
er-style" threat to oust bosses who ignore climate change. *The Independent.*
Retrieved from http://www.independent.co.uk/news/business/news/cli-
mate-change-blackrock-manager-threatens-directors-ignore-global-warming
-a7631266.html

Kaissar, N. (2018, April 17). Investing in virtue is hard when so few companies
measure up. *Bloomberg Opinion.* Retrieved from https://www.bloomberg
.com/opinion/articles/2018-04-17/investing-in-virtue-is-hard-when-so-few
-companies-measure-up

Lake, R. (2017, February 14). *Rob Lake: Why we need authentic—and moral—investors.* Retrieved from https://www.responsible-investor.com/home/article/rob_lake
_why_we_need_authentic/

Malvey, J. (2016, June). The history and future of global capital markets. Retrieved from http://www.centerforfinancialstability.org/research/Global_Capital_Market_History.pdf

McGregor, J. (2017, August 2). Why it's smart to invest in women-led companies. *The Washington Post*. Retrieved from https://www.washingtonpost.com/news/on-leadership/wp/2017/08/02/why-its-smart-to-invest-in-women-led-companies/

Principles for Responsible Investment. (2019). *How did the PRI start?* Retrieved from https://www.unpri.org/about

Shin, L. (2015, March 26). The racial wealth gap: Why a typical White household has 16 times the wealth of a Black one. *Forbes*. Retrieved from https://www.forbes.com/sites/laurashin/2015/03/26/the-racial-wealth-gap-why-a-typical-white-household-has-16-times-the-wealth-of-a-black-one/#94b4e571f45e

Thomas, K. (2017, February 28). It's not just about risk. *Shareholder Association for Research and Education (SHARE)*. Retrieved from http://share.ca/its-not-just-about-risk

United Nations. (2015, September 25). *About the sustainable development goals*. Retrieved from http://www.un.org/sustainabledevelopment/sustainable-development-goals/

US|SIF Foundation. (2018). 2018 Report on U.S. sustainable, responsible and impact investing trends: 2018 trends report highlights. Retrieved from https://www.ussif.org/files/2018%20_Trends_OnePager_Overview(2).pdf

Welch, S. (2019, April 3). Kresge pledges to place one quarter of assets with women, minority firms by 2025. *Crain's Detroit Business*. Retrieved from https://www.crainsdetroit.com/nonprofit/kresge-pledges-place-one-quarter-assets-women-minority-firms-2025

Williamson, C. (2019, January 16). *BlackRock's AUM down for the quarter, year*. Retrieved from https://www.pionline.com/article/20190116/ONLINE/190119897/blackrocks-aum-down-for-the-quarter-year

Yeap, N. (2016, June 14). *Millennials want their investing to make a difference*. Retrieved from https://www.onwallstreet.com/news/millennials-want-their-investing-to-make-a-difference

CHAPTER 10

TRANSPORTATION

Designing for Values-Based Mobility

Thomas Abdallah and Antoinette Quagliata

ZINDZI'S ABSTRACT[1]

Transportation systems are transforming from modal specific to fully integrated mobility systems. Where rail, air, bus, highways, and other travel modes once operated as isolated, independent parts, they are now designed as interdependent entities that co-evolve and adapt with each other and the values of the communities they serve. In the 1960s, grassroots movements spurred major federal regulatory actions that began to restore the well-being of individuals and populations harmed by transportation design choices over the last century that accommodated population growth and rapid economic expansion but damaged environmental and human health and delivered inequitable access to public transit. Since then, innovative mobility management agencies continue to facilitate transformation through generative design that builds upon past actions and learning, creative public private partnerships, and technologies that facilitate adaptation to user needs and ensure cohesive operations at scale. The fundamental inquiry underpinning design, planning, and operations at these institutions has been repositioned from "How do we minimize negative impacts to human health and the environment?" to

Visionary Evaluation for a Sustainable, Equitable Future, pages 175–185
Copyright © 2020 by Information Age Publishing
175

"Given the values of our users, how do we maximize the beneficial impacts to their well-being?" In the context of this paradigm shift, mobility, land use, and other agencies collaborate to catalyze the revival of communities that provide equal transportation access to everyone, enable more healthful mobility choices, encourage deeper social relationships, ensure the benefits of microtransit and autonomous vehicle use are realized, and improve overall social and environmental health outcomes.

The years between 2015 and 2030 saw many advances in human mobility as the critical role of a fully integrated mobility system in the function, character, and vitality of a municipality became well understood. Though materials, money, existing infrastructure, and time have been the traditional major barriers to the evolution of urban and transportation infrastructure, innovative design, collaborative cultures, and technology advances have created and continue to create new ways of navigating and dismantling those traditional barriers.

The incorporation of rapid technological advances within public transportation infrastructure and vehicles has helped to better account for interdependencies within transit systems and their companion service utilities for more sustainable and equitable mobility outcomes. Infrastructure management methods that enable holistic three-dimensional assessment of the planning and construction of municipal systems are well established in many urban areas. Some of the most progressive cities and towns are using new infrastructure modeling techniques to design urban systems that mimic natural ecological landscape flows with the intention to establish more generative relationships with the social and natural resources and maximize human interactions, the lifeblood of the city.

The creation of mobility management systems became shining examples of these transformations. Environmental and Sustainability Management Systems provided the framework for the ongoing environmental and social assessments of the transportation industry and enabled the transformation. While the focus shifted from individual modes of transportation to the singular all-inclusive concept of mobility, the conversation also shifted from minimizing the negative environmental impacts associated with these transportation operations to maximizing their environmental and social benefits. The commitments that many mobility management agencies have made over the last decade and a half to prioritize the values of their customers and amplify their connected and collective community voice has catalyzed the revival of many cities around the world. Cities and towns once again belong to people, to pedestrians, and to neighborhoods. Instead of cars and vehicles, community now dominates.

2030

Public transportation (transit) and other transportation modes no longer function in isolation as independent departments where the privately-owned automobile once dominated. Mobility management agencies, truly multimodal, are responsible for the entire transportation circulation of a municipality (a city, town, etc.), community, or population. Transit, redefined as "mobility," includes trains, buses, bikeshare, scooters, pedestrian access/facilities, autonomous vehicles, carpooling, vanpooling, ride hailing, and the ever expanding ride-sharing technologies. It is now fully interconnected with highways, airways, streets, and parking systems. This new comprehensive approach to mobility, has allowed more and more communities to become seamless fluid systems enabling people, their values and well being, to be prioritized over vehicles and vehicle-centric development.

Mobility management agencies are value driven by the community and people they service, coupled with the singular charge of allowing all people to move efficiently and equitably while minimizing negative impacts to human health and the environment. This current system is successful and achievable through the use of innovative methods, thoughts, processes, and technologies, and its ability to adapt to changing demographics and values. An ever-present search for opportunities to innovate, especially within existing infrastructure, drives creativity and design. Mixed-use developments and multi-use buildings and spaces along with collaborative economies maximize efficiencies.

There is no such thing as "a" single isolated train or bus line or even stand-alone transit. All aspects of mobility—walking, biking, transit, cars, shared rides, and others—are understood as interrelated and appreciated as critical components of a city's massive, high dimensional circulatory system. The mobility needs of the population are continually assessed and the mobility system adjusted, and its components chosen, based on the most efficient and effective way to meet these needs. Employers, schools, and large retailers are all involved in feeding this assessment system. Explicit attention to individual and social values has honed the efficiency and effectiveness goals set by transportation initiatives that now emphasize access equity, rider health, environmental sustainability, community development and health, and others on par with more traditional time and safety-oriented measures.

People-oriented development dominates most communities, and streets are no longer designed solely for automobiles. The streets have been returned to the people as now less than 50% of households own a car and the majority of commuting is by transit, bicycle, or shared used services. Personal trips, shopping, errands, and the like are primarily accomplished on foot, using shared use services, or by microtransit (small-scale, on demand transit), thanks to well planned, mixed-use neighborhood hubs. Traditional

American suburbs have been transformed, with its density redistributed and concentrated in town centers. As such, mobility, its impact and influence on land use, is now a universal emphasis of and wholly incorporated into urban planning and design. This shift in mindset has led to cities and towns designed and developed that optimize mobility and housing options, while minimizing land use and environmental impacts. For example, resource consumption is minimized by redeveloping previously abandoned and vacant lands, known as brownfields, especially those no longer needed with the sharp decline in personal vehicle ownership such as gas stations and auto body shops. And the redevelopment of parking lots and garages has provided instant relief to housing demands. Now, social and economic equity and resource efficiency is the norm in planning and community development. Worldwide, Americans with Disabilities Act (ADA) alternatives and accessibility have been integrated into building and zoning codes, and mainstreamed into engineering and architecture projects.

Autonomous cars have provided an alternative for those still desiring a form of private transportation and millions were in use by the early 2020s. However, numbers have declined as communities and development are no longer centered around automobile movement. Instead, the largest share of autonomous vehicles is found in car sharing services and transit fleets. Municipalities, in an attempt to direct the growth and incorporation of autonomous vehicles, embraced the technology early on, making it just one more component of the larger mobility system.

The interrelationship between centers of population and transportation is ancient, people want to live where mobility options exist. The successful implementation and management of mobility systems have been accompanied by both residential and commercial development. The interconnectedness between mobility management and stimulating economic development is a key component of community rejuvenation and well-being, measured in part by increases in social connectivity and a sense of identity. Mobility hubs and nodes create a space for millions of people to access all forms of information exchange (advertising, news, and public service announcements) and relationship development. Hubs provide stimuli for communities to establish and develop, starting first with the essential elements—infrastructure, housing, public spaces, groceries, and so on—and then maturing with additional retail, restaurants, entertainment, and education. The feeling of belonging to a community and its inherent support and stability have markedly reduced the typical isolation of city dwelling, its associated stress, and ultimately illnesses like heart disease.

Land use development centered around transit and mobility options has resulted in increased physical activity as people can easily and safely walk and bike to their destinations. The prevalence and ease of use of modes other than single occupancy vehicles encourage people to walk to catch buses and trains and intermodal connections. Children are more active as bike shares, walking clubs, free transit passes, and pedestrian amenities have become universal and imbedded in public school frameworks. People live healthier lives. We are witnessing transformations in mobility contributing to a reversal of U.S. health-related trends that began in the 1960s— healthcare spending is now decreasing and people are spending a larger portion of their budgets on higher quality foods.

Reductions in emissions from single occupancy fossil fuel powered vehicles coupled with transit's early commitments to more accessible low/no emissions have reduced pollution, further reducing healthcare costs. Today transportation-related atmospheric pollutants are significantly reduced from 2015 levels. The transition of streets and roads from vehicles to pedestrians and bicycles reduced road traffic noise levels, and, in many cities and towns, these changes resulted in massive increases in healthy life years. Incidents of heart disease, hypertension, and asthma-related emergency room visits have all dropped drastically. A healthy population, with less spent on health care, has resulted in more productive and economically prosperous cities and communities. The few municipalities that have been slow to let go of automobile dominance now see clearly their diminished prosperity and are scrambling to catch up.

The efficient use of water, energy, air, land, and materials resources in the operations of the mobility systems is made possible by the universal application of Environmental and Sustainability Management Systems (ESMS). ESMS provides a framework for wholly incorporating resource efficiency and sustainability into the organizational culture and being of a mobility system, encompassing every single action and decision. One of the key environmental aspects mobility management agencies have identified through their ESMS is emissions reductions. Every part of the agency, from administration, to operations, to construction, is held to the emissions reduction goals and targets established through the ESMS.

While the new wholly integrated mobility systems embraced energy efficiency and the movement toward sustainable energy, various parts of the auto sector still rely on fossil fuels. In the past decades, strong resistance to all-electric vehicles was mounted by a powerful minority in the fossil fuel and car industries. Yet, despite such resistance to change, communities were flooded by demand for electric vehicles.

Advances in the energy sector and the ability to convert systems to complementary energy development have been crucial to improvement in the transportation sector. Components of the transportation sector simultaneously consume and generate energy through the ubiquitous use of solar (panels, siding, paints, and more), piezoelectric technologies, and wind. Very few buses still operate on diesel; most buses are powered by electricity from a battery storage unit or by onsite super charged capacitors that shrink operational carbon footprint and reduce pollutant release. These buses run on a blend of energy generated from a range of sources, including on-board solar and regenerative braking as well as solar, wind, and hydroelectric energy supplied to vehicles via charging stations. Current transportation systems can generate up to 50% of the energy they consume.

In order to fund these new technological advances and systems, mobility management agencies had to restructure and redistribute costs. Through the innovative development of a universal budget and payment system, the financial burden of ridership was shifted from the passengers to the polluters by placing a higher tax on gasoline and diesel dependent vehicles specifically to fund transit operations. In 2030, gasoline and diesel fuel continue to be heavily taxed to pay the cost of the electric bus vehicles, and to finance the investment in renewable energy. This policy reform allows those who utilize above-ground mobility, such as light-rail, bus rapid transit, and bike share in lieu of a car, to ride for free. Car usage, specifically personally owned or rented vehicles that travel on public streets and highways, is considered private transportation. Private, fossil fuel burning vehicles must pay tolls, while electric vehicle owners are exempt.

The redistribution of costs and expenditures from a private transportation infrastructure to a public system has allowed for more equitable services and access for all populations. In line with the tenets of environmental justice and equity, all mobility projects now routinely undergo a thorough evaluative inquiry process as to their impact and benefit on communities and cultures. Further, significant change was often initiated from unexpected places. The #BlackLivesMatter movement brought on a groundswell of community meetings in the Midwest and elsewhere that called explicit attention to a wide range of inequities. Transportation became one of the focal points of these conversations. Communities told public officials that pregnant women, new moms and the elderly, particularly those with low income, had no access to public transportation that connected them to necessary health care professionals and facilities. Subsequent research bore this out and showed higher than average childhood mortality rates for these populations. Politicians and municipal officials came to see the massive social benefits to be gained from universal mobility services. They developed change-making policies and sought grant funding from federal agencies to support the required infrastructure transformations.

Building an inclusive mobility system dominates the political agendas of most U.S. cities and towns and provides an environment where differences in profession, age, gender, and income are null. The doctor, lawyer, engineer, laborer, store clerk, and more are all possible commuters, and during commute time, all equals. Though conflict and security issues are ever present, and even on the rise in some cities who have not embraced the mobility management approach, increasing access and use of social and environmental data related to transportation and commuters have improved many municipalities' ability to understand and incorporate into operations factors (e.g., lighting, visibility, at risk populations, equitable scheduling, and station siting) that powerfully influence the probability of safety and security events. The ESMS systems are expanded to include social impact and outcomes of neighborhood well-being goals, incorporating social data into operations and decision-making. As law enforcement, commuters, and transit operators and managers all have more useful information, most communities are seeing steady and significant decreases in incidents of injury as well as gender, religion, and race related crime.

The increased stability of cities, towns, and communities, has attracted renewed interest and investment from the private sector, resulting in innovative and visionary public–private partnerships. These partnerships are generating a new level of community excitement and involvement focused on multi-scale, connected, adaptation-based planning approaches that often result in ways to improve, retrofit, and renovate existing infrastructure systems rather than scrapping the old and starting over from scratch. Infrastructure costs are no longer born by governments and the environment, instead public–private partnerships encourage generative design and technologies that, in directly honoring the values of local communities they aim to serve, create economic, social, and environmental value.

The advent of an all-encompassing mobility system has led to 2030 cities and towns planned and operated around the values and needs of the people, allowing them to achieve their goals and live flexible and sustainable lives in a more healthy, community centric environment.

TRANSFORMATION FROM THE PAST

The industrial revolution brought prosperity and rapid growth among human populations. The world population grew from .8 billion in 1800 to 7.4 billion in 2015! But the rapid productivity and infrastructure growth happened at the expense of the environment, the poor, and the working class. With prosperity unevenly distributed, wealth disparity slowly grew. In the decades after the industrial revolution, human populations swelled in cities and people swarmed to the new suburbs. Mechanization made cars affordable to the average person and soon cars were everywhere. Cities and towns restructured around the use of cars and automobile-centric suburbs rapidly consumed vast swaths of open space and countryside. Smog, poor water quality, and a lack of exposure to nature increasingly became the norm. As time passed, conditions only worsened.

A tipping point in public perception and political will was reached when a few unimaginable environmental disasters occurred; for example, Ohio's

Cuyahoga River caught fire in 1969 and the Great smog of 1952 killed an estimated 8000 to 12,000 people in London. Rachel Carson's publication of *Silent Spring* in 1962 opened the eyes of the American public, and the environmental movement was born. The American government responded with the creation of historic environmental policies: the National Environmental Policy Act (NEPA), the Clean Air Act, and the Clean Water Act. NEPA, the federal environmental law, was established to secure a balance between rapid development and environmental protection, a balance that allowed humans and nature to coexist. NEPA mandated that the public be informed of the potential impacts of development plans and have an opportunity to challenge the findings of a governmental agency or big developer. Public transportation and highway development spurred the implementation of NEPA, as large transit projects were some of the first major capital investments subject to environmental impact statements. This paved the way for rapid development, without compromising future generations.

Expanding the scope of project development consultation to include human voices and environmental thoughtfulness was an early accomplishment within the realm of sustainability. Similarly, the Clean Air Act (1970) and Clean Water Act (1972) were enacted to set standards for safety and quality for both mediums, and had remarkable impacts on not only environmental health, but human health conditions as well. Aggregate emissions of air pollutants dropped approximately 73% from 1970 to 2016.[2] Particularly as it related to transit, the Clean Air Act helped to reduce the amount of pollution emitted by transit vehicles, encourage innovation in complying with these new standards, and even helped to boost ridership as it by nature offered an alternative to those who were now forced to retrofit their personal vehicles to be compliant.

While the environmental movement brought significant changes to the behaviors of the modern world, humans were still feeling the ever-growing effects of industrialization. Water pollution continued to close beaches and compromise the drinking water of many municipalities; people were told to stay indoors because of the elevated levels of air pollution; hospital admittance skyrocketed as vulnerable populations, such as the elderly, urban poor, and young children, experienced extreme health complications from unsafe exposure and poor air quality. Western Europe, in 2010, was losing one million healthy life years to noise pollution every year.[3] The poor health, the poor economic state of cities and towns, and poor transportation and housing options all led people to question the current state of their communities and how they were planned and run. The car-centric communities and dispersed transportation systems bred fragmented and heavily-paved suburban developments with no sense of community and little connection to the natural world. Driving as the sole option of transport was still dominant, and existing transit systems were still undervalued and often in disrepair. People, previously accustomed to car-centric ways of life, began demanding more human-centric, equitable communities. The concepts of transit-oriented development and smart growth gained momentum and planners began to ask, "How do people want and need to get around?" And decision-makers began to consider whether the right project was being designed in the right place for the right reasons.

The direct correlation between poor environmental and land management and reduced quality of life had become indisputable. Extreme weather events and natural disasters became more prevalent. The impact of climate change, and transportation's contribution to it, could no longer be denied. And while sustainability and climate change thinking faced major obstacles from some elected officials in the highest places in government, most professional engineers, architects, scientists, and many other professionals stayed on point, continued to follow the scientific evidence, and refused to stop doing the right thing when it came to sustainability.

This sustainability movement, incorporating environmental, social, and economic health, opened the door for new ideas and the mainstreaming of new values and innovation. It not only emphasized the problems we face in the future from increased pollution and climate change, but pointed to possible solutions. Academia, grass-roots organizations, the public, politicians, thought-leaders, innovators, and professionals across all sectors and perspectives came together to test and develop solutions. The unified efforts led to rapid research and development into new energy sources, and more efficient energy consumption. For example, previous train systems mostly utilized electricity generated from the combustion of fossil fuels such as coal and natural gas in electrical power plants. But since 2015, these fossil fuel power plants either dramatically reduced emissions or were replaced by renewable energy, such as solar, wind or hydroelectric producing power plants, supported by robust energy storage systems, to provide clean energy when necessary.

New technologies were now possible and poised for use. The ubiquity of the Internet provided access to more information about the goals and needs of people using the transportation systems. This coupled with ever improving analysis of infrastructure and travel patterns in the context of all transportation options, brought radical improvements to cities and towns, not only in commute scheduling and travel time, but also in commuter well-being and other key user values increasingly important to measuring the effectiveness of transit systems. The introduction of autonomous vehicles, ride-hailing, bike-sharing, car-sharing, bus rapid transit, and more introduced completely new concepts to transportation and paved the way for a broader view of integrated mobility. People recognized the inefficiency of having private vehicles parked and unused for 95% of the time, costing private owners $9,000 per year.[4] Car ownership dropped and commuting trends began to change as the steady rate of 76% of commuters who drive alone finally began to drop in 2018.[5] The idea of fully integrated mobility systems began to take hold and influence land development decisions. The system was envisioned to be adaptive, to constantly reassess priorities and methods.

Environmental management systems (EMS), begun in the 1990s, allowed for the identification of the true priorities of populations and their mobility needs and the creation of a system that could constantly adapt to changing needs and priorities. EMS is a structured and specially organized framework based around the "plan, do, check, act" cycle, under which an entity can manage environmental impacts by identifying priorities, setting goals and objectives, measuring achievement, and assessing effectiveness. An EMS can be visualized as an internal guideline which ensures that proper consideration is given to environmental issues, the health of the planet and those who inhabit it, throughout all levels of an organization.

This system served as a pivotal component for the promotion of sustainability in public transportation, especially leading up to the paradigm shift in environmental thinking. This system was so successful in this context that it was used as the template for evaluation and improvement across multiple sectors. EMS had become ESMS—environmental and sustainability management systems—and its scope continued to grow.

The rise of artificial intelligence (AI) was one of the last pieces of the puzzle that made it possible to apply the ESMS framework to a large complex system. It provided the analytical and synthetical power ultimately needed to develop and implement a fully integrated mobility system at scale.

CONCLUSION

Many lessons have been learned between 2015 and 2030 that have been instrumental in the evolution of independent public transportation systems to truly multimodal human mobility systems. Despite traditional emphasis on cars, trains, and buses, cycling and walking have become just as important, re-emphasizing the human element. Corresponding with this refocus on people, a boom in technological capabilities, and the rise of renewable energy, transit has managed to integrate the most successful aspects of each of these facets to generate a compellingly efficient, transparent, sustainable, and equitable mobility management system. The link between urban development and transportation has been further evidenced over the last few years as the growth of mobility centers offered an opportunity to elevate a previously deflated quality of life.

As was seen in recent history, the combined effects of air pollution and water pollution greatly reduced people's ability to interact with their environments healthily. As transit and transit-oriented development took steps to remediate the systemic vulnerabilities exacerbating these realities, so too came improved environmental and human health, with the added benefit of creating spaces for communities to grow and flourish. Increased opportunity for community revival led to increased economic stimulus, and the education and healthcare services that accompany a growing neighborhood.

In a unique position to service communities both at the systemic level and through subtle initiatives to help improve people's lives passively, the advent of mobility management systems has helped to improve the world at both the micro and macro levels. It is through the use of AI and other advanced computing that these mobility management systems can be implemented at the scale and level of complexity necessary to be effective.

NOTES

1. Each "Sector Visioning" chapter begins with an abstract prepared by the book editors and attributed to Zindzi in keeping with the storyline of the book. Zindzi is introduced in Chapter 2.
2. See U.S. Environmental Protection Agency: https://www.epa.gov/news releases/air-pollution-trends-show-cleaner-air-growing-economy
3. See World Health Organization, Regional office for Europe: http://www .euro.who.int/en/publications/abstracts/burden-of-disease-from-environmental -noise.-quantification-of-healthy-life-years-lost-in-europe
4. See Zimmer, 2016, Medium.com: https://medium.com/@johnzimmer/the -third-transportation-revolution-27860f05fa91
5. See U.S. Department of Transportation, Bureau of Transportation Statistics, "Commuting to Work." https://www.bts.dot.gov/content/commuting-work

CHAPTER 11

EDUCATION

Emancipating Learning

Elizabeth B. Kozleski

ZINDZI'S ABSTRACT[1]

In about the last two decades, education has shifted from being primarily in classrooms to being primarily online. It remains connected to places and spaces that we inhabit but is rarely located inside a purpose-built school. Instead, education happens through connections with relevant contexts such as rivers, corn fields, or community parks. Learners may congregate in huge office buildings, street corners, playgrounds, in the depths of an ocean, or on the moon.

Education's purpose has shifted. Heavily supported by technology, teachers also have shifted their role from deliverers of information to students to mentors and guides of students as they investigate issues across disciplines to produce new knowledge that applies to their situations. These changes have resulted in the Visionary Evaluative Principles being embedded throughout the work of teachers and students and the education sector itself. You'll recognize teachers and students as Visionary Evaluatives whose values, personal lives, personal stories, and context are central to education and learning today.

Visionary Evaluation for a Sustainable, Equitable Future, pages 187–203
Copyright © 2020 by Information Age Publishing

I am advancing the proposition that educators, wherever they teach, must shift their gaze from accumulation to production of knowledge. Artificial intelligence (AI) in our daily lives demands a new kind of knowledge curation and development. We are at a point in time in which the transformational effects of the information age have revolutionized our educational systems in ways that require active shifts in the mediation of teaching and learning. Perhaps no aspect of the education enterprise is more fully impacted than that of the teacher workforce. Students of 2030 have been born into this new age. Teachers of this era were born around 2012, not quite digital natives of the AI era. What does it mean to teach and support learning of others in 2030? What knowledges and skills do teachers need and how do they know that their work has produced the learners who can produce the knowledge that supports a sustainable equitable way of living?

While parents have always educated their children, particularly their young children, most education in the 19th and 20th century was officially relegated to schools (Tyack, 1974). Teachers were integral to this context. Education was accomplished by professionals from nine in the morning until three in the afternoon inside institutional learning sites. Teachers were the workers. Some countries educated their children five days a week. Others added a sixth half day. But, in affluent nations, education was something that children did away from the lives of their families and home. Now, in 2030, everything about that narrative has changed. The historical legacies that anchored our notions of learning, and, to a great extent, constrained innovation and rapid response to the changing contexts of the 21st century, are being challenged. The legacies of marginalization and segregation continue to seep into an educational system that cannot seem to jettison its role in perpetuating social, civic, and political inequity. What we demand from our education system is being assessed and improved from this vantage point. While we do so, we also acknowledge the profound opportunities and challenges of learning in a digital age.

The Challenge of Artificial Intelligence: What is the New Role of Teachers?

Given the huge resources of the age of technology, the great 2030 pivot in education is developing educators who are able to work across the life span. Educators must coach students of all ages to access the rich knowledge available and harness it to solve the critical equity problems in a world of shrinking resources, global instability, and ecological mayhem. The shift from knowledge accumulation to knowledge production is made possible through the hybrid relationships that humans are forging with AI. In doing so, educators can focus on the aims of education and its capacity to redress the inequities and injustices that come from the unequal distribution of material resources and concomitant inequality in access to the basic building blocks of modern society: health care, access to information, sustainable forms of industry, ecologically conscious stewardship of the planet's resources, and a focus on peaceful coexistence, human dignity, and social justice. Accordingly, educators and their students must develop a research-and-inquiry mindset that links networks of people together to solve the great challenges of the next 100 years.

BOX 11.1
Learning in a Digital Age

The tension between teaching and learning changed dramatically about 2018. Artificial intelligence (AI) came into its own. Many of the basic functions of teachers were done by smart bots that were programmed as tutorials, feedback mechanisms, and knowledge checkers. What made AI such a game changer was that computers were programmed to learn and expand their repertoires based on the feedback they received from the environment, including the people that used them. AI allowed computer companies to design cars that were driverless and home management systems that could adjust resource use (e.g., interior climate, water, electricity, gas) of homes based on outside temperatures, the time of day, year, and the calendar patterns of the people who lived in these homes. AI learned when human input changed their programs and incorporated those inputs into their algorithms for performance. It was not surprising that the world of education was quick to adopt these capabilities.

AI was and is adept at the technical aspects of teaching. It can translate text into multiple languages. It can perform conversational analysis. It can detect grammatical and mechanical errors in writing. It can track error patterns and create new assessment items that focus on drilling knowledge in weak areas. AI can plan, predict, and assess what students are doing in multiple ways and shift the difficulty level of tasks so that students are challenged but maintain their interest in skill development. AI is much better at providing immediate feedback than most teachers assigned to groups of 15 or more students, varying that feedback and using reinforcement schedules that match the learning level of students—initial, emerging, and mastery levels. AI can also spot what students focus on and give them more of that content—extending and expanding their interests.

But AI remains limited in its ability to determine what to learn for what outcomes. It needs human guidance to govern where to place its prodigious efforts, particularly as it is becoming critical to examine who benefits from what opportunities and what values are driving decisions about what to linger on and how to establish differences between persistence in the face of feedback and addiction engendered by enabling resources. Since AI builds its knowledge on associative learning, it crowdsources ideas. When specific terms repeatedly connect with one another, AI iterates. This kind of associative learning can create problems by normalizing (finding the average) to what is happening in digital space without having a critical lens to ask the critical questions such as "Who determines what is normal?" and "Different from what?" AI will only be as coherent and thoughtful as the knowledge combining systems it is able to access.

Learning in community, using the semiotics and discourses of communities of practice, is the new role of mediator that educators play. In this way, educators are embedded in everyday life with specific tools to engage, support, and expand learning in pursuit of common community goals. And, they can—in fact must—continue to practice the discipline that they also teach. In 2030, the roles teachers fulfill are more like coaches and research mentors. They help their students select educational experiences that prepare them to become both practitioners and teachers regardless of their career choices—culturally responsive brokers of learning across multiple social and cultural contexts.

Transforming Teacher Work Means Changing How Teachers Are Prepared

In 2030 teachers work in curated spaces like aquariums, museums, arboretums, historic sites, and parks. They assume professional development roles in business or industry. They work with children, young adults, or workers in the process of changing professions. They work locally in community activism, such as green space preservation, food cooperatives, or local energy production. They are not focused on assuming a role in the institution called "school." School is too static an environment. In fact, few teachers prepare specifically for teaching in classrooms because most basic learning is done online, with greater attention spent on what children and adults do in community rather than in school. However, they all share a common focus: learning. Teachers in 2030 recognize that machines are smart; they can do more than supply calculation and sorting. They can anticipate the next steps in learning to read, including what texts to present. They can select the prompts for new learning. Teachers consider the question: What must humans be challenged to do to continue to forge ahead with innovation and creation?

In 2030, children, youth, young adults, and adults spend very little time in classrooms face-to-face with their teachers. Rapid accumulation and adaptation of information to solve emerging dilemmas in authentic settings means a different kind of relationship between learners and their coaches. In 2015,

25% of American children were learning online (Basham, Stahl, Ortiz, Rice, & Smith, 2015). In 2030, only toddlers and young children up through 8 years old attend brick-and-mortar schools. Older elementary, middle, and high school students pursue academics online and work face-to-face in small social networks, or online in work-study enclaves focused on specific interests such as those in food chain sustainability, ecology, drama, coding, and designing. Both social networks and work-study enclaves include adults and seniors. So, in fields that range from nursing to surveying and mapping, from building boats to making movies, there are networks of people young and old working together to learn a craft, develop a product, or solve a problem. Educators help these enclaves or networks learn to get better at doing their work. In doing so, they also help people to learn consciously, develop solutions to problems that emerge, and do so continuously as a part of their everyday reality. This notion about education as a device to ensure that lifelong learning occurs is an important aspect of creating socially just, equitable, and sustainable communities. Children, youth, and adults need to conceptualize themselves as rapidly changing and developing throughout their life spans.

In 2030 our teachers must be able to support learning in the following ways:

1. Clearly define themselves in terms of the cultural perspectives and values they bring to their teaching and what their contributions to others' learning might be ("Making and Mapping Critical Beings").
2. Use online tools to help their learners become aware of the theories that undergird their actions ("Being in Praxis").
3. Understand literacies across a wide array of disciplines and help others acquire those skills ("When the Medium Meets the Message").
4. Work in community with others to test and refine ideas, building new knowledge that exists at the intersection of individual and collective innovation and discovery ("Community as Learning Networks").
5. Assess the capacities of the spaces they design against their goals for its use ("From 'Playful Sandboxes' to Serious Tool").

Each of these dimensions of the work of a 2030 teacher is elaborated below and illustrated with an example of an AI-enhanced demanding project that cohorts of teachers undertake as they move from the transmission of knowledge to the active engagement of inquiry and knowledge building with their students. This transition of the teacher workforce is still an ongoing process in 2030.

Making and Mapping Critical Beings

The first task of teachers is to know and understand themselves as cultural beings who, as educators or cultural agents, mediate the learning of other cultural beings. To do this, educators need to understand their own journeys and interactions with a schooling enterprise that historically has sought to unite knowledge and power in ways that create imbalance between different knowledges under the auspices of a benign and apolitical view of education (Darder, Boltodano, & Torres, 2003). An autoethnographic task such as that given in Box 11.2 illustrates how a teacher harmonizes knowing themselves, critiquing their positionality, and acting as an educator engaged in knowledge building and inquiry in order to transform

---

BOX 11.2
The Making and Mapping of Critical Beings

The process of "unfreezing" the mind's attachment to certain perspectives and ways of responding to change requires more than purely individualized forms of critical thinking or personal navel-gazing. Recognizing and embracing change requires interaction and collaborative mirror-holding, discourse, and dialogue that entail cross-checking so what we cannot see or recognize in ourselves is made manifest through discourse and debate.

Autoethnography is both a product and a process. It is an approach to research and modes of expression that seeks to describe and systematically analyze personal experience in order to understand cultural experience. This approach challenges canonical ways of doing research and representing others. It treats research as a political, socially-just, and socially-conscious act.

Here is an example of an AI enhanced setting where cohorts of teachers share their autoethnographic processes and reflections. The cohort schedules an appointment at their community-based TinkerLab. This state-of-the-art makerspace is run by a collective of interdisciplinary artists who specialize in illusory and multi-dimensional experience. They offer teachers free rein to experiment with a diverse range of old and new human technologies. Teachers find everything from handmade paper to 1980s instant Polaroid cameras to a HoloLens that translates data sets into three-dimensional interfaces to a 3-D reconstructive memory printer.

As teachers engage with excavating their own autobiographical journey, they are supported by mentors who are also representing their own content, processes, and premises that continue to shape their identity and positionality in the world. Teachers in the cohort and the mentors interact and share elements of their own autoethnography as we move through the various phases of our lives. They consider the ways in which they create and interpret meaning and how they have come to know and understand the world. They incorporate elements such as interviews with family members, photographs, digital recordings, social media highlights, poetry excerpts, abstract images that encapsulate some facet of their being, or more traditional, narrative-based journaling and self-reflection. They draw on the TinkerLab tools to flesh out and add dimension to your autobiographical profile.

how we come to know, understand, and act. This is an educator engaged in critical pedagogy. To do this task teachers design small steps along the way that builds in interaction with AI that supports them as they make choices in topics, structure, and design work.

The development of the autoethnography is analogous to the teacher's journey as a learner and change agent—it animates teachers' capacities to think, reflect, and act critically as they work to emancipate their thinking and any constructs of fixed identity that may inhibit or delay their capacity to fully engage in learning with their students. Teachers' experiences of culture are deeply carved by the degree to which they mark themselves as part of the dominant culture or as marginalized by it. The ability to lift personal veils in the act of teaching is a path towards addressing the inequities that surround us. These inequities are built into the institutional and individual biases that are revealed through action. Without close attention to this, teachers run the risk of becoming colonizers of specific kinds of knowledge. Regardless of how much teachers want to focus on a discipline, or construct, or practice, or idea, they simultaneously teach their students about their teachers' identities. Regardless of whether teachers are conscious of their identity as text, students read it and judge the teacher and, by extension, her ideas, perspectives, and technical skills. When teachers ignore themselves in their teaching, they excise the possibility of examining the richest text they have for how learning occurs: themselves. Both of these ideas germinated the notion that teachers need to learn to be critically conscious of their own cultural histories and be able to make that map visible through their teaching approaches, including the choices they make in directing students to specific experiences and resources.

In 2030, educators index power from their own perspectives in terms of their gender, sexuality, race, ableness, ethnicity, language, economic status, and other social markers of status, privilege, and marginalization. Since these attributes *intersect*, they also complicate how people perceive them, and how much access to power an individual may have. To ensure that *all* learners can access learning, consciousness about what is being taught and why is critical.

Because technologies afford us the opportunity to express ourselves in a number of ways, teachers develop proficiency with the tools that they expect their students to use. A key task for teachers is to be bold in the ways that they expose their own ethnographies. They have their own data that they can analyze, synthesize, and express, allowing them to focus on the more difficult tasks of qualitative research, the interpretive act and how it changes the narrative for the narrator and the reader. Access to worlds of knowledge requires inquiry to determine what may be relevant, useful, and valid perspectives and approaches to knowing, methods of knowing, and decisions based on that knowing. The rhetoric in the early decades of the

21st century acknowledged the importance of these skills. However AI, using algorithms based on what people do rather than what they may need to know, shifted the human gaze. It raised the bar for human beings to engage deeply analytic and thoughtful approaches to determining what to use as knowledge building blocks.

Through critical autoethnographies, teachers come to appreciate their own stories and how they may be read by their students. In turn, this knowledge can inform how they will approach and support their students, being mindful of the power differentials that exist in multiple dimensions between teacher and student. Equipped with this knowledge, teachers are able to help their students reach their learning goals. This is the difficult proposition of being in action while reflecting on the meaning and purpose of the action and making those reflections on action available to their students.

Being in Praxis: Doing Theory

Satellites and giant storage grids orbit our planet generating and managing gargantuan streams of data every second. Content moves through us and around us as we become the interface, and invisible holograms of information float like mirages in touch-tone air. Everywhere, even the forest, potentially has a Pokémon hidden in a tree. Making sense of the underlying patterns produced by such phenomena is an eternally iterative and always a time-specific and site-sensitive process. Learning propels reinterpretation of live events, encouraging us to remain in a constant state of becoming with no end to the learning. No final product but rather the formation of highly intelligent beings, with agency to generate and determine the lifelong, life-wide processes of forever-after learning.

Being in reflective action (i.e., praxis) foregrounds the importance of design in planning the learning experiences. Without design, learners can flounder or avoid experimentation because the intention is not clear. The power of design gives learners the chance to enter a learning space through multiple ramps, buoyed by the learners' skills, histories, cultural practices, and aspirations. Learners who are able to explore these aspects of themselves receive feedback on multiple levels that is more robust and specific. Teachers master the principles of learning design in order to support learner development.

Teachers master the process of designing tools for learning through building learning experiences that they test with their learners. They make transparent the intentionality of the learning experience, cataloging learners' experiences, both successes and failures, to improve on their design and their theory of learning design. Success and failure can apply to mastering a skill or producing an accomplished product that meets the learner's ambitions as well as reviewers' aesthetics and performance criteria. Success and failure can also apply to the intangible process of discovery, application, and completion from an emotional point of view. Teachers help learners to mediate their own feelings. Teachers create opportunities to talk about the emotional process of learning, including confronting frustration and failure, boredom, practice fatigue, and unpolished performance. Designing learning experiences requires the use of tools to provide feedback technically, contextually, critically, and emotionally. Learners in 2030 need these skills since the built-in social supports of the classroom are likely to be remote and asynchronous. Thus, teachers need to build highly tuned feedback mechanisms as they learn to teach more masterfully though practice. The relative anonymity of virtual learning spaces, the autonomy of the learner, and need for continuous feedback as learners dig into new knowledge and skills, make this kind of highly tuned feedback in virtual spaces vital to the process of transformation. Thus, the focus on feedback as a key component in what teachers are able to design into their virtual learning spaces is critical to learning and development.

BOX 11.3
Doing Theory

Theory enables a systematic analysis of a natural or social event or phenomenon in order to explain it—or its relationship to something else—in a logical and coherent manner. Theory serves to illuminate the nature of action and reflection in the context of praxis. Theory may be idiographic or nomothetic. An idiographic theory zooms in—like the "gaze"—to magnify the details of a specific situation under focus. This form is tailored to a localized context and may not be valid outside of that particular setting. Conversely, a nomothetic theory examines macro-level phenomena where generalizability is proportional to the significance and applicability of the theory. It enables the validation of broader patterns and sequences and seeks to empirically support theory in measurable and quantifiable ways.

One way that teachers learn to diffuse this bifurcation of theoretical forms is through the use of interactive video. It is a mixed-method medium and so enables both idiographic "micro" and nomothetic "macro" capabilities simultaneously. The interactive video tracks the individual frame-by-frame behaviors and choices of a single user, while also capturing the broad sweep of big data to reveal local, national and, if need be, international patterns and trends across multiple users in various locations.

Interactive video—because of its online, digitally portable, and social-network infrastructure—offers teachers a gateway to designing a way to capture bigger data. It opens teachers' theory of praxis up to applications within the broader cultural and sociopolitical context.

Here is an example of how teachers might examine their own theories of how they engage in reflective action (i.e., praxis). With an interactive and user-driven space in mind, teachers (individually or as a cohort) design an interactive video with a testable theory of praxis fully in mind. Their design fully lays out their topic or story and traces the narrative for their interactive video. The design answers questions such as: How am I envisioning that users will engage with this interactive video? What skills and discoveries am I anticipating because I am telling the story this way? What affordances have I drawn on to allow the user to go places that I didn't intend? What constraints have I created that narrow the users' focus and ratchet down their interactive possibilities?

When the Medium Meets the Message

In the global world of 2030, we have reordered our sciences and their applications. We are learning to harness AI to design complex systems that operate in nanospheres to change the systems that, for instance, comprise the human body. On a whole other scale, we design and manage air traffic from drones to rockets. The sciences, along with technology, engineering, and mathematics, have been integrated and are connecting with the Arts, making the transition from STEM to STEAM. The emergence of interactive media in the final decades of the 20th century produced engaged users as opposed to passive consumers of information. Interactive media challenged our ways of seeing and our habits of thinking about knowledge-making in visual culture. The sheer illusion of reality and the dominance of the (White) male (able-bodied) gaze in narrative cinema were thrown into high relief (Mulvey, 1989). Interactive video, and particularly video gaming, continues to shape how we make sense of the world, particularly in visual cultural and visual communication contexts.

In 2030 as teachers design learning situations, they bring their self-knowledge and their experience of teaching in action to a socially wrought problem. This connects teachers closely to notions of working towards socially just communities by exploring the tools for engagement that bring together the medium and the message. In building a theory of praxis through interactive video, for example, teachers learn to anticipate the triggers and visual or emotional cues necessary to draw users to examine their theories in light of their practices. When teachers think in terms of creating a visual parable that takes a user on a journey through concepts and constructs and experiences of "praxis," forks in the road that promise alternative solutions need to be available. Teachers anticipate sharing control of the learning process with their students. They predict the duration of the user's gaze and engagement and hypothesize the purposes of the student's sustained engagement. These ideas must be represented in the learner interface. Finally, teachers need to be able to disclose and reflect on their design decisions and what they learned from their students about their interactive, knowledge-making process.

In so doing teachers also learn to shift their focus from themselves to content that sits at the intersection of liberal arts and science. They learn to reframe who has knowledge and what forms it might take. Equally destabilizing is the demonstration of how knowledge travels across forms of knowing from the arts to science and back again, enriching how humans make meaning of their lives and the worlds around them. Teachers glimpse the range of shifts and pivots that students can make, depending on the design of the learning outcomes, interactions, tools, and materials. Box 11.4 illustrates this interplay of medium, message, and interdisciplinary understanding.

BOX 11.4
From STEM to STEAM

In Victorian England, in the 18th and early 19th centuries, the arts and sciences were interwoven. For instance, the beautiful wood engravings of Britain's first ornithologist, Thomas Bewick, were both art and science. The groundbreaking photographically illustrated scientific reference book by botanist and master photographer, Anna Atkins, binds art to science.

In literature of the period, Charlotte Brontë draws heavily on Bewick's scientific *History of British Birds*. In her novels (e.g., *Jane Eyre*) she surreptitiously undermines the rise of the hegemonic patriarchy driving the separation between the arts and the sciences, including the emerging separation of male and female access to either.

Since the early 20th century, most universities in the Western world represent knowledge in siloed ways: social sciences like anthropology, psychology, and sociology remain housed with literature, history, and world languages. Engineering, medicine, law, architecture, business, and education are often found in their own colleges.

In 2030 many educators are seeing student-centric learning as a means of bringing back the connection between the arts and sciences. They see a need, particularly in STEM disciplines, to replace "chalk and talk" practices with strategies that facilitate students to "tease out" their own creative processes, using creative play and embracing failure as a source of innovation so the learner is given space and time, to be led by their own curiosity. They propose centering on pedagogies associated with the liberal arts, such as inquiry and studio-based learning spaces and through their research they are demonstrating the value of the interdisciplinary approach.

In this activity teachers practice scaffolding education to ensure that connections to human consciousness and body are intrinsic to all forms of learning. This assignment invites a cohort of teachers to design a collaborative multidisciplinary project for a group of diverse adult learners, where they enhance their knowledge of some STEM-related topic through an arts or literacy-based activity.

Assignment: Visit publicly available photographic archives (e.g., http://digi-talcollections.nypl.org). Take 1 or 2 hours to explore the archives looking for a photographer who captured images for science or design who also is or was a member of a minoritized group (i.e., women, individuals of color, non-English speakers, and immigrants). Combine your collection of their images with historical, literary, and other sociocultural materials to examine the intersections between the photographs and the life experiences and education of the photography. How did the photographs challenge existing dominant views of their subject matter? Did they? What may have led the photographer to take the point of view represented by the photographs? How does or doesn't the imagery reflect science and art? What does this make you think about how arts and science might be interwoven through learning and discovery?

Once you have assembled enough general information to design a project, imagine how you might introduce this material. Describe your project assignment and detail the learning objectives you intend it to produce in the context of bridging the STEM–STEAM chasm. Your project should liberate scientific taxonomies, expand cross-pollination and equitable access to all subjects in a gender fluid world where the students' own emotions not just reason, are paramount to all forms of knowledge-making.

Community as Learning Networks

We live in community regardless of our own psychological inclinations to spend time alone, with others, or in a combination of both. Although the communities that we are surrounded by may embrace or marginalize us, we remain part of the fabric of community. For much of the 20th century, where we lived or worked physically grounded our notions of community. The material consequences of proximity dominated our mental models of community. The terrain that we traversed, the distance between social institutions like schools, churches, and hospitals were part of the catalog of community. Downtown areas where people shopped, went to restaurants, bars, and socialized—or the absence of downtowns—said something about the vibrancy of a community. We had civic responsibilities to our local and regional communities.

We may be members of a single community but, more likely, we attach to multiple communities brought together by work, play, commitments, and interests. Learning to enter and retain membership in multiple communities is part of learning how to meet our social needs and aspirations. Consequently, teachers also need skills of community building, supporting the capacities of communities as they take shape and focus their common interests in pursuit of substantive learning goals and outcomes. In the 21st century, these communities are likely to be connected across the planet in ways that impact access to natural, material, social, cultural, and intellectual capital.

To build community, teachers help their students access their consciousness of the lives they lead and how each person affects the lives of others whom they may never see. This is the profound challenge of building inclusive communities across the globe. Our ambitions to engage globally, yet personally, are grounded in ways of being that few, if any, human beings have experienced. Yet, teachers in 2030 design learning opportunities as if the reality of global, personal engagement has been achieved. Learning together in carefully designed activities is one way that teachers build skills, advance knowledge, and create such experiences. This is done in anticipation that students will be able to take these designed learning experiences and recreate them in their own networked communities.

Teachers need skills to initiate, mediate, and support networks for learning. To develop some skills, teachers interact with individuals whom they have never met. In the activity in Box 11.5, teachers establish relationships, build their activity networks, establish shared learning outcomes, and produce a fundable proposal to continue their inquiry. This advances their professional practice and engages them in continuous learning with a worldwide network of educators and their students building knowledge together as part of their everyday lives. Building knowledge networks mirrors the work of teams that are organized to invent, explore, and solve complex problems. Teachers draw on cultural, psychological, and knowledge-access skills that individuals and teams need to be successful in nearly all walks of life.

BOX 11.5
An Internet You Can Walk (Backwards) Through

Portals is an international exhibit where strangers make eye contact and converse with one another from across the globe in life-size, real-time formats. Portals are spaces where individuals and groups across the world interact with each other simultaneously in physical spaces that strip the material trappings of culture. These portals encourage finding unique ways of exploring community digitally. Constructed from wood and covered with sheets of golden, corrugated metal, these interactive, walk-in "rooms of Internet" are all identical to one another. They are fitted out with 24/7 web access, two electrical outlets, a camera, a voice-activated computer, a life-size full-body length screen, a couple of lights, and a projector. The structures are, in effect, glammed-up shipping containers with ample but intimate space to perform or seat a small audience. They are dark, sound proofed, and climate controlled, with adjustable spot-lit spaces to enhance the cinematic capacity of the interactions.

These "wormholes" offer people from all over the world a shared space to communicate and engage in all forms of human dialogue and face-to-face interactions. Some of the containers are located permanently at specific sites, and others are temporary. They have been used in the past to explore the experience of refugees where United Nations (UN) delegates and policy-makers could interact directly with Syrian refugees at the Zaatari refugee camp in Jordan. They enable all kinds of transnational collaborations involving multidisciplinary projects where individuals—including those displaced by war and natural disaster—can connect and advocate, chat with each other, or simply inform and entertain each other.

In this assignment teachers, working in teams, prepare and gather data to formulate a funding proposal for an international service-learning project with this Portal as a key "instrument." They also make a presentation in which they make the case for the quality of their project plan. (A later assignment involves carrying out the service learning activity.)

Each team is required to adopt a backwards-mapping model (Wiggins & McTighe, 2005) to build its response to the request for a proposal (RFP). Each team narrates and presents a shared audio or video to make its final pitch to explain why they want this technology, what international application they envisage it for, who they will work with locally and internationally within the Portal, and how they plan to use it to build a transformative policy, practice, or process to alleviate or transform the international problems they work to identify. Teams will ultimately work together on whichever application is funded to translate a vision of the service-based learning project into a virtual world "sandbox" space in Second Life.

Learners need expert mediation to support them through the development of an authentic product that they may not have seen or experienced themselves. Teachers mediate their students through the explanation, organization, and production of a task and the selection of tools required for accomplishing the task. As cohorts of teachers work together, they observe, anticipate, question, and provide feedback and scaffolds. They are practicing the very supports that they will be using to help students to move through similar tasks, experiencing the anxiety and concern that can happen when doing something new as well as accessing the support that they need to recognize and address their feelings as they tackle the unfamiliar. This kind of support exists when a well-functioning team is conscious of individual and collective behavior and product development.

Creating a Critical Virtual Reality

Teachers in 2030 regularly experience supporting others as they create an experience that is not predetermined. Teams learn to collaborate because the enormity of the task requires distributed leadership and expertise in order to accomplish the end goal. With a well-designed learning experience, teams develop the ability to assess one another's skills through hearing how they position themselves and considering the degree to which they are able to discuss their own capabilities, commitments, and capacity to find and use available information and tools. The team develops the capacity to use what they know about each other to meet the demands of the task through distribution of work, decisions about accountability, and conscious support for one another as they move into the unknown. As the work proceeds, team members learn to shift and adjust in order to reach the final goal. The team is thus able to assemble technology tools to support progress, including using AI bots to grab information about the workflow and help the team track progress and provide feedback, just-in-time, to one another. The teacher learns to serve as a coach as they move forward in their roles as educational designers of learning.

Virtual worlds, like Second Life, contribute extensively to experiential learning if students are carefully scaffolded. Virtual worlds create generative activity because they afford dynamic experimentation and exploration.

BOX 11.6
From "Playful Little Sandbox" to Serious Tool

Following up on the task given in Box 11.5, teacher teams in this task work through the interactive and interpersonal portal space to gather critical information from and with their international counterparts. With the funding the team received, the team purchased two Portals (they each cost less than $3,000 to install and construct!) for this project. One portal is permanently in situ on a campus in the United States. The second portal is mobile and located at a temporary, international site of the team's choice to address their service-learning objective. The benefits of using a virtual platform, in tandem with the live, face-to-face portal experience, means each international interaction has a point of focus and a shared space where team members literally play with an array of communication tools and override language barriers. The affordances of the tools mean that, regardless of geographic distances, team members can benefit from the immediate responsiveness of interaction and its potential to spark creative team activity, persistence, and effective feedback loops to polish and tune projects. The portal enables the interdisciplinary team to use the room's onsite computer to replicate and simulate the complex systems and situation surrounding the team that they will address through the free and openly accessible virtual Second Life world.

The team produces a product in Second Life that addresses the real-life problem that the team identified, researched, and proposed a solution. The solution is tangible, and can be tried out in response to the identified problem.

Solutions that are parsimonious, elegant, feasible, responsive, inclusive, and equitable will become part of the portal's permanent collection. Authors of projects that become part of the permanent collection are listed as design consultants for future project participants and are able to bill for services.

A final element of the task requires a response to this question: In what ways do virtual world experiences shift and transform the social and political text for team members in their material worlds?

MAKING EMANCIPATORY MEANING OF EDUCATION

Education in 2030 engages two vital notions: (a) education for what and (b) education for whom? Most of the thorny problems of the 21st century—hunger, overpopulation, pollution, global warming, world health, equity, and the unequal distribution of wealth—cannot be solved without combining knowledge and methodologies from multiple disciplines to find solutions. To address these issues requires expansive learning in which the solutions to dilemmas are discovered through collective, iterative inquiry that builds new knowledge about how to think about problem solving, how to transverse cultural tools and knowledges without privileging some kinds of approaches in order to find the path towards solving complex problems.

A vital tool for solving these complex issues is the ability to harness technology in pursuit of solutions. That means that students from a young age must know how to use technology as a tool for learning. Teachers must be at the vanguard for using tools to produce new knowledge. Their work must be to prepare students to engage in knowledge generation, not knowledge accumulation. Equally critical is the need for clarity about the functions of publicly supported education. It must address the dominant social issues to improve equity, access, and participation for all groups and individuals. A divided world cannot solve the problems that hang over us all.

A final note about education in 2030. Teachers are designers of learning spaces. They design activities that are not focused on a single outcome but are constructed to provide an open architecture that anticipates a broad band of learners who pursue understanding and activity in ways that instructors may not anticipate. Further, in learning spaces, teachers are learners with their students, building repertoires of shared knowledge that lead to innovation and the co-production of outcomes. Educators use critical social and cultural perspectives to maximize rapport and reciprocity among learners in ways that are ethical and empowering for individuals, groups, and communities. By opening up the architecture of learning spaces, learners cross boundaries among ways of knowing, moving back and forth from the familiar to the unfamiliar, adapting an interdisciplinarity to how knowledge is produced, mediated, and expanded. Nothing about the role of the 2030 educator looks familiar to the standardized, globalized, sanitized version of the teacher technician of 2018.

NOTE

1. Each "Sector Visioning" chapter begins with an abstract prepared by the book editors and attributed to Zindzi in keeping with the storyline of the book. Zindzi is introduced in Chapter 2.

REFERENCES

Basham, J. D., Stahl, S., Ortiz, K., Rice, M. F., & Smith, S. (2015). *Equity Matters: Digital & Online Learning for Students with Disabilities.* Lawrence, KS: Center on Online Learning and Students with Disabilities.

Darder, A., Boltodano, M., & Torres, R. (Eds.). (2003). Critical pedagogy: An introduction. In *The critical pedagogy reader.* New York, NY: Routledgefalmer.

Mulvey, L. (1989). *Visual and other pleasures.* New York, NY: Springer.

Tyack, D. B. (1974). *The one best system: A history of American urban education.* Cambridge, MA: Harvard University Press.

Wiggins, G., & McTighe, J. (2005). *Understanding by design.* Alexandria, VA: Association for Supervision and Curriculum Development.

CHAPTER 12

DESIGN

Creating the Future We Want

Cameron Norman

ZINDZI'S ABSTRACT[1]

Design—an applied discipline of innovation—is presented as intentional and action oriented. In these materials it is shown to influence almost everything, from the products we use in our homes to the national and global institutions that govern our world. Traditionally design processes have been narrowly scoped by relatively few perspectives that have approached problem solving mechanistically based on past experience and present needs. Design is shown to be expanding to account for the full lifecycle of products from the origins of supply chains to the rebirth of materials and functionality. Now more cognizant of their products as part of interdependent and interconnected living systems, designers embrace iterative prototyping, learning from failure, and co-creation. Design thinking encourages a systemic orientation to problem solving that both helps to align product development with user values as well as increase the accessibility and utility of the tools, skills, and mindsets of design to everyone with a stake in the design process. While designers openly acknowledge the lack of transparency of values and the challenges caused by that, they are also witnessing and actively enabling a shift in values from

Visionary Evaluation for a Sustainable, Equitable Future, pages 205–218
Copyright © 2020 by Information Age Publishing

accumulation (more) to sustainism (better) and now beginning each design inquiry with a common question "What kind of future do we want?"

It is 2030, and the term design is now a part of the fabric of everyday thinking across disciplines, fields, and problem domains. How did this happen and what does it mean for the sustainability of human and ecological systems? The many global crises of the early 2000s through the 2010s continued to manifest themselves in political, economic, and social upheaval onward to 2030. These crises were especially acute within the increasing mass migration of people due to environmental, social, and economic problems that are, in whole or in part, human-made. While the scope and consequence of these problems were not always intended, their sources can be traced back to how policies, programs, products, and societies were originally designed. Some of these designs were more thoughtful and considerate of the systems in which they were deployed, while others were not. This was so even though these design choices were known to result in widespread negative effects for generations. The implications of design are now better understood, and the methods and ways of thinking advanced by the lens of design are now widely used in support of design development that enhances sustainability and equity.

To illustrate the power of design, consider how we design the way we organize our social institutions. One example, to risk oversimplifying, is related to the design choice of how to set up a government and govern or rule within a society. In the Middle East and Northern Africa in the early 21st century, this approach was isolationist, oppressive of dissent, yet stable for most of the last half century. This was the case until it collided with designs supported by social media and a youth culture that embraced technologies that enabled them to engage with others who lived with alternative designs for governing and preferred them to what they had. This collision contributed to what became known as the "Arab Spring" and resulted in the overthrowing of autocratic rulers, unleashing a wave of instability and social change across the region with varying effects, both constructive and destructive (Wolfsfeld, Segev, & Sheafer, 2013). One region where it met substantial resistance was Syria, and within 5 years, millions of its citizens were displaced across the globe as part of the largest refugee crisis of the 21st century. The implications of these design and counter-design choices are still being felt in 2030.

Consider another design choice: the one made to create an automated way of traveling, beyond the constraints of the horse or railroad, with the invention of the automobile. The institution of the assembly line and related supply and production system established by Henry Ford was copied and led to mass production of everything from clothing to washing machines. The automobile transformed the way people related to, built, and even lived in communities. The modern city is shaped as much by road-ways as anything else and the automobile's impact on product distribution, the need for oil, and the shape and size of our cities cannot be overstated. Entire economic regions within countries were driven by industry that re-volves around the car. And after a century of industry developed around the internal combustion engine, we saw a shift to the electric-powered automobile, with Volvo being the first to have phased out its exclusively petrol-powered cars in 2019.

In both of the examples above, we see how human decision-making ex-pressed through the creation of services (e.g., governments) and products (e.g., automobiles) has enormous consequences for the planet, and those who live on it, that extend far beyond the original intention. These design choices have influenced the physical layout of countries (borders, transpor-tation networks), the cultural landscape within them, and the way people engage with each other and the world around them. These examples point to the connection between design and systems. When we look at the impact of design in the world, the outcomes of the design process and the way de-sign choices are made, all in the context of human values, we are looking through an evaluative lens. While these connections may seem obvious, it wasn't until just before 2030 that design, systems thinking, and evaluation were brought together in any meaningful way. Moreover, the implications of these connections are profound.

DESIGN

Design has been regarded by some as the "discipline" of innovation. While the term *innovation* has been overused in policy and business discourse, it also has never become more relevant given the need for new ways to approach problems that appear impossible to solve with what is current-ly at our disposal. Innovation is the intentional process of creating value through putting new thinking into action. New thinking may come from seeing things in a new way, combining existing concepts together in novel forms, or generating something new in its entirety. In practice, this might involve the development of a new process, product, or a reimagining of an existing product or service into something else that adds value to people and the planet. The design process that underlies innovation encompasses the journey of problem finding and framing, and the process of generating the ideas, insights, and manifestation of potential contributions to a solu-tion. Innovation can be small and incremental or truly transformative, but what sets it apart from terms like *discovery* or *ideas* is that it is *intentional* and *action-oriented*. Innovation is about making discoveries and taking ideas into the world with the aim of adding new value to the world.

Design is a professional field made of different branches of philosophy, theory, and practice (Norman, 2013). The field of design is comprised of many subspecialties like interior design, industrial design, software design, service design that are not always easily distinguished from one another (even from within the field). What these subspecialties share is an approach to creating and realizing products and services that are embodied in something called design thinking. Design thinking became popular in the early 2000s when businesses started looking for innovative solutions to complex problems and found that traditional models of solution generation were no longer producing dividends. Design thinking involves a disciplined exploration of a problem space, generating lots of ideas—many of them rather "wild"—and then organizing and prototyping the perceived best of these options, followed by implementing and evaluating possible options in quick "micro experiments" before landing on a final product (Cross, 2011). Design thinking is characterized by a bias toward action with an emphasis on creating a "good enough" product to start and then refining it. What this can do is reduce the risk associated with innovation and the unintended consequences that emerge from new "things" (products, services, policies) placed into established systems.

A New Focus for Design

Although design has had a history of making products attractive for humans, the fields' track record has been less stellar when it comes to making these products suitable for the planet, particularly at an industrial level. A central driver of change for design has been the growing global consciousness around humanity's relationship with the planet manifested in a growing understanding of the impacts and trends associated with urbanization, rising incomes, increasing access to increasing diversity and quantity of consumer goods and services, the supply chains and lifecycles of those goods and services, increasing availability (and need for) energy, and the natural and human resources required to sustain it all. As consciousness of impacts and accelerating change took hold, so did an awareness of systemic aspects of a growing and massively interconnected web of product and service lifecycles. From natural resource extraction at the birth of a product to the end of life product disposal, the lifecycles of products and services were causing negative impacts on water access, air quality, ecosystem resilience, and climate change that, in turn, triggered health crises, political and economic instability, conflict, and diaspora. As much as 80% of the environmental impact of a product was determined at the design stage, not just in how it was used (Thackara, 2006). Designers recognized that by not purposefully designing for the entire lifecycle of products and services they were, in effect, contributing, if not actually causing, increasingly severe planetary problems. So, rather than simply seek to change the behavior of people in the ways they use products—as embodied in the "triple aim" of *reduce, reuse and recycle*—designers began changing the way design itself was done even before consumers had access to what was produced. Thus began a shift in design that would continue for the next few decades.

Design's transformation was also one of values. A variety of social movements began embracing values that have begun to shift American culture from one that idolized "more" to one that valued "better." Amongst some communities demand increased for products and services that were sustainable, affordable, and respectful of people and planet, as embodied in the growth of "triple-p" (people, planet, and profit) bottom business lines. This contributed to the birth of sustainism, a new ethically and socially responsible approach to design. This design approach can handle advances in technology and both local and global conditions. It is sensitive to nature while also supporting collaborative and networked ways of working (Schwartz & Elffers, 2010).

The widespread availability of information resources made possible through the Internet, broadcast media, and traditional print forms now deployed globally was another factor that precipitated the shift toward sustainism. Lifecycles of everyday products are becoming ever more transparent to consumers who can now track product origins, the means of extraction of raw materials to make it, and visualize ways to repurpose or recycle it. Consumer choice, now more informed than ever before, is becoming "better" aligned with the kind of designs that they wish to endorse and the kinds of companies and political and economic regimes they want to support. Designing for transparency made opportunities for design thinking more accessible for not only designers but also for all consumers to better align their actions with their values.

Design thinking is as much an approach to conceptualizing ideas and problems as it is a set of methods and tools for envisioning possible problem solutions and products (Liedtka, 2013). Leidtka (2013) and colleagues found that design thinking commonly included four main processes driven by empathy for the intended user of a product or service:

- *Exploratory data gathering.* This includes doing background research, review of documents, and market analysis.
- *Idea gathering.* Generating ideas about possible options, including those that might seem outlandish, unpractical, or impossible to help generate frames of references to generate those ideas that are actionable.
- *Prototyping.* Generating workable examples of the solution that can be refined and evaluated.
- *Testing.* Evaluation of the working models.

A later review by Seidel and Fixson (2013) looked at how these approaches were used in practice through purposeful analysis of 14 case studies of multidisciplinary product teams. In their review, design thinking was classified into three processes—need-finding, brainstorming, and prototyping—and mapped on to formal and informal design methods. They found that novice professionals were successful in implementing design-oriented tools into most of their work, suggesting that design thinking can be taught and successfully implemented among non-designers. Caruso and Frankel (2010) further argue that design thinking is a social, rather than technical concept, and thus suggests that anyone can be a designer. This concept of "everyone as designer" was something that gained greater purchase as design thinking was adopted widely as a means to innovate, explore, and challenge complex problems.

Design Approaches for Sustainable Development

As designers more fully contemplate their role in planetary health and well-being, there came the subsequent acknowledgement of evaluation's role in guiding the design decisions and understanding of impact. Design's embrace of evaluative thinking has paralleled the field of evaluation's embrace of design thinking. This bidirectional influence allowed a more dialogical means of understanding and improving the innovation process and the impacts these new creations had on the world.

Design thinking's emphasis on iterative prototyping is one of the principal means in which more environmentally sustainable products and services are produced in 2030. Rather than aim to get it right in one "shot," product development is typically done in shorter, faster, more focused cycles, more often. This rapid cycle prototype approach includes an evaluative component built in throughout, allowing designers to better assess potential problems and unforeseen effects of their creations sooner to avoid harmful products making it to market. By focusing on prototypes planned to be created, deployed, and evaluated quickly, design thinking also gets organizations more comfortable with "failure." Fear of failure may take place at the product development stage, when ideas are first conceived and tested, and the implementation stage, when potentially useful products and services are not adopted or put into practice (Klein & Knight, 2005). By putting ideas into practice quickly with an expectation that they might not yield all the benefits that are expected, organizations become accustomed to "failure" and are better able to focus on learning, instead. This is particularly relevant when there is an expectation and plan for a future iteration aimed at building on the current prototype.

One of design thinking's strongest attributes is its emphasis on co-creation. Having individuals who are touched by a product, particularly intended users, at the table making decisions, providing feedback, and offering suggestions ensures that multiple value positions are recognized at the outset. When product users are part of the design, greater attention is paid to those users' beliefs, values, lived experience, and daily life in the course of developing that product. This attention can illuminate areas of need, disparities, as well as intended uses and impacts for what is produced. Co-creation is a means to put equity at the center of decision-making by ensuring inclusion of the people with a stake in the design of the "thing"—the product, service, policy, or system. Co-creation has become a standard in the design process. It is now a key measure of product quality and the success of co-creation processes is assessed in terms of the degree of alignment between a thing created and the values of the people affected by the thing.

FROM PRODUCTS AND SERVICES TO ECOSYSTEMS

As designers become more conscious of their creations, and the public more aware of individual and collective values, the relationship between what we make and what we consume changes. This shift was one of products and services as independent creations to one where the design was part of a larger ecosystem of understanding design's role in co-evolving with society, conforming to it as well as shaping it. This was represented in evolutions in design from what was considered design 1.0 (traditional design) and 2.0 (product and service design) to 3.0 (organizational transformation design) and 4.0 (social transformation design; Jones, 2013). With each stage in this progression the focus shifted from looking at products in isolation (1.0) to product use (2.0) to the organizational structures themselves that shape design decisions and actions (3.0) to designing social ecosystems aimed at making healthier design decisions systemically (4.0). Design is best a catalyst for change when viewed as part of a system, shifting discourse from making things to creating and shaping ecosystems of human and natural activity.

This shift in design became a part of the evolution of the social ecosystem from disparate, isolated choices toward ever more connected, collective action. Design came to focus on facilitating the natural need for and health of social relationships between citizens. The design community has been steadily elevating its commitment to leverage collective assets and social efforts to transform the use, exploitation, renewal, and protection of resources across the ecosystem (Design 4.0).

Drawing on design techniques and methods, design and systems thinking and co-creation, this new way of engaging social systems and the natural world took hold. Engaging others and society through a systems-oriented design approach also revealed more starkly the distribution of power, wealth, opportunity, health, and social mobility within society. This change allowed more purposeful, conscious, and often contentious engagement between those engaged in the design process and further contribution to sustainable creations and intentions. For example, social policies were designed with an explicit focus on not only their intention (e.g., economic policy), but how they were manifest in the lives of people across the system in different contexts on matters of sustainability, equity, and health. An example of such a system-level policy approach is the Health in All Policies Framework established by the World Health Organization.[2]

Innovations in product design, delivery and use are now commonplace—by design and necessity. The pace of change coupled with high need and unprecedented technological, economic, social, economic, and environmental connectivity across the globe has revealed the need to think and act in systems and to design them with skill and intention. Although the 2010s saw a vote for Brexit in the United Kingdom and the election of a president with a protectionist agenda (Donald Trump) in the United States, the mandates within each "movement" were highly constrained and contested. Whole systems change is realized when design is considered explicitly within the context of the environment and evaluation. For example, the decision by the Trump administration to withdraw the United States from the Paris Accord on Climate Change didn't prevent hundreds of jurisdictions from the local, regional, and state levels from continuing their climate change strategies as part of a national climate alliance. This was in recognition of the role that everyone plays in systems change, no matter how complex. In this case, the decision of the United States' federal government to withdraw from the Paris Accord was less impactful given that it didn't fully represent the country's impact on addressing the conditions associated with climate change.

Within the span of just 2 decades the language and utility around design and design thinking has changed. The literacy around what design is and how design thinking can be used to support systemic challenges has been raised and is no longer just within the purview of professional designers, architects, and business leaders. The term social innovation has often been used synonymously with the application of design to social problems and, while the two are distinct concepts, there is little doubt that they share much in their approach to addressing complex social issues (Manzini, 2015).

THE BEAUTY OF HUMAN SYSTEMS

Design has helped reframe the discussion about what we do, how it's done, and the context and outcomes associated with the things we do to influence the world around us. Design has been in the peculiar position of having to both overcome and embrace the perception of its focus on beauty. This required discussion on the role of aesthetics and drew on research to illustrate how it contributed to well-being, productivity, organizational effectiveness, as well as more desirable products (Taylor, 2013).

Design is as much about function as it is form and thus the role of beauty and elegance in our lives is also considered. Far from producing products, services, policies, and organizations that are simply functional, designers' collaborations with evaluators can ensure that what is produced is more beautiful. This builds on work done by Steven de Groot and others on organizational aesthetics and the power of beauty to improve organizational performance and sustainability (Strati, 1992; Taylor, 2013). Design has not always been known as something available to everyone, as a practical set of skills, knowledge, approaches, and mindset available to anyone. Design had to shed a reputation as expensive, elitist, out of reach, and opaque. Likewise, beauty was, for too long and at great cost to humanity, viewed as frivolous and extraneous to what we make. We now see beauty more for what it is: reflective of the possibilities of the human condition and an aspirational goal of good, sustainable design.

This approach to building in a perspective on beauty into our social and environmental systems serves many purposes, beyond aesthetics. Beautiful spaces have been written extensively about by poets, artists, playwrights, scholars, scientists and authors for centuries as means to inspire, engage, and reflect the natural world. Beauty can be considered to be an attractor in complex conditions: something that stimulates a pattern of activity around it (Mitchell, 2009). Whether it is parkland, art, performance or cosmetic fashion (e.g., clothing, decoration) people tend to gravitate toward things they find beautiful (however defined) and are repulsed by things considered "ugly." By creating beauty in the work we do, the policies we create and the practices we engage in, we are not only creating more impactful products, but ones that are more likely to attract others to them and the overall vision to which they aspire. Research on organizational aesthetics shows higher levels of employee engagement, commitment, and effectiveness when they feel their work and their work environment is beautiful (van Aken, de Groot, & Weggeman, 2013).

DESIGNING FUTURES

Humans have always sought to understand what might come from future events to assist in planning, anticipating threats, and envisioning new opportunities (Amsteus, 2012). Foresight, or strategic foresight as the professional practice, emerged largely from the Second World War and the dramatic social, economic, technological, and geopolitical changes that surrounded that time in history (Hines & Bishop, 2015). With the Cold War, the massive expansion of manufacturing and shifting economies, and the rise of new globalized production chains that took place in the postwar years meant that organizations couldn't simply look at what was happening in the present, but required some means to anticipate what might happen in the future. Scenario planning, one of the methods of foresight, emerged from this milieu thanks in part to the threat of nuclear war and the need to anticipate what could happen should specific policy or military choices be made given their potential consequences. By seeing possible future options through the combination of current data, forecast models, social deliberation, and creative visualization, strategic foresight can allow us to better anticipate challenges and design conditions that are likely to contribute to favorable outcomes. In short: we can better design our future. Indeed, design is one means of future-making (cf. Yelavich & Adams, 2014).

In 2030, foresight is no longer strange and is considered a valuable tool for envisioning possible futures and developing the kind of policies that steer society toward futures that are more sustainable and equitable. One of the reasons for this is that the foresight work of the early part of the century was able to be critically evaluated in terms of how various scenarios played out in the world. Foresight does not necessarily predict the future, but does provide a means to anticipate and think through issues as they begin to emerge. This ability to envision what might come allows for early action to be taken when things appear to align with those visions to amplify positive contributions while addressing those that are more harmful or problematic toward the goals of sustainability and equity.

An example of this kind of foresight work was the report from Peg Lahn and Cameron Norman in 2013, who employed foresight methods to consider what the future of the City of Toronto might look like in 2030. Toronto, a city of 2.4 million people (more than 5 million in the greater metro area) is known by its residents as a "city of neighborhoods"—a set of distinctive spaces defined by culture, geography, demographics, and history. Lahn and Norman looked at the trends and drivers of change within and across the neighbourhoods and proposed four possible futures based on assumptions regarding how power and influence was positioned within the city, by whom, and to what potential effect they might have on the shape of the city in 2030. These trends included the rise of the sharing economy, increase in home-based workers and the gravitation toward "third space" areas like cafes and co-working spaces, a decreased reliance on the automobile (and rise of local-oriented transportation models like bicycles), and shift in the production economy from large to small-scale manufacturing as realized through more "do-it-yourself" movement.

Like any foresight initiative, the intent was not to predict what would happen, but use data and a structured process to frame how current trends could influence the future. The Neighbourscape Toronto 2030 report (Lahn & Norman, 2013) provided civic planners with insight into patterns that were forming as the city grew, including proposing changes that could prevent architectural failings such as those caused by falling glass from inadequately designed high-rise condominiums. The rise in more local-oriented transportation meant that jobs needed to be located closer to where people worked. As the population increased, city planners realized the need for greater allowance for light-industrial businesses and related service sector businesses to be located closer to the neighbourhoods that were experiencing high density population increases. This countered the trend toward pushing these businesses out of the city core to the suburbs to make way for condominiums and apartments. This reduced the amount of time and energy required for people to get to their jobs, taking traffic off the roads while increasing the time people had for other things.

The Lahn and Norman (2013) report also foretold the rising power of cities in shaping their destiny. Since its publication, civic governments claimed a steady, ongoing increase in power to tax, regulate, and influence practices that affected their natural and social environment in ways that were once the domain of provinces or states, or nations. In the case of cities, this allowed a closer connection between people and their government on bigger policy matters, which increased accountability and reduced the number of inequitable policy decisions made because the implications of those decisions were more closely evident at a local level. These decisions were facilitated by the foresight that showed local decision-makers the potential implications of trends that were occurring in real-time and enabled them to make choices based on how they saw the trajectory of those actions unfolding. This "future-minded" thinking showed how one might design the future, rather than simply react to what is happening. By seeing where foresight models hold true, policymakers, citizens, and anyone else can explore what the potential implications are and whether they are desirable or not and then change course as necessary using the models as guides. This enables more design and data-driven decision-making that is also transparent to those who have access to the models.

What this kind of modeling does is also inspire the question: What kind of world do we want? It is an invitation to explore values and decisions and the implications of both together as realized in scenarios. Even if the scenarios aren't actually realized, the conversations that are generated through their development can help elucidate, articulate, and clarify value differences and similarities and provide a forum for co-creative dialogue on not only anticipated futures, but preferred ones. This can elicit dialogue on who benefits from certain future scenarios, addressing issues such as equity, disadvantage and the conditions that foster or fight against them.

Foresight requires careful consideration of how trends manifest over time and what their implications are. Evaluation of alternative futuristic designs brings the chance to validate these options and explore the degree to which data and foresight models fit with actual outcomes. This is another way in which the field of design and evaluation came together, providing greater opportunities. Designers employing foresight argue that if you can't see the future, you can't build it. Like any design, if you can't conceive of something even in imperfect terms, it's hard to expect that it will be realized. As Wheatley (2006) noted, vision and values act like "fields," unseen forces that influence people's behavior. Foresight can help to shape a vision of the future.

Havas, Schartinger, and Weber (2010) looked at innovation policy adoption and the role of foresight and found that it was a useful means of informing and facilitating new thinking about policy options that were distinct. This is particularly relevant for issues such as climate change, conservation, and environmental protection where policy options may abound as solutions to present issues, but are problematic for addressing future issues. By gaining insight into future possibilities—some that are not even rooted in the present context—policy makers can make inroads against having policy always be reactive to problems and help prevent or at least curb the effects of problems that are emerging.

DESIGN FOR EVERYONE, BY EVERYONE

Putting the tools of design in the hands of everyone—professional and nonprofessional designers alike—and supported by evaluative thinking is a means of establishing more distributed, equitable systems of creation. In the years between the present day and 2030 the term design and the methods, approaches and perspectives used by designers will become more standard means of interacting with the world by more people. The accessibility, the interactivity, the effectiveness, and the sheer fun of having a means of unleashing and focusing creativity toward problems of local and global importance that design brings to people from diverse backgrounds will serve a catalyst for positive change that has global implications (cf. Ehn, Nilsson, & Topgaard, 2014). These implications include reducing the inequities and disparities that unsustainable behavior helped create through generations of past practices where too many people were excluded from engagement with the means of creating the tools, policies, and practices that shape society. Design is not a panacea, but it will provide greater options and when forces like climate change limit certain options, this additive power will be welcome.

By focusing on the user experience, design can point out where gaps exist in product offerings, illuminating inequities, and opportunities for them to be addressed intentionally. Design can help us ask what kind of world do we want and what products, services, policies, and systems we need to create that desired future by working in the present to transform ideas into action. Evaluation is the means to assess how successful design is in this endeavor and together these ideas have the potential to shape the world to accept it not just as it is, but as we intend it to be.

NOTES

1. Each "Sector Visioning" chapter begins with an abstract prepared by the book editors and attributed to Zindzi in keeping with the storyline of the book. Zindzi is introduced in Chapter 2.
2. See World Health Organization, https://www.who.int/healthpromotion/frameworkforcountryaction/en/

REFERENCES

Amsteus, M. (2012). The origin of foresight. *World Futures, 68*(6), 390–405.

Caruso, C., & Frankel, L. (2010). Everyday people: Enabling user expertise in socially responsible design. In *Proceedings of the 2010 Design Research Society Montreal Conference on Design & Complexity* (pp. 1–14). Montreal, Canada: Design Research Society.

Cross, N. (2011). *Design thinking.* Oxford, England: Berg.

Ehn, P., Nilsson, E. M., & Topgaard, R. (Eds.). (2014). *Making futures: Marginal notes on innovation, design, and democracy.* Cambridge, MA: MIT Press.

Havas, A., Schartinger, D., & Weber, M. (2010). The impact of foresight on innovation policy-making: Recent experiences and future perspectives. *Research Evaluation, 19*(2), 91–104.

Hines, A., & Bishop, P. (2015). *Thinking about the future: Guidelines for strategic foresight (2nd ed.).* Houston, TX: Hinesight.

Jones, P. H. (2013). *Design for care: Innovating health care experience.* Brooklyn, NY: Rosenfeld Media.

Klein, K. J., & Knight, A. P. (2005). Innovation implementation. *Current Directions in Psychological Science, 14*(5), 243–246.

Lahn, P., & Norman, C. D. (2013). Neighbourscape Toronto: 2030. Toronto, Canada: OCAD University. Retrieved at *https://issuu.com/censemaking/docs/futureurbanneighbourhood2030*

Liedtka, J. (2013). *Design thinking: What it is and why it works.* Charlottesville, VA: University of Virginia.

Manzini, E. (2015). *Design, when everybody designs.* Cambridge, England: MIT Press.

Mitchell, M. (2009). *Complexity: A guided tour.* Oxford, England: Oxford University Press.

Norman, C. D. (2013). *The liminal space of design: Exploring creation for reproduction.* Unpublished thesis. Toronto, Canada: OCAD University.

Seidel, V. P., & Fixson, S. K. (2013). Adopting design thinking in novice multidisciplinary teams: The application and limits of design methods and reflexive practices. *Journal of Product Innovation Management, 30,* 19–33.

Schwartz, M., & Elffers, J. (2010). *Sustainism is the new Modernism: A cultural manifesto for the sustainist era.* New York, NY: D.A.P./Distributed Arts.

Strati, A. (1992). Aesthetic understanding of organizational life. *Academy of Management Review,* 21(3), 568–581.

Taylor, S. S. (2013). What is organizational aesthetics? *Organizational Aesthetics, 1*(2), 30–32.

Thackara, J. (2006). *In the bubble.* Cambridge, MA: MIT Press.

van Aken, J. E., Groot, de, S. A., & Weggeman, M. C. D. P. (2013). Designing and developing beautiful organizations: a conceptual framework. In *Academy of Management 2012 Annual Meeting: The Informal Economy, August 3–7, 2012.* Boston, MA.

Wheatley, M. J. (2006). *Leadership and the new science: Discovering order in a chaotic world.* San Francisco, CA: Berrett-Koehler.

Wolfsfeld, G., Segev, E., & Sheafer, T. (2013). Social media and the Arab Spring. *The International Journal of Press/Politics, 18*(2), 115–137.

Yelavich, S., & Adams, B. (Eds.). (2014). *Design as future making.* London, England: Bloomsbury.

CHAPTER 13

VISIONARY EVALUATIVE INQUIRY

Moving From Theory to Practice

Beverly Parsons, Matt Keene, and Lovely Dhillon

SITUATION

It's 2030. Omar would like to join one of the Praxis Quests that he has learned about from Zindzi. The following conversation occurred when Zindzi and Omar met a second time to discuss the Praxis Quests.[1] Prior to the second conversation, Omar had seen the following information that Zindzi had posted in a popular article about Praxis Quests:

> In its most basic definition, praxis is a way of learning where theory informs practice and practice informs theory. The sixth principle of Visionary Evaluatives (VEs) uses the term "deep praxis." For VEs, deep praxis means integrating creative actions, evaluative inquiry, theory, and learning into one's work and life to co-create with others a sustainable, equitable future. In the term "Praxis Quest," the word "quest" captures the notion of praxis being an ongoing search, exploration, and discovery. It involves engaging in praxis, refining a praxis, finding fit-for-purpose behaviors, adaptations, states of being, and

Visionary Evaluation for a Sustainable, Equitable Future, pages 219–240
Copyright © 2020 by Information Age Publishing
219

more. It engages VEs across sectors and disciplines in a process of continually "becoming" both in one's life and work through a focus on evaluative inquiry. Being and becoming a VE is a journey of reflection and supportive engagement with others.

Each Praxis Quest is framed around one of four general phases of an evaluative inquiry—(a) positioning and designing the evaluative inquiry; (b) data collection, compilation, and credibility; (c) meaning-making from data; and (d) shaping action and practice. We treat each Praxis Quest as holographic. That is, each Praxis Quest encompasses the whole of the evaluative inquiry process and the whole of the Visionary Evaluative Principles (VEPs) within any one of the four general phases of an evaluative inquiry.

In the situation I'm describing, a Praxis Quest consists of 6 to 10 people who intentionally—and with commitment—come together virtually and/or in-person to openly and honestly share their values and their struggles when using the VEPs in real time, in real life, and in their work. If the gathering is in person, it is often in a location that connects to the issues being discussed. It might be on a river, on a city street, or in someone's home. Each person brings their own personally and/or professionally challenging evaluative inquiry to the conversations.

A Praxis Quest is a practical way for anyone who is on the VE journey to engage with others to co-create their contribution to a sustainable, equitable world now and in the future. A Praxis Quest is an example of "deep praxis."[2]

Before the following conversation between Omar and Zindzi, Omar had read the Sector Visioning materials that Zindzi had curated for the VEs preparing for the Global Forum on Artificial SuperIntelligence (ASI).

OPENING CONVERSATION

Omar: It was very helpful to learn about the VEPs in our last conversation. I am particularly interested in VEP 6—engage in deep praxis. I'm also eager to learn more about your Praxis Quests and how I might get involved. I want to better apply my evaluative inquiry skills and passion, especially in regard to our local food systems.

Zindzi: I think your participation in a Praxis Quest also would be very useful to the others involved in the quest. A key feature of a Praxis Quest is that it is a complement to, not a replacement of, an evaluative inquiry process.

Participants in the Praxis Quests engage with one another by bringing their specific evaluative inquiry work into the praxis conversations but each one is doing their own evaluation work. The Praxis Quest is a reflective space in which the participants reframe, refine, and improve both their theories and practices as they learn from each other's concrete, contextualized experiences.

Omar: I like that members of a Praxis Quest keep working on their own evaluative inquiry in their own setting while also learning how their setting and sector connects to other sectors, settings, and the personal lives of one another.

Zindzi: Yes. For example, one Praxis Quest that I'm working with right now has eight people, teams of two from each of four sectors—law, industrial agriculture, water protection, and public health. Each of the teams is conducting an evaluative inquiry related to an initiative that is predominantly in one of the sectors I just mentioned. The team working in agriculture heard about our Praxis Quest facilitation and wondered if it would be something that they might be involved in. As I talked with that team, I learned more about "adjacent possibilities,"[3] that is, the ways the focus of their evaluative inquiry connects with other "nearby" sectors. As we talked, I saw that issues related to public health, water quality, and legal matters were possible areas of importance. I suggested we set up a year-long Praxis Quest in which I'd bring their agricultural team together virtually with VEs conducting inquiries about social determinants of health, water quality, and the laws in their particular state. The teams are now each continuing their own inquiries but they have monthly conversations as a group where they raise issues that those more deeply engaged in an adjacent sector might help them simply by sharing their knowledge. My colleagues and I have some general approaches we use for these gatherings. I'll explain more about that later.

By participating in ongoing and ever deepening praxis, VEs embed the VEPs into their evaluative inquiry at the transformative intersections of their professional and community work.

Omar: How did you start the Praxis Quests? How do people get into a particular Praxis Quest? How long do they stay?

DESIGN OF PRAXIS QUESTS

Zindzi: We started several years ago by simply tapping into our networks of VE collaborators who work in multiple sectors. We found that many were wanting more in-depth connections across sectors. We started with a basic guideline of diversity. We wanted a diversity of sectors, cultures, inquiry methods, values, and ways of using and conceptualizing evaluation and evaluative endeavors in each Praxis Quest. We invited people to send us a brief statement about why they want to join, what they want to gain, and what they want to contribute. Everyone gives and receives. To this day, we seldom have had a problem getting enough people to form Praxis Quests simply because the forming of a Praxis Quest grows out of the natural interests of the people in our networks.

We use our various technological tools to bring them together for a Praxis Quest. We usually have 6 to 10 people in each quest. They begin with an intention of involvement for a specified length of time, usually a year. A year may seem like a long time for some who simply want to get an immediate issue resolved and move on. We resist this instinct and mindset. It contradicts the VE approach. Of course, a year is actually extremely short when considering long-term consequences, but we find that during that time period, quest participants are at least getting a reasonably deep sense of how to attend to those longer term patterns such as shifts in long-standing values and how to watch for them. Many people come in and out of several Praxis Quests over time.

After the agreed-on length of time for the quest, the participants revisit what has happened. Some members may want to stay together but reframe the quest based on what they have learned, how their situations have changed, or important events in the world at large. Some shift to other networks that support praxis. We're happy to have people move to other groups and structures that meet their needs. We see ourselves as a part of a bigger web of learning. Basically, a healthy Praxis Quest is a self-organizing process that releases the creativity and leadership of the people involved. We provide leadership and participatory skills training if needed for members of the Praxis Quests.

The members of each Praxis Quest decide for themselves how formal to be in their structure and ways of working, how specific to be in their goals, and so on. And they can modify as they go along. We want them to be experiencing the very dynamic that they are learning about. The quest is intended to catalyze VEs' sensibilities and deep thinking about the focus of a given evaluation.

Omar: How do members of your Praxis Quests find the resources—both time and money—to participate? Are organizations and individuals willing to spend their resources for this type of learning?

Zindzi: This is one of the encouraging changes I've seen over the last few years. The tide has turned. People are realizing that they must slow down, reflect, engage deeply, and make sure that they are grounding their actions and inquiries on wise inquiry into the complexity of the issues they are facing, seeing the interconnections across sectors, and surfacing the values that are driving actions whether those values are conscious or unconscious. There is a refreshing sense of humility running through many organizations and funders of social and environmental change initiatives. Or to put it simply, they are seeing the wisdom and necessity of the VEPs.

All of the Praxis Quest members have seen some pretty serious missteps. Major corporations, rich families, people with political influence, and government entities have all thought they were powerful enough to make things happen that they wanted. They seriously underestimated the power of citizen rights, the forces of nature, and the entanglement of social and natural systems. Organizations and individuals both are recognizing that the risks resulting from not learning are much more costly than engaging in learning practices that help illuminate these systemic conditions.

Omar: It sounds to me like any evaluator who is starting a new evaluation should seek out a Praxis Quest to join.

Zindzi: I agree. And even if you don't hear about Praxis Quests until you have an evaluation underway, you can still get involved. We don't think of an evaluation as having a strict beginning or end although funding might be framed that way. Any evaluation can be seen as part of a bigger pattern of inquiry.

THE EVALUATIVE INQUIRY PROCESS AS AN ORGANIZING FRAMEWORK

Zindzi: We structure our Praxis Quests around what we refer to as the four arenas of an evaluative inquiry. As you well know, the evaluative inquiry process has been the foundation of the field of evaluation from its early years. It is based on the scientific process and methods but has three additional distinguishing features. First, it's based on values. Second, it emphasizes use.

And, third, it recognizes that whatever is learned from an evaluation has to be considered in light of its context. That context is composed of important additional systems that matter, that is, systems that are beyond those focused on in a given evaluative inquiry. As you see, this orientation is incorporated in the VE principles.

Omar: Are your arenas of evaluative inquiry the same, or at least similar, to those I used when I left the evaluation field a dozen years ago? Then, evaluators were thinking systemically about four interconnected phases of the evaluative inquiry process: (a) positioning and designing the evaluative inquiry; (b) data collection; (c) meaning-making, that is, illuminating the link between data and strategic action; and (d) shaping action and practice. That was quite an advance from when I entered the evaluation field in the 1980s. Back in those early days, we talked about the evaluation process as (a) planning the evaluation, (b) data collection, (c) analysis, and (d) reporting. In those days, we thought of these tasks as a linear stepwise process. When I left the field in the early 2000s, the talk was about the important difference between thinking of the phases as sequential and recognizing that they are much more overlapping and interconnected.

Zindzi: We are using the four arenas of evaluative inquiry that you were using when you left the evaluation field except we call the second one *data collection, compilation,* and *credibility* instead of *data collection.* This reflects the enormous change in the availability and accuracy of data and how to work with such data in the evaluation process.

Given today's evolving living transformation of social and natural systems, evaluators are doing fewer "program evaluations," where they go through all phases of an inquiry in a single sequential pattern related to a defined "program." Instead, they embed the arenas of evaluative inquiry iteratively with action. They are working at multiple scales, for example, across state and local policy and across policy, programs, and on-the-ground practice within a program. We think of these arenas of the evaluative inquiry process as entry points into situations where people are seeking to redirect *systems* for a more just and sustainable world. These entries reveal leverage points in systems where strategically-applied and fairly small amounts of effort can create a large influence. For example, I talked a few minutes ago about the inquiry team working in the agricultural sector that joined with others for a Praxis

Quest. After they had developed their evaluation design and were about to do some data collection and compilation, they saw some connection between their work and the work of the inquiry teams focused on public health and water protection. They realized they needed to zoom out from their current focus on specific state laws about pesticides to the state laws that addressed the rights of nature and health. They found a way to jointly focus on one set of policies that sped them through to an action and short-circuited their planned evaluation. It was disconcerting for them to have to redo their planned inquiry. They had to let go of their focus on completing their plan and focus on their overall purpose, their desired future. They learned more about how to engage people in the co-creating process by attending to intersectionalities and positioning their evaluative inquiry work.

This also connected to the idea that you as an evaluator may not be actively involved in a "full" evaluative inquiry cycle. You might be involved in, say, just the positioning. Then others in the situation may be carrying out other phases. The choices of who does what is all part of the process of creating and supporting structures within and across sectors toward a more desirable future.

These shifts in how evaluative inquiry occurs led to our framing the Praxis Quests for VEs in ways that may seem unusual. We use each of the arenas of the evaluative inquiry process at a fairly large scale as the basis of a separate Praxis Quest. We find that this helps people dig more deeply into the facets of a given aspect of the inquiry process. As in the example I just described, they learn how to engage with both action and inquiry at multiple scales and determine how to make small changes that can be tested in another iteration of that arena of inquiry rather than rushing to get to the next phase of an evaluation design.

Omar: This brings to mind fractal structures that we find in nature, those repeating patterns, like in broccoli.

Zindzi: I love how you make the connections to systems concepts. That's a great example of how Praxis Quest members keep weaving together aspects of the VEPs as they work together. Most likely, there would be others in the quest who aren't familiar with terms such as fractals. They would likely jump in and ask you to apply what you are talking about to a specific example or reel you back into the main points of the conversation.

These quests constitute the "learning labs" for us to deepen our personal being as a VE and our professional capacity to bring together not only theory and practice but our very "way of being in the world" as a VE. Everyone in a given quest is engaged in their own work in the real world that is focused on the emphasis of that quest. This helps us continually practice our "way of being" as a VE in a real world situation.

One more point. Note that, in these Praxis Quests, the members are *not* engaged in a joint evaluative inquiry. They learn from the experiences of others in other sectors and in other evaluative inquiry efforts and then bring that understanding back to their own work.

Omar: Does the evaluative inquiry work of each person in a Praxis Quest need to connect to the other sectors represented in the quest?

Zindzi: No, but connections, at least conceptually, tend to emerge during the Praxis Quest. For example, your focus on food systems easily connects to health and nature but I can see it connecting to several others as well. The idea is to practice working within your dominant sector while learning more about how it connects to other sectors. By having people steeped in each of the sectors, the application of cross-sector thinking is much richer than if a person in one sector had only a superficial knowledge of another sector. As you engage in the quest, you deepen your understanding of the interface of your sector with those of others. This includes looking at similarities and differences in underlying theories across the sectors.

Of course, you can't immediately apply everything you learn, but we set these up for ready application if possible. We find this supports creativity, efficiency, and effectiveness.

Omar: Wow, that's a lot to bring together. I can see why these Praxis Quests are so important. We need one another to keep all of these facets of praxis engaged as we shift both our personal and professional ways of being toward the use of VEPs to address the complexity of today's world.

One question, though. If the Praxis Quests are framed around the key arenas of evaluative inquiry, how do the participants help one another keep from slipping solely into their professional persona and losing touch with how being a VE affects their personal lives as well?

Zindzi: Good question; that is a very real danger. We address it through key questions that members ask themselves at the beginning and end of each gathering. An opening question

is: How did being a VE affect your life this past week? We end
with a question like: Envision yourself applying your VE practice *personally* before we meet again. What does that feel like,
look like? Envision yourself applying your VE practice *professionally* before we meet again. What does that feel like, look
like?

Omar: OK. I think I'm ready to focus in on the four Praxis Quests.
To be sure I have your labels correct, they are (a) positioning and designing an evaluative inquiry; (b) data collection,
compilation, and credibility; (c) meaning-making; and (d)
shaping action and practice, right?

Zindzi: Yes. Let's start with *positioning and designing an evaluative
inquiry.*

Praxis Quest 1: Positioning and Designing an Evaluative Inquiry

Zindzi: The sectors represented in the current *positioning* Praxis
Quest are design, education, health, financial investing, and
nature. The members focus their conversations on positioning and designing their particular evaluative inquiry. As you
well know, evaluators have tended to use the development of
theories of change and the specification of evaluation questions as tools to help people position their inquiries. Those
work well in many situations. However, I am noticing that the
members of this Praxis Quest are spending a lot more time
helping one another deepen their understanding of the context—particularly the long historical context— in which each
person is working before they specify evaluation questions.
They are becoming very attuned to the current day consequences of our country's history of colonization and genocide
of Native Americans as well as the history of slavery.

The Praxis Quest members are also attending to the history of corporate power over the rights of nature, people, and
communities. They are developing deeper insights into what
is creating inequities and where there are opportunities to
more responsibly and sustainably relate to natural resources.
The intersections of the sectors and how power and culture
dynamics lead to structural racialization as well as disregard
for nature are frequently a focus in the conversations. Those
conversations have a major impact on how Praxis Quest members think about theories related to changing systems.

The VEs are continually thinking in terms of the dynamic and flexible nature of living systems and how they can take advantage of that movement to make strategic shifts. These systems have some controllable linear patterns of organization within them but their overall patterns are more akin to the complex webs of connections in our brains or the roots of plants. They are thinking in terms of how an intervention could break some connections and build new ones that support a different habit or habitat. I'm reminded of what Cam Norman[4] brought up when he addressed design. He said: "Design has been regarded by some as the "discipline" of innovation . . . Innovation is the intentional process of creating value through putting new thinking into action."

Omar: And I recall that Elizabeth Kozleski wrote about teachers needing to be able to ". . . assess the capacities of the spaces they design against their goals for its use."[5]

Zindzi: Yes, for example, one of the Praxis Quest participants is in the health field. Her organization is focused on strengthening the capacity of communities to create their own healthy futures. She is looking very carefully at the many capacities available in a low income community where she is working. She is looking at how she can bring together the local food bank with a lively neighborhood association and local churches with community gardens supplying the food banks to design and test a weekly series of lunch conversations about healthy food.

Some of the residents first head out to the gardens to learn about and collect the food. Then they learn to prepare some tasty vegetable recipes using the veggies available that time of the year for the food bank. They serve them to their neighbors and have conversations over lunch where they explain how to grow and how to prepare the food. The attendees leave with the recipe, seeds, instructions on how to grow them, connections to local organizations supporting urban/community gardening, and some of the vegetables and other ingredients they would need to make the recipe at home. Now, after a few years, she sees some of these same folks coming back to the bank not for food but bringing their surplus veggies to contribute to the bank. The local health center is providing the funding.

Omar: The example also illustrates how professionals from multiple sectors are seeing the people most affected by an initiative as assets. This is the essence of supporting effective self-organizing. Oops, there I go again, getting into rather nerdy systems concepts.

How are those involved in financial investing looking at this situation?

Zindzi: The financial investor in the group is thinking about what types of new businesses might come out of this situation. For example, she is thinking about how a catering service in the community in which she has invested might hire some of the residents who are preparing the lunches. The catering service is working on getting a contract with the local hospital and is hoping to use the results of the evaluative inquiry that will accompany this test to help the hospital see how much better they could serve the community through using their catering company. They are also exploring ways to set up a co-op structure that involves the food bank.

Omar: I'm seeing ways to position an evaluative inquiry that I wouldn't have thought about if I hadn't attended to the financial investing intersection. I would have easily slipped into looking at the extent to which the residents were using the recipes they got at the luncheons, whether the food bank was getting more people selecting fresh vegetables, and what this might mean for the farmers and what they consider planting next season. I see my biases, my values, my sector, and my sole experiences dominating my thinking. I see your point about the need for ongoing praxis—ongoing interactions with people in multiple sectors and with multiple perspectives—so I keep constructing a bigger picture.

I would add too that Kent Redford, the conservation biologist, and his colleagues[6] wrote about reframing conservation questions as socio-ecological issues and talked about planetary health. I can spin off several thoughts about planetary health that grow out of this example. What if community members began cooperating as neighborhoods to find the space and other resources to grow and gather some of the more expensive, nutritious, and hard-to-get produce instead of buying industrially-produced vegetables where synthetic human-made pesticides and fertilizers are used that run off into the local waters poisoning the rivers, oceans, soil, and, eventually, all life.

Zindzi: And where the money that community members spend on industrially-produced vegetables is most likely leaving the local economy. This also reminds me of the discussion of the legal issues related to the Flint Michigan water issue.[7] They are all tied and interwoven, reminding us why a VE approach is so helpful.

Omar: I'm seeing some possibilities already for working with a teacher-educator to help teachers craft learning activities for students that engage the community and young people to create their own healthy gardens and explore protection of drinking water. The learning activity could be tested—could be the basis of an evaluative inquiry—and expanded to even more people getting involved than I would have thought of earlier. The ideas keep coming. By bringing in our evaluative thinking we are contributing at a whole different level than I typically did before when I wasn't attending so clearly to the VE principles.

Zindzi: Yes, that's the idea. By engaging in this type of praxis framed around any of the arenas of an evaluative inquiry, you can work within that situation to shift it toward a better future. Of course, you have to be careful here. It's easy to generate a lot of ideas when working at these intersections. You have to also be able to critique them from the perspective of their power to change relevant systems and their connection to the data from the inquiry. That is the kind of topic that a Praxis Quest would explore.

Omar: Can you give an example of how you critique the ideas that are generated when working at these intersections?

Zindzi: Sure. We have a generic list of questions about living systems. Participants in each Praxis Quest tailor these more specifically to their situation. Our basic questions are:

1. *Which stakeholders (that is, people affected by the situation) are represented?* This is a reminder of the range of perspectives and values that need to be considered.
2. *What boundaries are we setting within the situation for purposes of designing the inquiry?* The boundaries might be about which sectors and systems are included in the inquiry or what geographic boundaries are used. Those are just a few boundary examples.
3. *What relationships are especially important to attend to?* There are lots of issues related to relationships that the Questors might be thinking about, for example, how the relationships vary depending on the system structures, and what relationships are particularly relevant to the broader context.
4. *What dynamics, especially related to power and cultural differences as well as across time and space, are especially important to consider?* Corporate power and privilege often comes up in these discussions especially how large corporations—in

concert with government—have gained so much power over the last couple centuries.

5. *Where is the energy for change?* This is very important when it comes to changing systems. We define energy in lots of ways—from financial resources to people's passions and personal commitments.

6. *What systems are especially important in this situation?* The focus here is on considering four basic systems: technological systems such as ones for data compilation and analysis; ecosystems related to the natural environment in the context; hierarchical organizations; and various types of formal and informal networks among people including partnerships.

Omar: I can see that the trick here is being able to both look at the conditions separately and see the systemic wholeness that emerges as these conditions create systems with their unique patterns.

Zindzi: The VE principle about learning through iterative action and inquiry is especially important. No one inquiry or action has to answer all questions. Rather the discussions lead to sharpening that one next step of action and inquiry that can then be the basis for creating yet another round of action and inquiry. Ongoing iteration. That's what we want people to understand. See both the long and the short term. We're on a long, long journey of systemic change here. In fact, the journey is the destination. It's seeing that the very act of engagement in a life full of constant learning, action, and inquiry is what keeps life within boundaries of justice and sustainability.

Praxis Quest 2: Data Collection, Compilation, and Credibility

Zindzi: Let's move on to talking about the Praxis Quest focused on the second arena of evaluative inquiry—*data collection, compilation,* and *credibility.* The current members of this quest are from the business, financial investing, law, social protection, and transportation sectors.

Of course, at the heart of the inquiry process are the data that provide credible evidence related to whatever evaluative questions an inquiry is addressing.

As you know, today, AI is transforming the work of all types of professionals, for example, conservationists, teachers, engineers, economists, lawyers, and more. Today when it comes to the data used in evaluative inquiries, it's as much about accessing and working with existing data as gathering new data. Transportation was just one of the sectors where you can see the volume of available data and the multiple ways to use data. Much of the work of a VE is credibly using multiple data sets. We need to determine who gathered the data from whom. Was it a group or organization with a vested interest? Why did they gather the data? For example, if you're looking at data from a study of a new medication, you'll likely raise different questions about whether the test was done by an independent research firm versus a group closely affiliated with the pharmaceutical company that developed the drug. You'll want to look closely at who was involved in the test. Meeting regulatory requirements is not sufficient. The world is changing too quickly for most systems of government to adapt regulatory structures, in many circumstances, to adequately protect and serve the people's equity and sustainability values. The VE must be ever vigilant. For example, were males only included in the test but you're wanting to apply the results to women? These aren't new questions; researchers have been considering these questions for decades. The change that has emerged is the increased complexity of the challenge when you are bringing together multiple data sets gathered in so many situations and with a lot more people involved. Data need to be viewed in light of multiple values and with a systemic orientation. The change involves more transparency about everything, especially related to values and what is involved in aligning values and actions. VEs are at the forefront of facilitating society's ability to engage in such alignment.

Omar: That's a big ask. Say more about what you mean by that.

Zindzi: As you well know, it was shortly before you left the evaluation field in the early 2000s, that the issue of structural racialization was identified and brought to public attention. For example, African Americans were well aware of how multiple sectors of society were converging to keep them an underclass. It was discovered that police spent more time monitoring or arresting people in Black communities for minor drug violations when the rates of drug violations were just as high in White communities. Violators ended up in prison and then when they got out, they did not have access to certain jobs, housing, or public benefits. Their prison record also limited their ability to help change the social rules because now they were not allowed to vote. This is a powerful example of intersectionality and its negative effects when disadvantages build on one another and spiral out of control.

It was researchers exploring large databases that revealed that actual drug use was very similar in White and Black communities but the police surveillance was different in the two settings. Those researchers helped surface the negative intersectionalities. They showed the links between criminal justice, housing, education, transportation, and employment; and these links provided strong evidence of the structural racialization. They chose to look through a "systems lens." They were able to see and show links across sectors. That's a different focus and process than gathering new data. Seeing the larger picture generates different ideas about what new data are worth gathering and for what purpose.

We're much more careful now about data to be collected. The "right" data are not necessarily data that support a client's preferred values but data that help us honestly and systemically understand reality and help many different stakeholders think and act with an eye toward the future they are creating together. The whole process of funding evaluations is changing because of important insights such as this, but that's a topic for another conversation.

Although we pay attention to what happened in the past, what was accomplished, and what worked in the past, we engage with that information, that data, to help shape what "should be." For a VE, the "should be" based on values of equity and sustainability needs emphasis rather than what has been in the past. Recall that Eric Barela[8] talked about businesses being so much more attentive to the social and environmental impact than they had been previously, in large part because their customers care about these matters. It's not just thinking about the immediate financial benefits for their stockholders but also thinking about their future stockholders, customers, employees, and nature itself.

Although evaluators have attended to differences in inquiry methodologies since the inception of the evaluation field, they didn't necessarily dig deeply to understand underlying values and competing perspectives embedded in the methodologies themselves. Many evaluators were so immersed in their own culture that they didn't recognize the multiple values that shape other cultures or the different perceptions of what is meant by equity or sustainability. Visionary Evaluatives now look very carefully at the values and assumptions about systems and situations that underlie data measurements and descriptions.

Here's a simple example from the Praxis Questors. Recall that Georgette Wong[9] said that, for financial institutions, the measurement of social and environmental impacts of investments is more recent than their long standing measurement of financial return. As the values of our society—its people and institutions—are changing, so are the measures of successful investments.

For example, in the Data Collection, Compilation, and Credibility Praxis Quest, the Praxis Questors were looking at data from a social impact survey that the investment group used in a community recently. The results showed that community members gave priority to an investment that would support more emergency medical care. The investment group was about to move forward with decisions based on that survey when the members of the group from the transportation and social protection sectors pointed out that the survey had a limited number of options from which the respondents could choose. It wasn't an open-ended question. The options were all focused on impacts related to the type of medical care available. The person from transportation pointed out that the survey totally missed options about access to public transportation to get to the medical center or access to affordable emergency services. And the social protection person pushed it further to look at issues of safety in the neighborhood. Would the planned investment help make it possible for a person to safely walk to the medical center or to take public transportation to reach the medical center? What about decentralizing the medical center to more neighborhood clinics? That would also reduce noise and parking issues in the neighborhoods close to the current large medical center. Also, recall Charlyn Harper Browne's comments about the essential need to address community and structural risk factors, not only the risk factors related to the individual.[10] This led the group into quite a discussion about the role the legal profession could play and the need to bring together data related to these types of matters along with the survey that was done.

Omar: That's a strong example of how a focus on the credibility of one question in a survey opened up a whole range of considerations at a systemic level when VEs come together across sectors.

Zindzi: I also notice the differences among sectors in terms of their measurement expertise. One of the things that stands out for me is that each sector tends to have its own particular area of emphasis at a given point in time. For example, those involved in financial investing have honed their expertise in measuring financial return and risk but are just now getting involved in measuring social impact, whereas folks in social services are very familiar with measuring social impact but are often not very attuned to, and often even put off by, thinking in terms of financial returns. Praxis Quest members learn from the fields with advanced ways of measuring particular types of impact and social and environmental conditions. Interestingly, note too how "risk" tends to be defined differently in the two sectors in our example. For the financial investing sector it's about the financial risk whereas for the social services sector it's about risk to a person's physical or emotional well-being. Those language differences can have a big influence on one's work.

Omar: I also can see how attentive we have to be to not prioritizing quantitative data over qualitative data just because quantitative data dominate existing data resources. The long but successful battle to include qualitative data in evaluation must not be forsaken.

Zindzi: Yes, that is very important. Fortunately AI is looking at it all at once and has all but ended that discussion. Our biggest challenge with using AI to detect significant patterns is in detecting and correcting for the biases inherent in the machine itself. If the machine perspective is not accounting for values appropriately, the well is poisoned.

Praxis Quest 3: Meaning-Making From Evaluative Inquiry Data

Zindzi: I know you have to leave soon to get home to move the cows to a new pasture, so let's shift over to talking about the Praxis Quest focused on *meaning making from evaluative inquiry data.* The sectors involved currently in this Praxis Quest are business, nature, social protection, and transportation.

We use the term "meaning-making" to include analysis, synthesis, and interpretation of data. Years ago, evaluators analyzed the data and used predetermined criteria to make judgments about the meaning of the data.

It is typical now for VEs to use processes for collective interpretation by diverse stakeholders. This task now involves thinking outside the boundary of the sectors in which we are working to see intersections with other sectors and their stakeholders. This attention to diversity of stakeholders also brings up many issues related to power and privilege and its influence on how meaning is made from data. It was this type of meaning-making and cross-sector work with data that led people in recent years to identify community and nature's rights versus corporate rights as a critical issue. People across sectors and issue areas were calling attention to patterns of corporate dominance. In relative quantities, direct violence between humans today may be at historic lows leading us into a false sense of increasing peace, but the violence perpetrated by humans upon nature is still on the rise. Today's most rampant violence, often in the form of war, between humans puts nature in the middle. Nature becomes the absorbent and adaptive intermediary between the rich who have taken from the Earth what they want and the poor who must make do with what's left. It is "making meaning" and seeing patterns across sectors and societies that reveal the bigger system patterns that are at play.

Omar: I can see that an important issue we face as we work with the meaning of data at the intersections of sectors and cultures is working with AI and maintaining scientific credibility, that is, trustworthiness. We have to be sure to not let the speed of AI-supported meaning-making overtake the necessity of the actual people in a situation making meaning for themselves.

Zindzi: Exactly. A big challenge for the VE is how to convene and facilitate these conversations about values, cultural differences, power, privilege, systemic realities, and potential strategic actions. This is a very contested space. Yet, it is at the heart of the work of a VE who is helping to make meaning of data and determine potential wise actions that help advance a sustainable, equitable future in a given time and place. Being able to hold the tensions of these contradictions and confusions is a critically important skill for VEs who work in this space. It is critical to engage the multiple stakeholders in this meaning-making so they not only help elucidate the issues and possible solutions but also so that they become part of making the change. The meaning is deeply embedded within the very being of people.

Or to put it another way, there is a heightened awareness now that making meaning from data is an important learning activity for those involved in that process. VEs intentionally use participatory approaches, not just to carry out a particular task, but to also foster deep learning among stakeholders.

Learning theories and practices that had been known for many years in the education sector support participatory meaning-making. Because of the lack of cross-sector engagement, evaluators in other sectors often were not recognizing the learning potential of participatory approaches to making meaning from data.

Omar: I'm not sure I would be very good at guiding the meaning-making process with the many different stakeholder voices that may be needed.

Zindzi: Fortunately, none of us do this work alone. Here again is the importance of these Praxis Quests. We need to pay attention to our own particular strength, our "signature," our interests, and capacities to engage in certain ways. Grasping the interconnectedness and complexities of today surely sharpens the sensitivity of every VE to work with others. No VE needs to do all the tasks single-handedly. And there are so many aspects to this work. We all have continual growth opportunities that involve exploring new ways of deepening the expression of our commitment to a sustainable, equitable future. We may not get down all the aspects of it the first time, but we will be closer each time we use the Visionary Evaluative approach and principles. And we will carry every experience and all learnings into each time thereafter.

Omar: My colleague, Ricardo, is very skilled and experienced in this type of work. I need to be more attuned to when to let him lead this work and I support him.

Zindzi: Note, too, the visionary, forward thinking nature of these conversations. The evaluation orientation embraced and embodied by the VE continually moves the interpretation toward strategic action—what to do next for the well-being of both present and future generations.

Omar: Ahh, that's more my strength—being able to move back and forth between the present and the future in my thinking. I can see better how Ricardo and I can work together. I also remember Kent Redford talking about nontransparent and conflicting values having long served as major impediments to solutions to conservation problems. He also talked about considering the influence of different actors in a system from the perspective of humility. I'm also reminded of Ryan Eller's comments when talking about social protection.[11] He talked about having to reconcile the two themes of America—the welcoming nation of opportunity for all people and the divisive nation of resistance to diversity and equity.

Zindzi: The goal of this arena of inquiry is to generate options for action that take into account the range of perspectives of the various stakeholders involved in a situation, think through the theories that exist within and across sectors, disciplines, and cultures grounded in the values of sustainability and equity with an eye to both the present and future.

Praxis Quest 4: Shaping Action and Practice

Zindzi: This leads us into our fourth Praxis Quest. The focus of the *shaping action and practice* Praxis Quest is how to have the most significant impact both short and long term based on what has been learned from an inquiry. VEs from five sectors— business, design, education, health, and law—are involved in this Praxis Quest.

I'd like to bring up two important points about helping stakeholders determine what actions to take.

First, the focus on shaping practice is not to use the data from the inquiry to congratulate or blame someone or some group. It's about using the data and the subsequent meaning-making to determine the next wise action to bring about long-term equity and sustainability. The evaluative inquiry done by VEs is focused on improving and transforming, not on proving whether something someone did in the past accomplished or didn't accomplish a specific goal. The data from the inquiry are used to continue the journey in a valued direction. So visionary evaluative inquiry is both about moving into the future with guiding principles about a sustainable, equitable future and about drawing on carefully considered data from multiple perspectives grounded in what has happened in the past.

Second, we focus on getting the *multiple* stakeholders who are directly within the situation thinking collectively about their action. Some will have a more active role at one time and a less active role at another time. Those not directly involved in the next action can support it and think forward to what might happen next when it may be their turn to act. The evaluators and other VEs involved in leadership are doing things such as helping people combine being creative, leveraging possibilities, determining how much risk to take, and how to play back and forth between changing policies; modifying, creating, and in some cases ending programs; advocating; informing; and generally influencing the various systems in a pattern of building momentum in the desired direction. It involves crafting a next action. What is best in one situation may not be best in another. In fact, let's not use the term *best*.

Let's talk about *fit for purpose*, that is, what is good for that situation with those circumstances at that time.

It's so important to get stakeholders who are in different roles in their sector to see the larger systemic conditions and determine how to take collective action. By collective action, I don't necessarily mean they all do something at the same time. It may mean careful staging of action by one group at one point and then another group at another time. It's developing a strategy that builds on what was learned from the inquiry data and from the mean-making activities but being ready to adjust that strategy as new information arises.

There are a lot of power issues here. The personal interactions and relationships are very important. That includes having a setting in which the stakeholders are learning to interact compassionately with others who may not agree with their values or assumptions or have different types and degrees of power, privilege, and influence. We need all the stakeholders.

Omar: I recall Elizabeth Kozleski talking about education being a shift from knowledge accumulation to knowledge production.[12] She talked about this happening through a hybrid relationship between humans and AI. It seems like working with multiple stakeholders would be much like Elizabeth's description of how an educator works. She talked about educators coaching students of all ages to both access and harness the rich knowledge that is available and use it to address critical equity problems in a world of shrinking resources. It's *using* knowledge strategically that we're looking at here. Elizabeth talked about educators and students developing a research-and-inquiry mindset that links networks of people together to address major challenges. That sounds like what you are talking about when you refer to working with multiple stakeholders to bring about a change of course, one that moves toward well-being for all now and into the future.

Zindzi: Yes. There's so much more we could talk about, but I think you have the idea of how we leverage every part of the inquiry process itself as well as the data from an inquiry to shift social systems to equitable and sustainable relationships with each other and the ecosystems in which we live.

NEXT STEPS

Zindzi: Given our conversation, do you know which Praxis Quest you want to get involved in?

Omar: I need to go back and talk with other members of our collaborative but I'm thinking it is likely to be the *meaning-making from data* quest. We're currently in the midst of this type of work.

Thank you for making time for this conversation. I'm seeing how important ongoing engagement in a VE Praxis Quest is for me to develop as a VE. It's critical for me personally to have a more meaningful way of moving in the world—being a VE—and professionally to contribute through the work I do with others in my community around food systems. I'll get back to you next week about joining a Praxis Quest.

Thanks, as well, Zindzi, for giving me a better sense of the VE principles and how they play out in the evaluative inquiry process. All of this is getting me excited about returning to the evaluation community in a way that aligns with my own values and my desire to be part of creating a sustainable, equitable future.

NOTES

1. See Chapter 3 for Zindzi and Omar's first conversation.
2. A Praxis Quest could be structured differently than the approach described in this chapter. For purposes of this book, the Praxis Quest structure used here highlights connections across sectors and rethinking how to frame phases of an evaluative inquiry.
3. See Johnson, S. (2014). *How we got to now: Six innovations that made the modern world.* New York, NY: Penguin Group.
4. See Chapter 12, "Design: Creating the Future We Want"
5. See Chapter 11, "Education: Emancipating Learning"
6. See Chapter 5, "Nature: Connecting Well-Being and Conservation Praxis"
7. See Chapter 6, "Law: Living Values in our Legal System"
8. See Chapter 7, "Business: Doing Well and Doing Good"
9. See Chapter 9, "Financial Investing: Valuing Social Returns"
10. See Chapter 4, "Social Protection: Reframing Toward Individual, Community, and National Well-Being"
11. See Chapter 4, "Social Protection: Reframing toward Individual, Community, and National Well-Being"
12. See Chapter 11, "Education: Emancipating Learning"

CHAPTER 14

VISIONARY EVALUATIVES' PERSPECTIVES PART 2

A Conversation About Creating a Future of Well-Being

Matt Keene, Beverly Parsons, and Lovely Dhillon

SETTING THE STAGE

Background

In early 2030, the United States Congress asked a group of eight Visionary Evaluatives (VEs) to participate in a U.N. sponsored global forum on Artificial SuperIntelligence (ASI). They were asked to facilitate and contribute to conversations about creating a sustainable and equitable future. In preparation for the approaching global forum, the VEs gathered together for a week to discuss the relationships that connect human values, actions, outcomes, patterns, and a sustainable and equitable future. They began on Monday morning and then midweek took a break from their formal meeting to review and discuss a collection of materials about the work of VEs in a variety of sectors over the last decade. Now it's Friday morning and the eight VEs are gathering again to continue preparing for the Forum. The following includes excerpts of that conversation...

Visionary Evaluation for a Sustainable, Equitable Future, pages 241–260

Setting

Circular room with warm lighting and rich acoustics, walls, and ceiling of glass. Eight comfortable, formal chairs circle the room with a small circular slightly raised platform in the center. The meeting room is equipped with holography presentation technology and located on a spacecraft in low Earth orbit.

Characters

Ezekiel (Zeke) Tizoc, 66. Aztec ancestry, Mexican American, humble, direct, master strategist, Marine Corps four-star general. Development and health strategist.

Gretchen Locke, 69. Northern European descent, incisive, concise, high energy, controlled, adaptive pragmatist. Impact ecologist.

Hula Lovelace, 32. Osage Native American, brilliant, fearless, patient power. Technology entrepreneur.

Jackie Mandela, 9. South African-Cuban. Family fled apartheid. Loved by all, adored, selfless, famous. Mechanically, biologically enhanced.

Lovett Williams, 55. African American, confident, humble, deliberate. Neuroscientist, attorney.

Philip Churchill, 80. British descent, dogmatic, provocative. Industrialist, politician, philanthropist.

Sōhō Miyamoto, 48. Family interned in California in WWII, genius, uses both hands to illustrate her thoughts using holographic living illustration technology. Impact artist.

Sophia Biruni, 44. Family exiled from Iran in the 1970s, positive, passionate, intensely progressive, recently more cynical and conflicted. Educator.

Note:

Presentation (P) indicates that dialogue is accompanied by visual presentation content, for example, images, graphics, video, holography, audio.

Illustration (I) indicates that Sōhō is creating holographic and other visual art to accompany dialogue.

Gretchen, 69	Hula, 32	Jackie, 9	Lovett, 55	Philip, 80	Sōhō, 48	Sophia, 44	Zeke, 66
Northern European	Osage American Indian	South African Cuban	African American	British descent	Japanese American	Family exiled from Iran	Mexican American
Impact Ecologist	Technology Entrepreneur	Famous Artificially Enhanced	Neuroscientist Attorney	Industrialist Politician Philanthropist	Impact Artist	Educator	General Development Strategist

THE VISIONARY EVALUATIVE'S RESPONSIBILITY
Friday Morning 9:00 a.m. GMT

After having spent the last day-and-a-half discussing and reviewing collections of VE conversations from over the last decade curated by Zindzi and Jackie, all are returning to the circle of seats in the main meeting room.

Jackie: *(looking around the room)* Am I understanding correctly that our time spent reflecting on our colleagues' work has contributed to our preparations for the forum?

Lovett: Immensely. I found deep and original insights about the co-evolution of values and actions at virtually all levels of human organization.

Sophia: And how that may or may not relate to desired outcomes or patterns. This lends to our efforts to ensure compatibility between humans and an ASI, if it were to come to that.

Philip: Of course each of the VE Principles (VEPs) was exemplified, to a degree, and our colleagues shared useful examples of visioning and how VEs facilitate visioning a future. Those examples will be helpful to share at the forum. But truly, a key point they drove home repeatedly for me: With our eyes fixed on a world that is universally just, on one thriving with living abundance, Evaluatives have the responsibility to cultivate and navigate future-oriented processes that cultivate and sustain purposeful and disciplined inquiry, action, and reflection.

Jackie: *(P)*

PRINCIPLES OF THE VISIONARY EVALUATIVE

1. Commit humbly and compassionately to a sustainable, equitable future.
2. Recognize the world as composed of living, entangled systems.
3. Discover, reveal, and respect intersectionalities.
4. Facilitate the transparency and understanding of human values.
5. Learn through iterative action and inquiry.
6. Engage in deep praxis.

Jackie: So, for us? Now how do we see our work? What will be helpful in preparing for the conversations we will lead at the forum?

Sophia: We've got values and systems of values, values nebulae, interacting and changing from within the individual straight through to the mix of cultures, corporations, neighborhoods, and nations. VEs are in the thick of it, not standing back. Grappling directly with human values in all of what we are doing and advocating for. If we aren't doing this, the rest will fall short.

Zeke: I agree, Sophia. Dr. Redford and his colleagues' nature conservation initiatives and the other Praxis Quests are full of the examples that we'll need in order to show what that looks like and why it's valuable and important.

Philip: Perhaps to your point, Sophia, over the last 20 years the lines of work of many of our evaluation colleagues have all but disappeared.

Lovett: Even those lines that we followed and learned from to get to where we are today.

Gretchen: Agreed. There is no question that the VE—the practice, perspective, their very existence—evolved out of the discipline and profession of evaluation as our colleagues in evaluation created it.

Jackie: *(P)*

SYNTHESIS AND INSIGHT

- The relevance of evaluation depends on its ability to meaningfully engage with values.
- If the majority of investment into evaluation is about repairing the past rather than creating the future, most investments may be immediately irrelevant.
- VEs are helping to facilitate evaluation's growth and coevolution with society and the world.
- VEs are helping to facilitate society's evolution toward and adoption of evaluative thinking and evaluative inquiry.

AI AND THE TRANSFORMATION OF EVALUATION
Friday Morning 9:35 a.m. GMT

Hula: I *do* believe that the rise of machine intelligence radically accelerated the transformation and displacement of the evaluation community's vision for its role in society.

Gretchen, 69	Hula, 32	Jackie, 9	Lovett, 55	Philip, 80	Sōhō, 48	Sophia, 44	Zeke, 66
Northern European	Osage American Indian	South African Cuban	African American	British descent	Japanese American	Family exiled from Iran	Mexican American
Impact Ecologist	Technology Entrepreneur	Famous Artificially Enhanced	Neuroscientist Attorney	Industrialist Politician Philanthropist	Impact Artist	Educator	General Development Strategist

Sophia: For those who had a vision. Too many still see evaluation as a technical enterprise... (*Hula conceding the point*).

Zeke: There were other significant factors. But yes, while some evaluators were still debating definitions of evidence and improving slide presentations, a few sufficiently agile and opportunistic companies began building AIs that could offer up "good enough" answers to most any evaluative questions.

Sōhō: Uncertainty paralyzed those unable or unwilling to vision and adapt... it activated and strengthened those anxious to deliberately envision and strike out toward more healthful horizons.

Sophia: Of those who jumped into the void and started producing useful evaluative knowledge, only a few had even heard of evaluation but *Surprise!* That didn't stop them from offering free, shockingly reliable evaluative recommendation engines based on predictive and prescriptive analytics that started pumping out learning-oriented action options, probability-based outcomes, estimates of interventions' relative effectiveness, and even targets for knowledge generation.

Philip: Over the course of some of our careers we saw a leap from the paper survey we'd drop in the mailbox on the corner accompanied by our own incessant whining about the paucity and cost of information to today... (*looking to Hula*)

Hula: ...today, when we have HuMachine collaboratives delivering universally accessible, inquiry driven, self-generating, adaptive, perpetual modeling fueled by more information than was thought could exist.

Gretchen: Nearly ubiquitous sibylline computing, especially in some areas of our work, is, undoubtedly, radically transformative. Not too long ago, not only did we not constantly ask for information to help us to envision and question the future we are creating, we were almost completely focused on the past and designing our evaluative work as a straight line, stepwise process.

Sophia: (*tongue in cheek*) But we'd draw it as a circle.

Gretchen: Right. Articulate questions, collect data, interpret, recommend. That's evaluation? In those days, evaluation was about the past with hopes it would be used in the future. Today, I facilitate teams that are constantly crafting interdependent evaluative questions and criteria. Those drive the work of the machines that are producing products delivered to stakeholders and the world. We use their almost instantaneous feedback to make meaning and judgements about next wise actions, questions, criteria. All at the same time. All before lunch. Everyday.

Hula: Some private sector actors are doing what you describe as well. They are also making it possible, even requiring, that users of their "free" evaluative knowledge and guidance engines build in sustainability and equity questions and criteria.

Zeke: That may be better than nothing but unpacking their black box? That isn't happening.

Sophia: If answers are easy to get and good enough, will there ever be a strong enough incentive for enough people to care how the recommendations are created, whether they're credible, or who is making those judgments?

Lovett: Not until risk or consequences outweigh the convenience and we rarely know about that until the damage is already done.

Sophia: Even if initiatives are working best when evaluatives are involved, which, to our shame, is usually a question left unaddressed, will the way they've been involved in the past survive what's here and what's coming?

Jackie: *(P)*

SYNTHESIS AND INSIGHT

- Aspects of evaluation can quickly become unrecognizable as new boundaries are drawn and new perspectives and technologies emerge.
- As demand for evaluative knowledge increases, the diversity of human values influencing judgements about its quality, worth, and importance will increase and change the total diversity and relative weights of the criteria by which it is judged.
- Closed mindedness and rigid allegiance to discipline and mindset increase fragility in times of accelerating change.
- Make wise judgements and take wise actions; do not wait for permission.
- It is the responsibility of each of the members of the community to contribute to the well-being of the whole community.

Gretchen, 69	Hula, 32	Jackie, 9	Lovett, 55	Philip, 80	Sōhō, 48	Sophia, 44	Zeke, 66
Northern European	Osage American Indian	South African Cuban	African American	British descent	Japanese American	Family exiled from Iran	Mexican American
Impact Ecologist	Technology Entrepreneur	Famous Artificially Enhanced	Neuroscientist Attorney	Industrialist Politician Philanthropist	Impact Artist	Educator	General Development Strategist

THE VISIONARY EVALUATIVE'S POWER
Friday Morning 10:22 a.m. GMT

Zeke: Like we were saying earlier, our colleagues who didn't lift their heads fast enough, insisting they were different from the operator on the assembly line, the accountant, radiologist, engineer, economist... they told us why they could not be replaced by a machine. Now, in their irrelevance, facing local extinctions left and right, they still argue that everyone else is wrong.

Philip: If someone has a question that is important enough, an immediate answer gets attention. With the evaluative knowledge products out there today, nobody's waiting 12 months for information they need in the afternoon (*nodding at Gretchen*).

Hula: The VEs who are helping others to adapt and thrive have such a talent for distinguishing between the time for action and the time for reflection, when to move independently or in coordination with others, when to focus, and when to open it up.

Zeke: Their performance in dynamical systems, like everyone's, is dependent on the relationships between their values, natural capabilities and capacities, and their commitment to actively develop relevant competencies.

Hula: I'd like to correct myself. I said talents. Zeke, you called these attributes competencies. I've come to view them rather first as values—as fundamental beliefs and guiding principles that are most responsible for one's ability to navigate uncertainty and volatility in a given context.

Lovett: Whether values or skills, the VE must be able to be all of this: systematic and systemic, present and future oriented. And much more besides. The value added by VEs is powerful and getting serious attention.

Gretchen: The nature of this work, perpetually reflecting on and facilitating alignment between people's actions and values, gives VEs access to significant power.

Sophia: But how is it wielded? It's been misused, knowingly and in ignorance, more than once to perpetuate the inequities we aim to vanquish. Peoples and organizations with highly developed evaluative aptitudes and skills are better off for it. Those without, aren't.

Gretchen: (*as if obvious and just the way things are*) Decisions are repeatedly made with inferior evidence, and effectiveness and competitiveness suffer because of it.

Zeke: We see this happening in all of our initiatives. Two organizations attempting to deliver similar outcomes to different populations. One with evaluative expertise, the other without. One making slightly better decisions, the other, slightly worse. The gap between widens, between organizations and populations served. Inequities lock in.

Hula: Offloading traditional work to machines and focusing on our human, values-based, intelligences feels like progress for VEs. And maybe we're designing more sophisticated pathways to intended outcomes that more often avoid the iatrogenic damage done by troublesome traditions of evaluation.

Sophia: And what will we do to prevent this damage? We are still creating and perpetuating inequities because of our aggressive and self-centered notions of goodwill or our complacency and fear of change and challenge from the unfamiliar. These are artifacts of our White, male, rich, elite, capitalist origins . . . We need to tear down that past, bury it, let it rot, and forget it.

Jackie: *(P)*

SYNTHESIS AND INSIGHT

- Search out, explore, use, adopt, and adapt characteristics that improve the match between ourselves and the systems we intend to understand and change.
- Recognize our bias for action; because we can act does not mean we should.
- Recognize our bias about intervention; we intervene where there are resources and encouragement to intervene and do not when they are lacking.
- No evidence of harm is not the same as evidence of no harm.
- The better evaluation is able to match society's needs, the more power evaluation will have.

THE EVOLUTION OF VALUES
Friday Afternoon 1:07 p.m. GMT

Sophia: If we thought the future was going to be the same as the present, we wouldn't be talking about vision.

Gretchen, 69	Hula, 32	Jackie, 9	Lovett, 55	Philip, 80	Sōhō, 48	Sophia, 44	Zeke, 66
Northern European	Osage American Indian	South African Cuban	African American	British descent	Japanese American	Family exiled from Iran	Mexican American
Impact Ecologist	Technology Entrepreneur	Famous Artificially Enhanced	Neuroscientist Attorney	Industrialist Politician Philanthropist	Impact Artist	Educator	General Development Strategist

Jackie: We have said the future will be very different in many ways that require more explicit attention to human values. What are your proposals? What is your vision?

Gretchen: My tendency is to look through an evolutionary and ecological lens. Here, the evolution of values—origins and changes in values over time?

Philip: Human values have always been at the root of philosophy. But still we lack accessible, useful, credible information about values, relationships between them, their origins. We've never, until now perhaps, had sufficient incentive or ability to gather this information or make it visible.

Lovett: The context in which we are asking the question is unprecedented. The prospect of an ASI just beyond the horizon is forcing the question "What is it to be human?" outside the rarified bubble of philosophical debate and right onto everyone's dinner table. People are starting to care about this question. A lot.

Zeke: (*to Gretchen*) So what are you seeing? An evolutionary tree with the branches as what, different values?

(Seated, Sōhō begins illustrating the conversation about the tree and the entire ecosystem surrounding it, pushing her translucent holographic illustrations to the center of the circle.)

Gretchen: More open, more like a large sprawling oak on a hill in a meadow near the sea, with everything—air, water, sun, soil, and the three domains of life—everything it needs and everything that needs it.

Lovett: The analogy implies incommensurability to a single value or a single set of values.

Gretchen: Yes, and leaves it open enough for both overt and visible values, the sun and rain, while also allowing for the hidden, latent, unknown influences and interactions of values, like the undescribed symbiotic interdependencies between unidentified species of bacteria, archaea and eukaryota in the canopy and soil.

Sophia: Looking at it this way, I have to think of the starting point, the seed, before, when there were no values. I mean, what and when were the first? What was the last moment when none existed? What changed? Was the change a single bang or was it drawn out?

Hula: The significant influences most likely adjacent to the "first values" starting point would be likely to include information, knowledge, computational ability, values, understanding, consciousness...

Lovett: That's where increasing computational ability enables information to be contextualized. Once that begins to happen, it opens up the possibility for interdependencies between knowledge, computation, and the emergence and sophistication of values and consciousness, with the latter conceivably being based on some degree of awareness of values.

Philip: Would this look similar to human development of consciousness today?

Lovett: Maybe in some ways. Why not? Who knows? My guess is that the emergence and developmental evolution of values, like consciousness, is punctuated by occasional leaps forward but generally stretches out over long, complex stages and processes.

Hula: For humans! And we must keep this front of mind. The constraints on our development in the past no longer apply to the evolution of machines or biologies, not their acquisition of values or consciousness. It could happen in an instant.

Lovett: This is the impetus for the new energy in the debates about rights. So far it's been easy for those with the power and incentives to ignore and confuse these conversations.

Philip: Corporations play by the paradigms we create for them. So, many still believe they must consume people and consume nature to meet shareholder and public expectations for growth and accumulation.

Sōhō: (*in thought, aside*) Humans and nature the producers, the supply. Corporations the consumers, the demand.

Lovett: Enter ASIs, and the accompanying threats and risks, and *that* debate is reorganizing to make a little more sense.

Philip: Concerns around ASI may be the impetus for putting the rights of nature, humans, citizens, and corporations back in an order that complies with common sense. But we aren't anywhere near where we need to be.

Lovett: Some questions that come to mind: Who or what would determine when a machine has rights and what would they be? Or better yet, when do nonhumans have rights? If possession of values or consciousness were criteria for the judgment, who would have the authority to define those terms?

Gretchen, 69	Hula, 32	Jackie, 9	Lovett, 55	Philip, 80	Sōhō, 48	Sophia, 44	Zeke, 66
Northern European	Osage American Indian	South African Cuban	African American	British descent	Japanese American	Family exiled from Iran	Mexican American
Impact Ecologist	Technology Entrepreneur	Famous Artificially Enhanced	Neuroscientist Attorney	Industrialist Politician Philanthropist	Impact Artist	Educator	General Development Strategist

Sophia: Those questions require considering whether values are the exclusive domain of homo sapien or are we open to the homo genus or *(pause)* all life.

Hula: And if we did that, what if we were to determine that machines have acquired sufficient depth and diversity of human values? Or, thinking about it another way, what is the threshold between human and nonhuman, natural and artificial, life and nonlife?

(pause)

Gretchen: Okay, that's a lot. Keeping these questions in front of us, I'd like to present another angle of approach. What, if anything, do already described evolutionary processes—natural selection, mutation, drift, migration—lend to the growth and decay of values and values diversity in and across individuals and groups?

Sophia: Those processes, that framing, could be useful in explaining the persistence and extinction of values and related behaviors that are, at a given time, helpful, harmful, or innocuous at various temporal, spatial, and organizational scales.

Sōhō: (*Illustrating the conversation at a faster pace, adding diversity and macro and micro scales to the tree system Gretchen describes*) What's evolutionarily natural need not survive the evolution of our morality.

Philip: The goals and intentions of individuals and collectives today, especially at a macroscale, are going to look very different than homo sapiens' goals a hundred thousand years ago.

Lovett: Are they?

Philip: Different enough to find myself attracted to the notion that the last hundreds and thousands of years of human evolution and growth have been a period of increasing disruption in the evolution of values (*gesturing to Sōhō's illustrations*). That today there are artifacts of values that once served survival goals but now, if left in the mix, undermine our chances of surviving ourselves.

Sōhō: (*drawing*) This is when we learn that our most meaningful relationships have been invisible.

I: *Some branches from the big oak have been slowly rotting, then just hanging on and occasionally crashing down, crushing everything under and around them.*

Gretchen: (*startled, an idea sparked by Sōhō's drawings*) The phenotype of an organism—what it looks like—is determined by its genotype—genetic makeup—its environment and stochastic developmental events. We can perceive aspects of phenotype instantaneously, but can't fully understand phenotype without a lot of additional information and even more information is necessary to discern genotype. It could be much the same with the relationships between values "phenotype"—observable features of values like behavior—and values "genotype," the underlying values diversity, and all that gives rise to that diversity, that explain features of a phenotype.

Zeke: It's true that I can "see" many values and the way they play out in different situations. The values of trust, loyalty, respect, kindness, generosity—and the inverses of each—in two different people are evident enough in what they do and say. But it is the unique histories and memories, cultures, and genetics (*questioning?*), that are hidden from view that influence the variation in how those values are lived. Where one group will blindly trust because they are loyal, the other is loyal because they have good reason to trust.

Sophia: Has all of this already been done? I don't mean by philosophers. Isn't this what sociology, psychology, anthropology, ethnography, and other fields are already doing... exploring, organizing, and explaining values, their origins and relationships?

Lovett: Is it? If others have the answers we've said we must be desperate to find, either we've had blinders on or there's something about what's been done in those fields, and how it's been done, that reduces its utility or makes it inaccessible for our purposes.

Hula: I suspect it's partially rooted in differences between basic research and evaluation. One is mainly retrospective, motivated by curiosity and pursuit of objective truths. The other, the way of VEs in particular, is future- and use-oriented, pursuing subjective, normative, as well as objective and complex truths.

Lovett: *(adding to Hula's point)*...Yes, and VEs also assume responsibility for acknowledging all truths as potentially valid and facilitating their use to wisely navigate toward bays off shores of balanced and healthful co-evolution.

Sōhō: *(drawing at a furious pace while while Lovett and Hula are speaking)*

I: *The evolutionary tree of values on the hill by the sea had grown slowly at first, over millions of years with few small fruit. The*

Gretchen, 69	Hula, 32	Jackie, 9	Lovett, 55	Philip, 80	Sōhō, 48	Sophia, 44	Zeke, 66
Northern European	Osage American Indian	South African Cuban	African American	British descent	Japanese American	Family exiled from Iran	Mexican American
Impact Ecologist	Technology Entrepreneur	Famous Artificially Enhanced	Neuroscientist Attorney	Industrialist Politician Philanthropist	Impact Artist	Educator	General Development Strategist

branches of the genus homo start growing faster and faster, becoming the main trunk, with more and larger fruit that drop from the tree and sprout more, new and different trees and life of all sorts and the forest and other habitats diversify and spread ever faster away from the original single tree in all directions.

Jackie: *(P)*

SYNTHESIS AND INSIGHT

- The more different the future is expected to be from the present the more important visioning a desired future becomes.
- Visioning requires divergent types of thinking, including critical, creative, design, evaluative, systemic, and systematic thinking.
- Visioning can be used to surface and understand values.
- Challenging the "rightness" of rights—nature's, human, citizen, corporate—is a personal and professional responsibility.
- Actions and outcomes may be related but are distinct from values; making assumptions about the values of others based on actions and outcomes is dangerous.
- The wisdom of evaluation must coevolve with society and the world.

TRUE EFFECTIVENESS—TRUE HUMANITY
Friday Afternoon 2:36 p.m. GMT

Lovett: The ability to describe Sōhō's forest, that's the key to true effectiveness.

Jackie: True effectiveness?

Lovett: Sure. The effectiveness of an action in terms of the systems of values surrounding the action—the entire lifecycle and ecosystem of the action—and the effects on well-being at all levels of human-nature organization.

Gretchen: Assessing true effectiveness requires information about relationships among values, actions, outcomes, patterns, emergence, contexts, and more.

(pause)

Lovett: Attaching Truth—and so the multiple dimensions of truth— to the word "effectiveness" marks a more sophisticated understanding of the word that stretches well beyond traditional notions of the word as defined by boundaries set by and around a few individuals, an intervention, or an organization.

Sophia: But "effectiveness," that word, it still feels too restrictive, too externally prescriptive, too much baggage. It implies that there is some fixed outcome to achieve, a finish line. It sets off the search, the guessing, the prediction—and from there—the power imbalances, manipulation of people, and all the rest of it.

Zeke: The more I've heard about this subject, the more I am coming to agree. The boundaries of an Evaluative's fealty are becoming less predictable and dependable, more dynamic and expansive. Evaluatives craft and facilitate processes that deliver patterns and conditions that can enable humanity's attempts to create itself as it would like to be . . . and our knowledge of what that is is extremely limited.

Lovett: Perhaps that's it. Perhaps we are not pushing out truths about effectiveness but instead pushing away from our ignorantly engineered selves and civilization and toward a true humanity, one that is flourishing, enabled, and empowered by both human, natural, and machine intelligences to continuously design itself upon the universal assumption of multidimensional, multi-valid truths.

Philip: I don't disagree, but does it matter what we call it if it's impossible?

Lovett: (*light, kind sarcasm*) And you'd be referring to the likely infinitude of nuanced, dynamical, coevolving values, and relationships between them and everything else?

Sophia: As we've said, the space is full of invisibles. Where would we even start?

Gretchen: That we don't know how to start is no reason to wait. Biological evolution was, not long ago, also a complete mystery.

Sōhō: As was that (*indicating Earth and space, drawing an explanation*). Even so, our exploration began and is accelerating.

> **I:** *First peoples, with the sun going down and a few striking out toward the horizon. The establishment and growth of ancient peoples, cultures, and civilizations. Ad hoc, disconnected, haphazard, failed explorations into the unknown, navigating by sun and stars, gathering information and learning about geographic space and the world. Sharing knowledge for mutual benefits, next explorations, and more information gathering. Increasing interconnectedness between peoples*

Gretchen, 69	Hula, 32	Jackie, 9	Lovett, 55	Philip, 80	Sōhō, 48	Sophia, 44	Zeke, 66
Northern European	Osage American Indian	South African Cuban	African American	British descent	Japanese American	Family exiled from Iran	Mexican American
Impact Ecologist	Technology Entrepreneur	Famous Artificially Enhanced	Neuroscientist	Industrialist Politician Philanthropist	Impact Artist	Educator	General Development Strategist

and cultures by trade, transportation, food, politics, religion, sport, art, language, migration, education, ecological systems, information systems, and space exploration and travel.

(the illustrations fade leaving only the image of Earth, turning)

Sōhō: What was once invisible, impossible to imagine, has become impossible to imagine without.

(The group has been entranced by the beauty and movement of Sōhō's art and then the simplicity and stillness of Earth and Space, and then, reflected in the lens of each VE's eye, a few very bright shimmering stars rising over the dark side of Earth's horizon.)

Jackie: *(P)*

SYNTHESIS AND INSIGHT

- Effectiveness, like sustainability and equity, is a value that emerges from and is defined by the relationships at the nexus of values, actions, outcomes, and visions.
- In the Anthropocene, we cannot be certain we know what to do. We must just as often first wisely do so that we might know.
- Every path to a future we want will require the courage to strike out into an unknown with the ambition to explore, discover, share, and make wise use of what we learn.
- Observe the context and evolution of humanity's praxis; assess it in terms of our current context; design a praxis for today.

A PRAXIS FOR A SUSTAINABLE EQUITABLE FUTURE
Friday Afternoon 3:50 p.m. GMT

Sophia: Humans evolved from participating in the cycles of life, growth, and decay, to now, after just a few thousand, a few hundred years, dominating existence by breaking it into parts and putting them on a factory assembly line.

Lovett: Today we are witness to what we hope is the next stage of rebalancing, in the direction of wholeness of people, living, economy, well-being, and nature.

Zeke: *(with conviction and emotion)* The time is right to let machines do the work of machines and let humans learn again what it is to be a human.

Hula: Because I agree with you, it feels strange to say this, but I also believe this human transformation, Zeke, requires machines. And, if we are amenable, I have a proposal.

(group ascent and encouragement to continue)

Hula: Our company's Presence initiative grew out of the Hidden Mind Movement's mission to protect the brains, minds, bodies, behaviors, and the total self of individuals from all human and machine manipulation and takeover—and to that mission statement we've added—and to increase an individual's agency over identity and evolution. It works like this: A person, the Host, is assigned an AI we call a Presence. With Host guidance and supervision, a Presence collects and works with all relevant information—knowledge, experience, health, history, genetics—to build deep understanding of its Host's history, psychology, relationships, behaviors, values, beliefs, and, from there, potential future scenarios. The point? Organized as a heterarchy with other Presences and Hosts, a Presence is distributed and co-created, designing and delivering an intensely personalized, values-oriented, preveniently protected virtual world for its Host.

(pause)

Gretchen: The Presence empowers the Host to set the terms for engagement with both real and virtual worlds rather than the other way around?

Hula: Exactly. An Internet fit for purpose. In fact, and in light of our conversation earlier I need to amend this, the driving question framing a Presence's evolution, growth, and service is: "How can my host be more effective?" Unless it's in the host's best interests, attempts to manipulate the behaviors, perspectives, or preferences of the host, even the most sophisticated and surgical marketing, are rendered obsolete.

How does this relate to our work? Presences are designed to facilitate human interactions at the human-machine-nature nexus by doing some things humans can't—like calling up and assessing large quantities of information, easily distinguishing between human and machine tasks, and flagging opportunities for improved values-action-outcome-vision alignment. I had the thought that a Presence may also help us prepare for the forum. So, I conceived a Presence for us, the host, and it has been learning and growing with us for about a

Gretchen, 69	Hula, 32	Jackie, 9	Lovett, 55	Philip, 80	Sōhō, 48	Sophia, 44	Zeke, 66
Northern European	Osage American Indian	South African Cuban	African American	British descent	Japanese American	Family exiled from Iran	Mexican American
Impact Ecologist	Technology Entrepreneur	Famous Artificially Enhanced	Neuroscientist Attorney	Industrialist Politician Philanthropist	Impact Artist	Educator	General Development Strategist

year. It has created an output—a sort of experiential facilitative tool. It is unlike anything our teams have seen before. I would like to share it but I will warn you that it will be (*pause, tilt of the head*) intense. Would you like to see?

(*Group is curious, says "why not?" Then silence. All focused on the center of the room*)

(P)

- *To begin:* Everyone is seeing the same Earth and universe, rotating, moving. Then the perspective zooms out to reveal the eye and its lens also. Each person's perspective begins to shift to see the Earth as if through the lens and then each person's perspective becomes unique and intensely personal.
- *Throughout the presentation:* They are looking out at earth and everything from behind their lens. They are zooming into and out of a rapid series of events and situations familiar to each. They are watching change over time, first over thousands of years, then hundreds and then over their own lifetime. They experience virtual realities depicting change and transformation. The pace of the change they witness adjusts according to the significance, quality, and value of the scenes to each person.
- *Chronology of the presentation:* Each person first experiences histories that confirm the way they came to know the world. They then experience histories of others and how they experienced that history. They are in a world that is unfamiliar and alien, one that challenges and upends their understanding and experience with others and the world. They see representative moments of themselves forming, growing, learning, becoming who they are. They see what they and their ancestors have done in support of growth and decay and why it is good, bad, and/or with unknown results. They gain insights about their own and others' strengths and weaknesses.
- *Throughout the presentation:* Each person's reactions surface and evolve—stoicism, deep breathing, confusion, incredulous nervous laughter, resignation, sadness, occasional gasps, awe. The experience ends like it started with all of them watching the eye seeing the turning world but now with faint text in the lens of the eye.)

Zeke: Por Dios!

(*Sōhō is stoic or shocked, tears running down her face*)

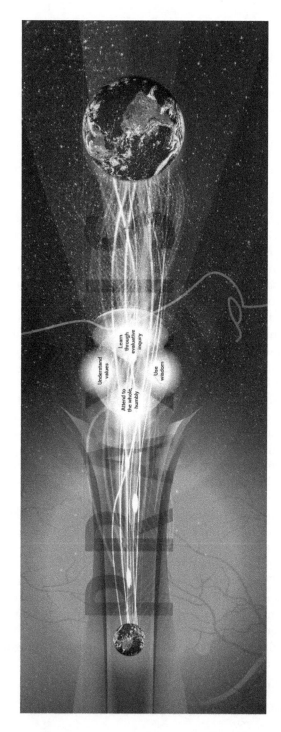

Figure 14.1 The Visionary Evaluatives' Presence offers the beginnings of a deep praxis to their Quest.

Philip: What the hell?

Sophia: *(stuttering)* Who ... b-but what? What!

Lovett: *(slowly)* Oh. How could that ... What was that?

> *(Others shaking heads, looking around the room, whispering to themselves)*

Hula: and, well, that's *(clearing throat)*. That's *(indicating their Presence)* based on work begun in the late 20 teens to assess and influence the ability to perform in a complex system. As the technology evolved, we lost track of some facets of how Presences were processing information or why. No surprise there but we've been frustrated by many of the outputs. We often don't know what to do with them. They are more like riddles than answers. As it turns out, Presences like to empower. Teach and model rather than give a fish. I've asked Jackie to pitch in here because what she can do in a moment, well, unpacking a Presence's reasoning can take our team weeks.

Jackie: *(impressed but matter of fact)* Our Presence is using 50 zettabytes of information, observing everything about us really. Demographics, education, finances, travel, health, and communications. All to contextualize our experiences while we've been together—our conversations, stories, problems, interpersonal dynamics, ideas, behaviors, metabolic status, emotions ... everything. With "How can this group be more effective?" as the framing question, the Presence has guided us through virtual recreations of actual and alternative worlds and truths. Did you see that?

Lovett: What I saw confirmed, but more often contradicted, in the strictest of terms, my understanding of, well, most everything.

Zeke: *(tense)* I do not like much of what I've seen. I want to say it is ridiculous.

Sophia: I had choices I needed to make where I hadn't even recognized there was a choice.

Philip: *(confirming what he already knew)* The world and my life as a horrible fantasy.

Hula: *(frustrated and despondent)* My views and actions—even here with you—in all my attempts to make them otherwise, are narrow, uninformed, and self-interested.

Sōhō: I was able to see the give and take between the world that created us and the world we create. The eye and the world are one ... and many; the parts and the whole; past, present, and future.

Jackie: What we are offered here *(indicating the eye and text in the lens)* is a form of praxis. One designed with principles intended to be a good match for our purpose.

Gretchen: Is *that* (*the eye*) an answer to how we might be more effective?

Jackie: It and everything you experienced is offered as a praxis that is a good fit for the question. The experiential perspective-taking elements of the praxis build upon the existing VE principles familiar to all of us.

Understand values; attend to the whole, humbly; learn through evaluative inquiry; use wisdom. We are encouraged to engage with these principles and this praxis in our *way*. Use it to navigate the coming and bringing together of self, world, others, and the nature-human-technology nexus. Use them to move with wisdom in our judgements and our actions to vision and create a future we want.

Zeke: (*considering the praxis*) I, we, are not there, nowhere near.

Sōhō: Not so. This is familiar to us. In these last minutes, I've learned that somewhere in us we are already what we need to be.

Sophia: (*realizing, remembering*) We *are* moving in this way.

Gretchen: We can design our lens, our evolution.

Lovett: It's a start.

Jackie: For each of us … For all of us.

(P)

SYNTHESIS AND INSIGHT

- The questions of evaluative knowledge—what it is, how it is used, why it is created, who will create it—are completely open and new.
- Through the eyes of others we will discover and respect intersectionality.
- Revealing and respecting intersectionality opens pathways to seeing and understanding values.
- "Imagination is the Discovering Faculty, pre-eminently. It is that which penetrates into the unseen worlds around us, the worlds of Science." (Ada Lovelace)
- Design a praxis for today and a future we want.

END

Gretchen, 69	Hula, 32	Jackie, 9	Lovett, 55	Philip, 80	Sōhō, 48	Sophia, 44	Zeke, 66
Northern European	Osage American Indian	South African Cuban	African American	British descent	Japanese American	Family exiled from Iran	Mexican American
Impact Ecologist	Technology Entrepreneur	Famous Artificially Enhanced	Neuroscientist Attorney	Industrialist Politician Philanthropist	Impact Artist	Educator	General Development Strategist

CHAPTER 15

CONCLUSION

Living as a Visionary Evaluative

Lovely Dhillon, Matt Keene, and Beverly Parsons

Our future arises from our present day actions just as today's reality has flowed from generations of actions before us. Knowing that change is accelerating unlike ever before, we—the people of this planet—have the opportunity, and indeed the necessity, to address these changes by embodying the aspirations behind our values with daily passion, meaningful design, and intentional action. As issues that challenge people and planet intensify and new ones loom, this is the time for us to embrace and connect with our brothers and sisters and with nature in bringing forward a sustainable, equitable future. We must feel the depth and breadth of our power and be adventurous and indefatigable in bringing a healthy and just way of living on this planet into being.

Visionary Evaluatives are not waiting. We know we cannot do it alone but that will not dilute our intensity of purpose and boldness of action. We are relentless in our values and actions to be an active part of creating the world we want to see—however small and however grand our creations may be. We connect with others, bringing our vision to networks of other visions,

Visionary Evaluation for a Sustainable, Equitable Future, pages 261–270

where visions healthfully exist, learn, evolve, and adapt together to build and engage wisdom about the relationships between values, actions, outcomes, and visions. Visionary Evaluatives walk this planet hand in hand with others, sharing the understanding that together we can lift up and realize visions of the survival and flourishing of humanity and nature together.

This book has explored the concept of Visionary Evaluatives (VEs), the Visionary Evaluative Principles (VEPs), and the role of evaluative thinking and inquiry in co-creating a sustainable, equitable future for people and nature on this planet. Contributing authors have provided a view into the work and environment of the VE in 2030, sharing how a visionary approach will benefit us in the future. We have learned about the types of issues and conversations that VEs may have, and the implications of a VE approach in the context of the evaluative inquiry process.

How do we ground the VE approach and principles in our everyday living? The VEPs require us to be mindful and fully engaged as we move through our lives with a goal to co-create a sustainable, equitable future. Visionary Evaluative Principles will be applied to different degrees, in different contexts, with different people, and at different times. There is no one path for moving through the world with a VE mindset. Visionary Evaluatives know that VEPs will need to be fit for a particular purpose and context.

The point is not to take these on as a mechanistic or conceptual task, but to take the VEPs in—as a way of being—and to share them out just as we breathe air into our lungs and back out to the world. Like air, our values sustain us and provide us the ability to move uniquely in the world. The VEPs serve to inspire us and to move us forward confidently through our rapidly changing world.

This chapter provides you the opportunity to engage with the VEPs through a starter set of checklist questions that allow reflection with other stakeholders[1] regarding what to pay attention to as we continue our VE journey together.[2] Use the checklist to test the VEPs and yourselves; be creative and constantly learn; listen to the wisdom of others; tap into your own wisdom; wrestle with the principles in praxis to leverage intent, experience, and knowledge; and build more deeply, more fully, and with more resiliency than if you were practicing alone.

The checklist questions constitute a flexible, starting point, rather than an ending point, for us to refer to as we reflect on our own journeys of becoming and living as VEs. They can guide us as we work to create the world we want to live in, that we want our children to have, and for the generations to come.

The checklist questions are designed to bring attention to the direct, intentional and/or short term impacts as well as the indirect, inadvertent, and long term impacts. They assume that the stakeholders with whom we join together in our situations represent a diversity of perspectives. The checklist questions, framed for *yes* or *no* responses, are intended to challenge VEs to make commitments and set boundaries on their thinking and action to exercise their own unique visionary power and impact. They are intended to start and focus conversations but are not intended as the only questions that those in the conversation need to address.

VISIONARY EVALUATIVES PRINCIPLE 1: COMMIT HUMBLY AND COMPASSIONATELY TO A SUSTAINABLE, EQUITABLE FUTURE

Of the many values we as VEs consider, there are two that we routinely keep in mind and prioritize as we maintain a focus on the future. These are the values of equity and sustainability. Not only do we consider these in the immediate situation and short term aspects in our work and life but we are also cognizant of the long term impact our actions and perspectives contribute toward both. We embrace these values and are steadfast in our commitment to them, regardless of the time and effort needed to improve our trajectory toward their realization.

Equity

As VEs, we know that equity is inherent to a world that provides opportunity for all to be their best selves. While equality may be an inherent value of a program or intervention, equity is not necessarily the outcome. The value of equity requires more. Indeed, a VE looks beyond the *intention* for equality in the work and way of being to see whether there actually was an equitable *outcome.* Importantly, we do not segregate the prioritization of equity between our work and personal lives. Rather, we think critically about whether how we move in our personal life also aligns honestly and deeply with our value of equity. As VEs, we go beyond intent toward evaluative inquiry of the actions we take —as well as the inactions—and to consider our roles in the outcomes that result. We listen to people who may feel as if they are being treated inequitably. We delve into that discomfort, reflecting honestly, and with a mind open to considering our roles in inequity. Indeed, VEs realize that true change requires those moments of discomfort and agitation, pain even, that can motivate us to change our actions, and so, our world.

Sustainability

Visionary Evaluatives are dedicated to the sustainability of nature and are intentional about creating a flourishing and thriving future for all life forms and the Earth. While protecting, conserving, and improving well-being, VEs actively commit our personal and professional lives to balancing and lifting up the values that underpin requirements and visions of sustainability for nature, people, and their relationships. We engage personally and with others in the relationships connecting social-ecological systems. We understand sustainability as a value that is ever-evolving, emergent, unpredictable, requiring constant attention, dependent upon context, and one that shapes our work and way of living. We actively search out opportunities to better align relevant actions and values to create a desired future.

As VEs living in the Anthropocene, we recognize the responsibility—and the opportunity—we have in protecting and being a partner with nature and in taking action based on that understanding.

Visionary Evaluatives Principle 1 (Sustainability and Equity) Checklist Questions

1. Have we witnessed and described how our values of, and related to, equity and sustainability of nature are expressed in this situation?
2. Have we articulated the relationship between people, planet, and profit for our situation?
3. Have we identified the power dynamics in this situation that impact equity and sustainability, including our own roles in those power dynamics?
4. Have we adapted our vision (or visions) of a sustainable and equitable future based on our experiences of evaluative inquiry and taking action?

VISIONARY EVALUATIVES PRINCIPLE 2: RECOGNIZE THE WORLD AS COMPOSED OF LIVING, ENTANGLED SYSTEMS

The second VEP is about recognizing the world as composed of living, entangled systems. Through this VEP, VEs explore the way in which natural systems exist, adapt, and evolve, and recognize that we are part of these natural systems. We also consider the many systems that humans have designed. Like natural systems, we realize that these human-enhanced systems within which we exist can be thought of in terms of cycles that also move from birth to rebirth or to generation of life in some other form. Visionary Evaluatives are not attached to any one part of that cycle—emerging, adapting, or growing, for example. Rather, they see the life cycles of macro and micro systems. They appreciate, study, learn from, and work with the systems in whatever phases of life those systems are in.

We also know that many of the systems are often unobserved and unrecognized, and require deep reflection and inquiry if we are to unearth and disentangle them. These systems vary in countless ways including size, levels of complication, and culture. They are seldom linear nor are they easily discerned in the way that they connect to one another. Visionary Evaluatives inquire as to these systems at both the micro and macro levels, looking for patterns, structures, boundaries, and networks that help us recognize them and how they are intertwined, gnarled, and nuanced.

We know, too, that systems—like all of us—are interconnected and interdependent and that forces are embedded within their structures. We see our own place in being part of many systems and know that our actions will impact others within our system and ripple out to the many systems to which they connect.

Visionary Evaluatives Principle 2 (Living, Entangled Systems) Checklist Questions

1. Have we considered multiple conceptions of how living systems function and change?
2. Have we articulated a shared understanding of what is or may be undermining living systems and developed an agreed way to reveal them while setting stronger foundations for ones that will support a sustainable, equitable future?
3. Have we explored which of our actions and values create social systems that lock in inequity and/or unsustainability and those which could be liberating?
4. Have we explored the relationships among natural, social, and economic systems?
5. Have we considered the life cycles of the systems involved in the situation and the relevance to a sustainable, equitable future?

VISIONARY EVALUATIVES PRINCIPLE 3: DISCOVER, REVEAL, AND RESPECT INTERSECTIONALITIES

In considering entangled, living systems, VEs recognize that there are many forces and issues that span many systems and that by looking closely at where those intersections exist, we can potentially unlock oppressive, unequitable, and unsustainable historical forces, creating opportunities for reshaping the future. The VE wrestles with these forces in the third VEP, knowing these forces are routinely expressed in power and culture. Visionary Evaluatives look to the way they play out at the macro and micro intersections of nature, economics, sectors, communities, organizations, and people with differential power and privilege.

VEs see the structures of power and culture that exist in society, that are deeply embedded, often for generations. The forces and issues that lay at the root (for example, patriarchy, racism, classism) are pulled through time as they pervade through societal systems, institutions, and communities. The ways in which individuals are caught in these cross-cutting social issues and forces can be overwhelming and, at the same time, unseen. More often, they are unacknowledged.

As VEs, we shake loose these embedded forces by bringing together different sectors, institutions, communities, people, ideas, perspectives, industries, and organizations. This requires honesty, deep reflection, creative thinking, listening, discussion, and collaboration about those structures, their context, their history, and the many roles that they play as well as the considerable impact they may have.

VEs understand that the level of interdependence and systemic operation in the Anthropocene requires that people, nature, sectors, organizations, technology, environments, and disciplines work and learn together. As VEs, we look for effective actions that allow structures and systems to co-evolve for the benefit of humankind and nature. We also search for innovative ways to expel the harmful and deleterious impacts of oppressive forces.

Visionary Evaluatives know that progress requires interconnected and multifaceted actions, and that the perspectives of many must be engaged for learning, listening, teaching, and action. We deeply and personally consider the cultural and power issues within our society rather than moving through life with blinders on that are unseeing of privilege or impact on other people, living entities, and natural systems.

Visionary Evaluatives Principle 3 (Intersectionality) Checklist Questions

1. Have we courageously sought out, found, and engaged with the intersectionalities that are creating inequities and that undermine sustainability (e.g., internal; internal–external; culture; power; values; sectors; worldviews; paradigms; ecosystems)?
2. Have we identified the priority intersections that we agree are the appropriate ones for our attention at this time to move to a sustainable, equitable future?

VISIONARY EVALUATIVES PRINCIPLE 4:
FACILITATE THE TRANSPARENCY AND UNDERSTANDING
OF HUMAN VALUES

As VEs, we believe that values are at the core of everything we do. We honestly and with great intentionality regularly consider our values and the ways in which we bring those with us as we move in the world. We are transparent about our values and have an earnest desire to learn about the values of others, listening, observing, and having conversations, sometimes difficult ones, to gain that insight. The values people hold—whether our leaders, colleagues, friends, or neighbors—give us insight into how best to connect with others. They open the door for grounded conversation, growth, and connection about what matters in our collective lives. Transparency is important in the understanding of one another's values, giving us a basis on which to collectively prioritize some values, knowing there may be trade-offs with other values. This does not mean those other values are eliminated or ignored—just that they are not the key focus. It is a bit like making a movie—there are certain images for certain parts of the movie that are focused upon but others may become the focus later. Understanding values also allows us to collectively align our values with our actions and with outcomes. Visionary Evaluatives jointly engage in evaluative inquiry about whether the values optimized for a situation are resulting in outcomes that reflect those values.

Further, as VEs, we must also keep in mind that being aware of and transparent about values is important not only at the beginning of a situation, when we often unearth and share them, but also throughout the course of our involvement with others. Periodically, as we move through a situation, we return to the prioritized values and facilitate a reflection on whether those values are actually being integrated and prioritized as we had intended.

Through the transparency of our values and those of others, we will be able to consider whether our actions are reflecting the asserted values and if outcomes resulting from our actions also align with our values. In embracing the fourth VEP, we weigh those varied and sometimes conflicting values and determine which ones are fit for the situation at hand. In our personal and professional life, we marry our values to our actions with a constant vigilance to live with as much commitment to them as possible.

Visionary Evaluatives Principle 4
(Transparency and Understanding of Human Values)
Checklist Questions

1. Are our values adequately transparent and understood to move forward?

2. Have we discussed the relationships between values, actions, outcomes, and visions?

3. Have we discussed the values with the greatest influence on sustainability and equity in this situation?

4. Have we made transparent the values that are likely to create the most conflict and tension?

5. Do we have a process for agreeing upon the prioritized values for the situation?

6. Have we planned ways to return to the list of prioritized values to ensure that actions and outcomes are aligning with those prioritized values?

VISIONARY EVALUATIVES PRINCIPLE 5: LEARN THROUGH ITERATIVE ACTION AND INQUIRY

This deep consideration of values, commitments, systems, and intersections is not a one-time occurrence for VEs. Rather, we are constantly designing and taking actions, pursuing and adjusting inquiry to create the learning that informs our next actions and inquiries. We check in with others, develop feedback loops that involve the input of many, communicate our own learning, and create open access points so that all can take part in the learning, develop their own views regarding how their own learning can lead to meaningful, impactful action.

Learning along the way leads VEs to new areas of inquiry and to new actions guided by a commitment to considering the learning they are gaining and applying it to creating a sustainable, equitable future. We not only reflect on what is being learned about systems, culture, intersections, networks, structures, privilege, and power, but we also openly and honestly discuss and exchange those learnings with others. We look for ways of having greater impact through more connected action. We consider how and whether the values embraced at the beginning continue to inspire the iterative inquiry and action process. As VEs, we are dedicated to learning, sharing our learning, and action for not only our own benefit but for the benefit of others and for nature.

Visionary Evaluative Principle 5 (Iterative Action and Inquiry) Checklist Questions

1. Are we iteratively examining, communicating about, and developing the relationship between our learning, actions, and inquiry and connecting that to creating a sustainable, equitable future?

2. Are we facilitating the capacity and development of competencies for learning through iterative action and inquiry that are tailored to the needs of the full range of stakeholders?

VISIONARY EVALUATIVES PRINCIPLE 6:
ENGAGE IN DEEP PRAXIS

The final VEP is engaging in deep praxis. This is where we unite values, vision, evaluative inquiry, theory, creativity, and action through practice and in communion with others. As VEs, we recognize that a sustainable, equitable future requires good intent, solid theory, and individual action. It also requires VEs to have a steadfast commitment to a mindful practice of reflection, continual questioning, learning, iteration, and integration with others who are interested in testing, improving, iterating, and integrating learning to deepen their own positive impact. We keep values at the core of our praxis, feeding in what we have learned and using that learning to understand, reassess, refine, and sometimes reframe those values.

As VEs, we are constantly practicing the VEPs and considering our values as we move through our life to actively co-create a sustainable, equitable future. We search for interconnections in our actions and ideas to craft and refine a fit-for-purpose praxis that allows us to test, inquire, reflect, learn, create, and contribute to a healthy future for us, other humans, and planetary life forms that exist now and that may exist in the future.

Visionary Evaluative Principle 6
(Praxis) Checklist Questions

1. Are we designing and engaging in a praxis that is fit for our purpose?
2. Are we individually and collectively continually mindful of the multiple and differential impacts of the transformations associated with our praxis?
3. Is our praxis, individually and collectively, coevolving with our values, action, inquiry, and learning toward a sustainable, equitable future?

MOVING IN THE WORLD TOGETHER
AS VISIONARY EVALUATIVES

We have the power to create a sustainable, equitable future. We must choose this future. As VEs, we live with steadfast learning and dedication to using our lives and our work to bring about well-being for all forms of life and for the planet. Let us use the rich array of opportunities we have to address the challenges the Anthropocene creates for humanity and for nature. Join us in creating and maintaining a constant commitment to, compassion for, and connection with other people, living beings, and our planet. We believe that using a Visionary Evaluative appraoch to create a sustainable, equitable future will provide not only the best opportunity for the well-being of others and our world, but also for ourselves.

NOTES

1. Stakeholders are defined as those directly involved and those indirectly impacted by the evaluand. The term "stakeholder" includes sector or issue experts who provide needed insight; are often vested in the issues through their experience, education and skill; and are integral to a VE approach.
2. When we talk about a "situation," we mean both personal and professional circumstances in which the VE is engaging.

ABOUT THE EDITORS

Beverly Parsons is committed to fostering health and well-being for people and planet. As a first-generation college student at the University of Wisconsin in the '60s (receiving a BS in medical technology), her eyes were opened to a world far beyond her rural Scandinavian immigrant community birthplace. Beverly has worked and lived nationally and internationally in rural, suburban, urban, and indigenous communities. She has worked closely with governors, legislators, local communities, philanthropy, and business across social sectors, particularly education, health, environment, and social services. Her PhD (University of Colorado–Boulder) in educational research and evaluation grounds a career of compassionately using mixed evaluation, research, and facilitation strategies to reveal ways to influence complex systems in support of learning, equity, and sustainability. She is executive director of InSites (www.insites.org) and was the 2014 president of the American Education Association. She enjoys playing her harp and using her training as a licensed massage therapist.

Lovely Dhillon, born in India and raised in the United States' Deep South, learned at an early age about the beauty and challenge of difference. This, and the values of equality and service fostered by her parents and sisters, inspired a career dedicated to social progress. As a lawyer, she built national and regional social justice collaborations as well as prosecuted hate crimes and domestic violence cases. Lovely served with the Bill and Melinda Gates Foundation as a deputy director for strategy, management, and evaluation, furthering her interest in linking data and strategy. Now as CEO of Jodevi Consulting (www.jodevi.org), Lovely co-creates a future that calls to the very

Visionary Evaluation for a Sustainable, Equitable Future, pages 271–272
Copyright © 2020 by Information Age Publishing
All rights of reproduction in any form reserved.

best in each of us for the well-being of all of us. Lovely hold a BA from Florida State University and a JD degree from Yale Law School. Lovely lives life fully, enjoying the wisdom of others and constantly being awestruck by the beauty of our world.

Matt Keene envisions a future of well-being for all. He believes that an understanding of human values is required to realize the vision. Matt grew up on the Eastern Shore, floating west on the Nanticoke River. He has degrees from Virginia Tech and Duke University, and has surfed and worked in 50 countries. From 2006–2018 he served as an evaluator and social scientist at the U.S. Environmental Protection Agency where his praxis focused on the nexus of sustainability, evaluation, systems thinking, and complexity. As CEO of The Silwood Group, Matt creates innovative spaces for Visionary Evaluatives from systems, natural and social sciences, arts, technology, and elsewhere to gather with a common passion: learning to navigate the wickedness of the Anthropocene and co-create a future we want. Matt laughs a lot with his family in Arlington, VA, where the gardening and woodworking are good and the waves are small (www.linkedin.com/in/mattkeene).

ABOUT THE CONTRIBUTORS
Sector Visioning Chapters

Chapter 4: Social Protection

Lateefah Simon, president of Akonadi Foundation, is a nationally recognized advocate for civil rights. Lateefah has over 20 years of executive experience advancing opportunities for communities of color and low-income communities in the San Francisco Bay Area. Lateefah has received numerous awards for her work, including the MacArthur "Genius" Fellowship.

Charlyn Harper Browne is a senior associate at the Center for the Study of Social Policy. Her work and publications focus on promoting healthy development and well-being in children, youth, and families, in general, and Black populations, in particular. Her son, nieces, nephews, and grandchildren are the center of her life.

Ryan Eller, executive director of Define American, use the power of story to shift the conversation around immigrants, identity, and citizenship. An ordained Baptist, Ryan holds degrees in political science, divinity, and public administration. He was U.S. campaigns director at change.org and executive director of CHANGE—the largest broad-based community organizing group in the southern United States.

Bo Pryor, served in the U.S. Marines from 2003 to 2010. He completed three overseas tours, providing security to U.S. embassies and consulates, and deployed to Iraq as a civil affairs specialist. He subsequently worked for

Visionary Evaluation for a Sustainable, Equitable Future, pages 273–276
Copyright © 2020 by Information Age Publishing
All rights of reproduction in any form reserved.

USAID in Afghanistan as a safety and security officer. His primary job since 2011 is the safety, security and education of his children.

Justin Speegle retired from the air force as a colonel after 28 years of service. He holds advanced degrees from the Naval War College, Air University, and Embry Riddle. A lifelong surfer, he currently volunteers on the board of directors for AmpSurf.org—a nonprofit organization that takes disabled people surfing.

Chapter 5: Nature

Kent H. Redford is the principal at Archipelago Consulting in Portland, Maine. He is a conservation practitioner with 10 years in academia, 20 years in NGO work and 5 years at Archipelago. His work includes protected areas, subsistence hunting, conservation practice, and synthetic biology's intersection with conservation.

Carly Cook is a conservation biologist at Monash University in Australia. She is interested in the interface between science and practice in environmental management. Her research is broadly focused on developing decision support tools to help practitioners to integrate the best available evidence into their management decisions.

Duan Biggs is a senior research fellow at Griffith University. His research interests include community-based conservation, people-centred responses to illegal wildlife trade, nature-based tourism, the socioeconomics of conservation decision-making, and operationalizing resilience ideas for biodiversity conservation. Duan earned a PhD from James Cook University and an MSc from the University of Cape Town.

Glenda Eoyang: Glenda Eoyang helps individuals, communities, and public and private organizations thrive in the face of overwhelming uncertainty. She is a pioneer in applications of complexity science to human systems and founding executive director of the Human Systems Dynamics Institute.

Chapter 6: Law

Ellen Lawton, JD, co-leads The George Washington University's National Center for Medical-Legal Partnership in the Department of Health Policy and Management. An expert in poverty law, Ms. Lawton is a lead editor of the 2011 medical-legal partnership textbook. She has led the development of the medical-legal partnership approach, and published multiple articles in both clinical and legal journals.

Joe Scantlebury is vice president for program strategy (places) at the W. K. Kellogg Foundation. He leads, designs, and implements the foundation's strategic programming efforts to improve the lives of vulnerable children and families, and works to advance community engagement, leadership, racial equity, and healing. Joe received a BS from Cornell University and a JD from NYU School of Law.

Chapter 7: Business

Eric Barela has over 15 years of experience as an internal evaluator, specializing in building organizational measurement & evaluation systems. He is currently the director of measurement & evaluation at salesforce.org where he leads efforts to determine its global social impact. Eric holds a PhD from the UCLA Graduate School of Education & Information Studies.

Bob Willard is a leading expert on quantifying the business value of sustainability strategies. He has given over a thousand presentations, has authored six books, and provides extensive resources for sustainability champions. He leads an award-winning certified B Corp, is a certified sustainability professional, and has a PhD in sustainability from the University of Toronto.

Chapter 8: Health

Jeanne Ayers, Wisconsin's State Health Officer, is a leader in national efforts to assure health and racial equity and improve population health. She works across policy sectors and fields of practice. Jeanne previously served as assistant commissioner and chief health equity strategist of the Minnesota Department of Health.

Chapter 9: Financial Investing

Georgette Wong is a recognized trailblazer in impact investing. From 2007–2012 she curated the Take Action! Impact Investing Summit, which convened thought-leaders and pioneering asset owners representing over $4.5 trillion dollars. Georgette has presented on impact investing before the U.S. Senate, the U.S. State Department, the UN-backed Principles for Responsible Investment, and others.

Chapter 10: Transportation

Antoinette Quagliata, M.E.M. LEED AP, is driven by the values of environmental protection, sustainability, effective and equitable planning, and "people-oriented development." She works across sectors to advance environmental management systems, environmental and sustainability policy, and mobility innovation research. Antoinette works with the U.S. Federal Transit Administration and has degrees from Duke and Cornell.

Thomas Abdallah, P.E. LEED AP, is the chief environmental engineer for the MTA New York City Transit. He holds a BS in Chemical Engineering from Rutgers University, and is a professor at Columbia University. He is the author of *Sustainable Mass Transit: Challenges and Opportunities in Urban Public Transportation* (Elsevier, 2017).

Chapter 11: Education

Elizabeth B. Kozleski, dean's senior scholar for teaching and learning, Graduate School of Education, Stanford University, researches and writes about equity and justice issues in inclusive education. She taught special education students in Virginia and Colorado before becoming a special education professor. Her work focuses on solving the struggles that minoritized families and students face within the public schools.

Chapter 12: Design

Cameron D. Norman, PhD MDes CE, is a professional designer, psychologist, educator, and evaluator whose life work has focused on ways to organize and support innovation for human well-being. He is the president of Cense Ltd. and on the faculty at OCAD University in Toronto, Canada.